# SEVENTY YEARS IN ARCHAEOLOGY

FLINDERS PETRIE

# SEVENTY YEARS
## IN
# ARCHAEOLOGY

*By*
FLINDERS PETRIE, Kt.
D.C.L., LITT.D., LL.D., PH.D., F.R.S., F.B.A.

GREENWOOD PRESS, PUBLISHERS
NEW YORK

*To*

**MY WIFE**

**ON WHOSE TOIL MOST OF
MY WORK HAS DEPENDED**

"It behoves all Men that labour to excel all other Creatures, to make it their chief Endeavour not to waste their lives in silence like the Brute Beasts. . . . We make more use of the command of the Mind than of the service of the Body. The one we share with the Gods, the other is common to us with the Beasts. For the Captain and Commander of human life is the Soul. If Men were but as sedulous in laudable Professions as they are eager in pursuit of things unprofitable they would rather govern than be governed by Fortune."

*To the mundane, by Sallustius the splendid.*

"Dare to look up to God, and say, Deal with me henceforth as thou wilt; I am of one mind with thee; I am thine. I reject nothing that seems good to thee; lead me whithersoever thou wilt, clothe me in what dress thou wilt. . . . If Death shall find me in the midst of these studies, it shall suffice me if I can lift up my hands to God and say, The means which thou gavest me, for the perceiving of thy government, and for the following of the same, have I not neglected. . . . I am content that I have used thy gifts so long. Take them again, and set them in what place thou wilt, for thine were all things, and thou gavest them me."

*To all men, by Epictetus the slave.*

# CONTENTS

The device on the cover is the motto of King Akhenaten—
LIVING IN TRUTH

# ILLUSTRATIONS

# FOREWORD

THE affairs of a private person are seldom pertinent to the interests of others, yet the rise of a great branch of knowledge in the archaeological discovery of man's development should be worth some record. The tracing of the various steps, moreover, which have led to results from small beginnings, may encourage others whose prospects would seem very insufficient for their aims in life. As a record of how we have learned the past, and how much may be done without influence or means to start with, it may not be amiss to put down an outline of what I have been permitted to do. All work is but an incompleted intention, so it is not irrelevant to state sometimes the aims, as well as the methods, which led to results.

From the mass of recollections, those have been chosen which influenced my life and work and which helped or hindered the final outcome of each endeavour. It is often the slight details which lead us on, the trifles which show character most truly, the close fitting of the patchwork of life which guides us at last to see the pattern of the whole. As memories of fifty years ago may lose precision, it is as well to say that full journals and letters have been read over, and often it has seemed best to put (in quotation marks) what was written at the time, with some abbreviation. This is only a record of the work, and of what led me up to it, and has nothing otherwise to do with the inner life.

For what end came I here? I could not say,
But step by step I have been taught to stay
And try to find the truest path I may;
The end I see not, and know not the way,
But take my marching orders day by day.

| | |
|---|---:|
| Born . . . . . . | 1853 |
| Began collecting coins . . | 1861 |
| End of tuition . . . | 1863 |
| Began British Surveys . . . | 1875 |
| First Publication . . . . | 1877 |
| Began work in Egypt . . . | 1880 |
| Work in Upper Egypt . . | 1891 |
| D.C.L., Oxon . . . . | 1892 |
| Professor, London University . | 1892 |
| LL.D., Edin. . . . . | 1896 |
| Marriage . . . . . | 1897 |
| Ph.D., Strass. . . . . | 1897 |
| Litt.D., Cantab. . . . . | 1900 |
| F.R.S. . . . . . . | 1902 |
| F.B.A. . . . . . . | 1904 |
| LL.D., Aberdeen . . . . | 1906 |
| War Years . . . . | 1914-1919 |
| In Egypt again . . . . | 1919 |
| Kt. . . . . . . | 1923 |
| Work in Palestine . . | 1926- |

# SEVENTY YEARS IN ARCHAEOLOGY

## CHAPTER I

## PREPARATION

THE first chance in life is ever being born at all, and a mighty uncertain affair it seems to us mortals. My grandfather, Captain Matthew Flinders, who died at forty, left two young friends who kept in touch with his widow and daughter for half a century. One was his cousin, a midshipman on his ship H.M.S. *Investigator*, John Franklin, of Arctic fame. From his childhood, John was always the heroic gentleman. One evening my great-grandmother, visiting his mother, rose to leave, saying it was getting too late; Johnnie, then four years old, at once said, "Never mind, Mrs. Tyler, I will see you home."

The other friend was William Henry Smyth, but for whom my father and mother might never have met. He was a man of wide interests, known as a literary sailor, as surveyor, astronomer, and antiquary. His sons were notable for rising to the top of their professions, his daughters for marrying men who, later, were equally successful. Some of their names reflected his tastes; Piazzi, the Astronomer Royal for Scotland, was named from the Sicilian astronomer; Rosetta, the wife of Sir William Flower, had her name from the Rosetta stone. Their house in London in the 'forties was a centre of many interests, and my mother, Anne Flinders, often stayed with them when up in town for meetings.

Piazzi Smyth had begun his career as an assistant to Sir John Herschel at the Cape, and thence naturally knew my grandfather, Petrie, who was head of a department there. He brought my father and uncles into the Smyth circle on their return to England. Amid the many friends who went to and fro there, it did not escape the eye of Mrs. Smyth that her eldest daughter, Henrietta, and young William Petrie were very intimate. Now she was a very careful mother, and knew her duties. She felt that my father had not that amount of worldly wisdom which she desired for her daughter's success, so Henrietta was promptly taken to Cambridge, and soon after married the sexagenarian Professor Baden-Powell.

Meanwhile William Petrie and Anne Flinders had been constantly meeting at the Smyths, and some years later my father and mother were married. So Mrs. Smyth was the agent by whom scouting and Egyptian archaeology took their present form. B.P. and I both speculate whether either, or neither, of those subjects would have been otherwise so shaped?

My parentage being thus determined, my first risk was being supposed still-born, and it was to an experienced old nurse that I owe my existence. Next, another nurse dropped me, and so punched in my skull, slightly marked on the temple to this day. The old past seemed all around me as I drank in the family stories. My mother had known her grandmother well, who was born in 1745 and knew Queen Anne's dressmaker; pieces of the blue and silver brocade and other dresses had come down to us. The old grandmother was thus a single life linking those who had known 1692 and 1892, when my mother died.

My great-aunt, who brought me up, talked of the college days of her father, about 1770, and was full of the stirring events of her youth, of the adored Nelson, and the watch, night by night, for the beacons on the

Lincolnshire coast which might signal Napoleon's invasion. The woes of Queen Caroline were a matter of yesterday, and I often passed the house at Charlton where she had lived.

My mother's grandmother was a sturdy old lady, a friend of Wilberforce; her first husband was Benjamin Chappell, grandson of a Huguenot refugee, and my mother had thence her small, alert figure, and very dark complexion, with a true reverence for her persecuted ancestors. The grandmother was closely contemporary with George III, and when he died she sat rocking to and fro and crying, "My king, my king!" It was her pride to have been born at York, "a citizen of no mean city," as she said.

My grandfather Captain Flinders' work, and his long, illegal captivity by the French in Mauritius, were naturally in the sanctum of family feeling. So long had passed without hearing from him, detained in Mauritius, that his wife had lost all hope, dressed as a widow, and wept over his miniature. They had only just been married before he left for Australian discovery in 1801; she was prevented from going with him, though Captains' wives were tolerated then in the Navy, *sub rosa*.

He returned in 1810, to work hard, on half-pay, at writing his account of discovery, and thus, worn out by tropical disease and work, he died in 1814, unconscious of his volumes issued in time to be laid upon his death-bed. I need say no more about his life, as it has been well written by Professor Scott. A passion for discovery I owe to my grandfather, though his was in space, and mine was in time. The fate of my grandfather's old middy, Franklin, was often part of our family talk.

In such an air of the past I began to understand things around me. The first puzzle was how could I be sure of the reality of what was told me about the world; was all that I saw a mere show and a deception? This was set at rest, when I was three, by the vast extent of a street full of people half a mile away; the disproportion to my little self was too great for it not to be a great reality. I cannot have been more than three then, as before four I knew places very much farther off, and the world seemed wide.

Children look for meanings much earlier than is credited; I saw my little son of two, eyeing the wavelets lapping the beach on a still day; at last he solved the why of it, "the wind is pushing the water up." The sense of duty also comes early; my mother called out to me that I was naughty in doing some trifling thing, so I gave myself the three slaps on the arm, which was the standard punishment, and then did the standard crying, to follow.

My first train journey was when my aunt took me over to see Greenwich Hospital, the Nelson relics and the painted hall; it was a tramp of over five miles going there, she at seventy-two and I not yet four. The return of my uncle from the Crimea in 1857, the launch of the *Leviathan*, the Great Comet of '58, the glare of Tooley Street fire, and the victories of Garibaldi in '60, were the excitements of life which I remember.

From six to eight years old, I had, as a governess, a favourite friend of my mother's, beloved and sufficient. She was succeeded by an injudicious woman. My mother's love of languages—of which she taught herself half a dozen, from Hebrew to Italian—led to its being thought quite natural to stuff me with English,

French, Latin and Greek grammars all together, at the age of eight.

The result was a collapse, and a doctor's order that I should be left alone for two years. I soon ravenously browsed on all sorts of books, and ran loose, mind and body, to great advantage. I was always fascinated with scales and weights and, whenever they were brought out, I weighed everything available. At ten, a fresh attempt was made upon me with grammars, equally futile. Later on my own account I strove hard, making, in all, ten starts in Latin and five or six in Greek, every one ending ignominiously in my forgetting the early lessons as soon as I got a little forward; never have I been able to hold any language grammatically, but only by the practice of necessary use.

As in the 'sixties such subjects were essential at any school, and as I had chronic asthma which kept me indoors half the year, it was hopeless for me to get any regular education, and I was cut off from knowing any other children, being an only child myself. My father intended to find an ideal tutor for me, who should be certain to keep in touch with his own beliefs; but as such would be rare to find, and a constant flow of fresh matters filled my father's attention, the tutor never appeared. Thus I was taught nothing after ten, till, when grown-up, I took an Oxford extension course in mathematics; this was mainly for algebra, as geometry and trigonometry I had picked up by myself. I always disliked the ungeometrical nature of algebra, like blind Samson grinding at the mill.

Being left to my own devices, I ransacked the marine store shops of Woolwich for coins, thus beginning archaeology when still accompanied by my nurse, at eight, and triumphing in finding an Allectus. My mother had inherited some coins, a quinarius of Vespasian (found in draining the fens, and taken to my great-great-grandfather as the learned doctor of Donington), also coins of Constantine and others; she had learned of them on her mother's knee, as I did on her knee, and she had collected many more, handed to her by officer friends at Woolwich when they "got the rout."

When I was eight, a little boy of ten used to come to visit us (later, Rev. Longley Hall, Director of C.M.S. schools in Palestine) and he described the unearthing of a Roman villa in the Isle of Wight; I was horrified at hearing of the rough shovelling out of the contents, and protested that the earth ought to be pared away inch by inch, to see all that was in it and how it lay. All that I have done since was there to begin with, so true is it that we can only develop what is born in the mind. I was already in archaeology by nature.

My mother had a fair collection of minerals and fossils, and had tried in the 'forties to raise interest in mineralogy by popular articles, based on the chemical arrangement. She had been stirred by lectures at the Royal Institution, by Faraday and others, which she heard when staying with an old friend, Miss Marston, afterwards my godmother. That good lady's life had been crippled by a deep attachment to the mathematician Sylvester; she felt the difference in religion prevented their marriage, and they parted, he to follow a meteoric course of bachelor wandering from one university to another, she to decline upon a lady companion, lap-dogs, charitable work and anti-vivisection.

From my mother's collection I soon knew a hundred minerals, and found garnet-granite and serpentine in the gutter-linings of the streets, which I howked up and chipped for specimens. I soaked in old Allan's *Mineralogy* till I knew every page of it, a delightful book not devitalised by abstract science. Minerals naturally led to testing specimens, and so to chemistry, and I collected the testings of every element I could get, to make comparative tables. I revelled also in dozens of pots and bottles with various messes, and in electrotyping, and tried everything that I could start on, out of Miller's *Inorganic Chemistry*.

In the summers, some weeks of fossil hunting filled the time. In this desultory, but very living, way, I gradually picked up many useful subjects. Though I dabbled in trigonometry, I did not get hold of Euclid till I was fifteen. Then I sat down in my cousin's garden at Puttenham, and feasted on a book a day with full delight, skipping all the propositions which were already axiomatic to me, and satisfied if I could visualise the reality of those demonstrations which were not self-evident. It was a joy like that of conic sections rather later, in the good old geometrical view so full of beauty, and not assassinated by algebra. This was unconsciously following Matthew Flinders, who taught himself geometry and navigation, so that he was ready for work when he entered the navy.

An external opening of a strange kind came at the age of thirteen, when I was wandering about Blackheath and Lee, where I saw a large tray of Greek copper coins, at twopence each, in a shop window. My mother went with me to look at them, and so we got to know the owner, Riley, a man of rare character. He saw we were fascinated with the hundreds of coins before us, and could not settle which we wanted; so he fetched a bag, poured them all in, uncounted, and told us—entire strangers—to take them home and pick out what we required.

That opened a friendship with an extraordinary man. His influence on all who knew him was remarkable. Above all, he taught one human nature, in rather a Socratic manner, with wits sharpened by all the shady practices of life in dealing and cheating, of which he had a withering contempt; he was the most absolutely honest and straight man that I ever met. His shop was piled with old instruments, books, furniture, pictures and antiquities; while a tempting workshop and lathe were in his back premises.

The place was a centre which all sorts of people frequented, drawn there by his shrewd sayings, his love of music and chess, and his considerable judgment of painting. He had always spent his spare hours, when in London, at the National Gallery, and had a sound taste. Blake was one of his idols, and he was not unlike him in some respects; there was much of the same kind of genuineness in both. His mainstay in life was cataloguing for auctioneers and attending sales. He had been used, as a little boy at Dover, to help in smuggling in the jewels for Queen Victoria's new crown, an innocent child who could run to and fro unsuspected.

I used to walk over to Riley once a week from Bromley, and when I began exhibiting antiquities in London he became my door-keeper and was my right hand in all the work. He revelled in the new discoveries, and used to show people round, enthusiastically. It was perhaps the greatest pleasure he could have had in life, to enter into the work of enterprise, and feel how much he shared in it. He taught me more of the world than anyone else.

I got a little insight on examinations by clerking for

a sub-examiner, to whom papers were sub-let at so much a hundred. The subject was geometry, and I proposed to simplify his work by making tracings of the right construction to be laid over the answer; if it did not fit, then, plucking was inevitable in a few seconds. After a batch done, he was told by the nominal examiner that he was assessing "like a father," and accordingly all later papers were rated much lower. I was enlightened.

Turning now to the influences on my father's side, there was a tradition of management and organization, his father and grandfather having been Commissary-Generals in the army. They were stubbornly incorrupt Presbyterians, and kept down the customary waste. They knew that "every army marches on its stomach," and my great-grandfather kept up the transport and supplies in the Napoleonic wars on the Spanish and Italian side. He left innumerable sketches and water-colours made in the Peninsula.

My grandfather was sent out to Brussels to wind up the accounts of the Waterloo campaign, which kept him there till 1817, when he married a daughter of the deceased goldsmith and banker, Henry Mitton, a former partner of Sir Richard Glyn. During a few years of peace in England, they were settled at King's Langley, where my father was born. After that, my grandfather was sent to the Cape; there he had to manage the material for the Caffre War. His family grew up there, the boys having a long ride into Capetown daily for school. This gave my father a hot-country disregard of English habits, which passed on to me, and served me well in the desert. Some facility in handling men and materials may also have come from the business ways of the older generations. But there were no

stories of family life and doings from that side, as my
father was singularly out of touch with relatives, owing
to his early life at the Cape. He never remembered
how many aunts he had or who they were; all that I
learned otherwise.

After loitering in Italy and on the Rhine, the family
came on to England for education, when my grandfather died suddenly. My father had started on medi-
cine, but methods in 1844 seemed so irrational and
unsatisfactory that he dropped it. As his brother said,
"William would rather stay out in the rain than shelter in an imperfect house." He had a longing for finding perfection, and for spending time in seeking it,
which always hindered success in a world of compro-
mise. He had done chemistry at King's College under
Daniel, and when the railway mania of 1847 was rag-
ing he turned to surveying.

His party were kept out in the open, surveying all
day, and then plied with hot coffee all night to keep
them awake to do the plotting, just getting an hour or
two on a sofa for sleep. Such was the race to get plans
completed in time for the day of final entry of Bills
before the Session. When the day came, unfinished
drawings or blank sheets were sent in, and later visits
"to compare plans," with a tip to the custodian, enabled the completed sheets to be substituted before
the Bill came up to the Parliamentary Committee.

When that fever was over, he turned to his old interest in electric lighting, and generating current by
rotating magnets. The work with a large battery
reached the practical stage of brilliant arc light on the
steps of the National Gallery, lighting all down White-
hall, and also on Hungerford Bridge. But the company
promoters who exploited the scientific work came to

grief, and nothing was seen of electric light till, over twenty years later, we had "twinkle, twinkle little arc; ugly, dull, expensive spark." In disgust at mis-handling of the business, my father, when he married, turned off to chemical engineering. From all this I gleaned much in long talks with him on all kinds of chemical and physical questions, schemes and speculations, and for twenty years soaked in all he had to tell. He was a literalist in his beliefs, and sought his longed-for perfection in primitive Christianity, certainly the reasonable course.

It was only natural, in a world so rapidly changing in knowledge and outlook, that each generation should see matters in a different light as time went on. As I am neither a Butler nor a Gosse, more need not be said on this score. I delayed writing *Egypt and Israel* till after his death.

A new stir arose when one day I brought back from Smith's bookstall, in 1866, a volume by Piazzi Smyth, *Our Inheritance in the Great Pyramid*. The views, in conjunction with his old friendship for the author, strongly attracted my father, and for some years I was urged on in what seemed so enticing a field of coincidence. I little thought how, fifteen years later, I should reach the "ugly little fact which killed the beautiful theory"; but it was this interest which led my father to encourage me to go out and do the survey of the Great Pyramid; of that, later on.

Stimulated by a bit of earthwork on Blackheath Common, where we lived, I made myself a working sextant with cardboard and looking-glass, and then my father let me have his sextant, and I began planning earthworks. In pursuing this, I followed a plotting process more accurate than had been used before, with three-point survey. The detail of this I published long afterwards in *Methods and Aims in Archaeology*.

At the age of twenty-two, I started off on long survey tramps of a month at a time, spring and autumn, working over a district to survey the earthworks and stone circles. I thus rolled up over a hundred and fifty plans of sites about the south of England. These are still the only plans of much of the remains, and I gave copies of the earlier ones to the British Museum Library. When settling a route, I got up all the county histories and marked the one-inch ordnance maps with everything which should be searched. The way was then arranged so as to take twenty miles a day, and end at some village where I could sleep. I started as soon in the morning as the village shop opened, laying in a stock of bread and cheese and some cake or fruit, then tramped till breakfast could be enjoyed with a good view, took another snack after noon, sometimes while walking, and then hunted up quarters at sunset, retiring to the church porch to eat my supper.

I used to spend five shillings and sixpence a week on food, and beds cost about double that. I learned the land and the people all over the south of England, usually sleeping in a cottage if I could find room, as the beery inn was loathsome. All this was the best training for a desert life afterwards. In those weeks I have seen barn-floor threshing with flails at Keston, and slept in a room at Cranbourne Chase which had not even an iron nail in it, all wood to the latch on the door.

From fifteen onward, I used to be wandering over the British Museum, in all departments open to me, usually once a week, till I knew it by heart. In those days all the upstairs Egyptian collections were housed in one room, and all the minerals in two rooms. Another attraction at that time, and for a dozen years after, was Sotheby's sale of coins and antiquities, and that gave a wide field for observation, and for noting the chances of forgery reflected in the prices.

I early began to nibble, with only a few shillings. Then, through a friend of ours, I had an introduction to Professor Donaldson, and saw some of his collection of architectural coins, in the oppressive gloom of a dark Bloomsbury room. He, seeing I was in earnest, gave me an introduction to the British Museum Medal Room, where I saw the august figure of Vaux, and was much encouraged by finding that some of my more puzzling coins were also new in that sanctuary. I took up more, and more were wanted. So I was asked if I would offer up the novelties—all ugly copper, for I could not aspire to silver—and to my delight five pounds was my return. I was thus launched on jackalling for the Coin Room, which was badly off in Imperial Greek and Byzantine. I was attracted to the out-of-the-way late Greek, as reflecting the condition of the fringes of civilization; the Crimea, Mesopotamia, Bactria, and that gorgeous name of Attambelos, King of Characene, fascinated me, as much as the remote tales of Herodotos.

I found that any large mixed lot of Greek coins, which had not been picked over closely, would contain enough prizes to pay for the lot; my last haul had in it the almost unique coin of Irene. With hardly any pocket-money to rely on, I managed to roll up a couple of thousand representative coins of all the countries, interpreted by the kindly help always granted in the Coin Room. This miscellaneous observation learnt thus has been of much use later.

Another line of work that seemed promising was the ascertaining of standards of measure which had been used, by comparing the dimensions of ancient buildings. For this, books of reference were essential, and as soon as I was of age and the British Museum Library was open to me, I collected all the measurements of buildings that were to be had. Such are generally unsatisfactory material, as being often taken at wrong parts, incomplete, and not very exact. A better resource, as far as England was concerned, lay in measuring the buildings myself, and many churches were worked over, to this end. The results of second-hand material were but tentative; by the age of twenty-four I had gathered enough to make up something like a general review of the subject, which my father then helped me to publish, as *Inductive Metrology*. Better materials have since superseded part of it.

The results are still often useful, however, in support of later conclusions; as, for instance, in the Byblos foot, recently obtained from a sarcophagus, agreeing with various examples of the Phoenician foot from my work fifty years earlier. The principle had not been regularly used before, and it is a sound means of advance, especially when accurate measurements can be made of parts likely to be controlled by measurement. The subject attracted some anthropologists, as E. B. Tylor and others.

In a different direction, I was preparing for Egyptian research. My father had intended to work at the Great Pyramid, and make accurate measurements, so I was arranging all the apparatus. We had a rare chance of getting a ten-inch theodolite by Gambay, which read by verniers to three seconds, and had an average error of 0.8 second in practice. My father de-

signed a steel standard scale of 100 inches, with zinc
thermometer, for invar was not yet invented. The
needful hand measures of all lengths I graduated from
our standard. A badly regulated five-inch theodolite I
adjusted till it was better than Troughton's. The reading arrangements for the Gambay I re-modelled by
adding efficient microscopes, and had by this time become quite familiar with the mechanical details of
instruments, questions of colour and amount of light
for readings, of average of estimation, and all the col-
laterals of work.

Just then Lord Rosse advertised for an observatory
assistant, and as I knew Brünnow's *Spherical Astron-
omy* pretty well, I ventured to think of switching on
to that line of work. I applied, was interviewed, and
without any further detail was asked if I had a degree
in Science. As I had not, the matter ended. The next
time Rosse and I met, we walked up together to receive honorary degrees at Cambridge.

I had a preliminary canter at accurate surveying
with my father at Stonehenge in 1872, and designed
for that a new steel chain which had very long links
and rhombic eyes. Hearing that the Society of Antiquaries were going to have a series of surveys of stone
monuments, I offered my plan, but it was refused on
the ground that the scale did not suit the series. Some
years later, after I had got well on my feet without any
help, St. John Hope met me, and remarked, "I don't
see why you should not be one of *us*," in a way that
made one reply, "I do not see why I should." My
Stonehenge plan is now adopted in the work carried
on by the Society.

When the plans of earthworks of my first season
were ready, in 1875, they were shown at the Archaeo-

logical Institute, and thus began my friendship with Flaxman Spurrell. He was a young doctor, devoted to archaeology, and when he found that my motive was study without regard for credit or cash, he joined me and had a voice and a hand in almost all I did. He so much disliked the personal working of most societies, and had such a contempt for the seeking of advantages, that he hardly ever took part in public things.

Where he felt confidence however, there could not be anyone more generous with his help. Suggestions and warnings he would give, stimulating one's work. With whole-hearted diligence, he helped my exhibitions of results from Egypt until 1896, working out various questions. To my deep regret his health, and unhappy melancholy, retired him to Norfolk, and only rarely did he appear for an hour or two and then withdraw again. I tried much to persuade him to join me in Egypt, but never succeeded. He was almost the only man with whom I was ever familiar, and I owe him more than I can tell.

There was yet another influence which must not be omitted. My grandfather Flinders had a favourite sister, closely kin to all his feelings. Somewhat of the family affection descended to the grandchildren of both, myself and my cousins the Harveys. Though the four little ladies were from twenty to thirty years older than me, I was very intimate with them, and especially with Susan, the youngest. Their cottage in Surrey was a restful haven of quiet, and in delightful taste, lined with fine engravings—the choice of their father, who himself engraved. The scientific and historical interests which I had at home were widened by the artistic feeling and knowledge of my cousins. Susan Harvey was one of three good women with whom I was mentally intimate in my youth, and who each supplied a different point of view. There is hardly anything that can be as helpful in forming perceptions as such companionships; the memory of them is holy ground in after life.

At last, as my father's affairs in helping other folks always put off his own preparations for Egypt, it seemed needful for me to make the first move, so in 1880 my start was made, at the age of twenty-seven, and my father was to follow in a couple of months. He never came. His undertakings at home always stood in the way. A quiet life of research was congenial to me; in a letter to Spurrell in July, 1879, I wrote: "I abhor all ceremonies and festivities, and all concourses of people; I want to be *doing*, instead of being and suffering. I would rather do a week's hard work than assist in a day's pleasure."

Looking back, I can now see how much I owed to my forbears; partly derived from my grandfather Petrie's handling of men and material, and his love of drawing; from my great-grandfather Mitton's business ways and banking; from three generations of Flinders surgeons' love of patching up bodies; from my grandfather Flinders' exquisitely precise surveys and his firm hold on his men; from my father's engineering, chemistry and draughtsmanship; from my mother's love of history and knowledge of minerals.

I had but a portion of all this, no match for the professional abilities which went before me. Yet the mixture was what was wanted for the work which was set for me to do in life. Not a single aptitude inherited, or a single year of the varied picking up of knowledge, was a waste. Any success in work was not due to myself, but to reflecting my ancestors. To them be the praise. "Poets are born and not made," and this is true, in the widest sense, of all *poiesis;* whatever anyone can originate is a faculty born with him, to which events can only give facility.

The state of affairs into which I emerged was in great transition. The recognition of flint implements had been the battle during my boyhood, and they were at last accepted. Layard and Newton and Schliemann had begun to dig up great things, but the observation of the small things, universal at present, had never been attempted. There was only a single plate of pottery published by Lepsius in the *Denkmäler,* and that was almost entirely wrong in dating. Dr. Birch, of the British Museum, begged me to bring a box full of pottery from each of the great sites, as, knowing somewhat of the history, a clue to its age might be found. He did not know the date of any beads, whether they were early or late, and asked for any evidence.

The science of observation, of registration, of recording, was yet unthought of; nothing had a meaning unless it were an inscription or a sculpture. A year's work in Egypt made me feel it was like a house on fire, so rapid was the destruction going on. My duty was that of a salvage man, to get all I could, quickly gathered in, and then when I was sixty I would sit down and write it up. That was a true forecast. Two months after I was that age, the War broke out, I was not allowed to take any part abroad, but was ordered to stick to my post at the University. Until then I could only write up the annual volumes of discoveries. During the War, however, I could do as I had planned, and begin to write up the results of observing and collecting, in the series of catalogue volumes, with discussions of dating, which is still in progress.

## CHAPTER II

## THE PYRAMIDS

At last I started off from Liverpool on a Moss liner, at the end of November, 1880. All my instruments and stores were on board safely. The weather was a horrid gale blowing up the Irish Channel, and I slept on the engine gratings behind the spray shields, as I was too ill to go below; I could not even touch a drop of water for nearly two days. By the third day the times were better, and with a box sextant I got out the latitude within 3′ of the captain's reckoning. The usual sights on the way were all new to me, and we landed at Alexandria on December 14.

By dint of hustle the boxes were all unloaded, through Customs, with instruments duty free, by order of Mr. Caillard; then up to Cairo, making friends with Dr. Grant, getting hold of Aly Gabry through him, getting boxes from the station, and finally settling in to Waynman Dixon's rock-tomb at the Gizeh pyramids, all within a week from landing. In all the intervals of the business I had rambles over the outskirts of Alexandria and much of Cairo.

Though I only had a very slight introduction to Dr. Grant, he and Mrs. Grant received me with the greatest kindness, and made me free of their house, so that for years it was my place of call in Cairo. In those days there was a relic of Muhammed Aly's times in a little French place, the Hôtel d'Orient, near the station. A bedroom at three francs, and feeding picked up at restaurants for five francs a day, were then possible in Cairo.

My position was that of independence of Mariette and the Antiquity Department. I was merely staying at the pyramids on an order from the Prefect of Police, and doing surface work of planning without any digging. For one season, the laying out of the triangulation, and getting fixed points marked all over the pyramid sites, was as much as I could manage, along with measurements of the inside of the pyramids.

Aly Gabry was a valuable helper; he had been a basket-boy in Howard Vyse's excavations of 1837, and served Piazzi Smyth and Waynman Dixon. He was very intelligent, and knew everything about the pyramid hill, and what had been done there; with much good feeling and manner, he was an excellent companion in all my work. As he was regularly in my pay, I was free of the place, and no guides or clamours for *bakhshish* ever disturbed me. Usually, measurements inside the pyramid were begun after the tourists had left at sunset, and continued till midnight so as to be undisturbed.

It was often most convenient to strip entirely for work, owing to the heat and absence of any current of air, in the interior. For outside work in the hot weather, vest and pants were suitable, and if pink they kept the tourist at bay, as the creature seemed to him too queer for inspection. After rigging up the rock-tomb with shelves, and re-making the old shutters and door, which had been left by Dixon, I found the place comfortable. The petroleum stove by the door cooked my meals, which I prepared at any time required by the irregular hours of work.

When the big theodolite was out, it was needful to

MY TOMB AT THE PYRAMIDS

THE SECOND PYRAMID AND GRANITE TEMPLE

finish a stretch of observing within the day, which left only time for a morning and evening feed, and I always reduced the observations every night. On days when work lay inside the pyramid, the morning was spent in writing up observations, and the hours of interior measurement ran from about five till midnight. A negro slave of Aly, and a little nephew of his, used to sleep in the next tomb, as night guard.

A notable figure in Egyptian matters was the Rev. Greville Chester, who was out that year for his thirty-eighth visit to Egypt, so he must have begun almost in the days of Vyse. He needed to winter in the East for his health and he went all over the Syrian coast and Egypt, picking up antiquities, and supplying the British Museum and many private collectors. He became my firm friend, till his death in 1892.

A striking man in many ways, his strong preferences and objections and his outspoken manner brought Dr. Johnson to mind. He felt for the fellahin and hated Ismail and his doings. He had many amusing ways of securing things; when he bought the throne of Hatshepsut for Jesse Haworth (since presented to the British Museum), he was having it carried along the narrow path by the river at Luqsor, and the bearers of the box held up Grébaut, who had to let them pass. The Greek consular seal was a valued protection, which no Egyptian official dared break for fear of diplomatic consequences. I never used such surreptitious help myself, as all I found was pledged to be shown to the Department under whose permit I worked, and the bought things were always passed by Maspero, unless so important that he required them.

The beginning of the survey of the Gizeh pyramids was the selection of points which should be in sight of each other and form good triangles. A single large triangle could just be arranged to encompass the Great Pyramid, and another around the second pyramid, so avoiding reliance on any chain of triangles. After securing positions, and putting down rock-drilled station marks, so placed that it was possible to get the head into positions for observing, the scheme of relative values of the stations had to be planned.

Some were far more important than others, and required therefore many more observations taken from them.   After assigning the number of observations to each point from each centre, they had to be woven together in such order as to detect any possible shift of the instrument. Thus the note-books were prepared in this fashion: From D observe A B C E, A B C E F, B C E F G, B E F G, B E F G H, E F G H, &c. If any shift was suspected, due to a flick of the finger or too rapid rotation of the telescope, the averages of all points before, and of all points after, were taken. If shift was proved, then the observations were treated as two independent sets.

First thing in the morning, I had to put up the signals over the stations for the day, which took two or three hours, often walking a quarter of a mile to and fro to arrange visibility against a background. Then the theodolite was set up, and Aly held a large screen over it, as the sun must never shine on the circle, to expand it unequally. The telescope I had guarded by a cork coating. Then observing went on continuously, according to plan, with four microscope readings each time.

It was often difficult to get into position, when perched on the top of a wall, or edge of a pyramid, yet needing to read on all sides of the circle. A set round one centre was always done in the day, and then in the dusk I ran round and collected all the signals. Choosing good days, with cool air, but no wind, the whole of the network of triangles was completed in the first season. All readings were reduced in the evening, so as to see that nothing was wrong or misunderstood.

My position was expressed in a letter to Spurrell, some months before I went out. "So much has been lost through not allowing for the possibility of a higher value existing—whether in accuracy of construction, or in care and regularity of dimensions—or by digging barrows over by the spadeful anyhow—that a radical change is required in the way of doing all such things, and I do not wish to rest until whatever care may have been bestowed on ancient work is brought to light. This is almost universally misunderstood, and I am accustomed to be accused of trying to find something that never existed, though a gold digger is not thought foolish for washing a pan of earth on the thousandth of a chance of finding a nugget. He does not expect it, but takes the only means of finding it, if it is there. So do I."

Besides the survey and measurements in the pyramids, the methods of construction were also examined. The sawing of the granite sarcophagi and the hollowing out by tube drilling were an entire surprise. The tube drill hole, with core still in it, is a perfect demonstration of the instrument, yet there are authors who vainly imagine that iron tools were used for such work. Facing plates were used to test flatness, as proved by the spots of ochre on the prominences of dressed work. Another result which contradicts modern theories was the finding of sunk surfaces all over the deep trenches east of the pyramid; this proves that they were lined with blocks of fine stone, and such a lining, of the usual thickness of blocks, would reduce the trench to a narrow passage, which could not contain a funeral barque.

While I was at Gizeh, workmen were sent to remove broken stone from the pyramid for road mending, this brought to light again the great casing stones found in position by Howard Vyse, and a large number of fragments of casing, from which I preserved those which showed the angle. From many of these together, a useful mean value of the angle could be ascertained for each of the pyramids. Of minor interest were the graffiti of visitors, of which over sixty were found to be earlier than 1700.

"Mariette is having some excavations made near the Sphinx, and the workmen are filling up all the clearing which cost so much to make on both sides of the Sphinx, in fact covering it up again; this, absurd as it seems, is all of a piece with the style of excavating here. Rubbish is always thrown over the nearest handy place, quite irrespective of whether it may be in the way or not, or what it may cover. I should like to have £100,000 to shoot all the sand and stuff off the pyramid hill into the plain below, and leave the thousands of tombs all clear and bare, instead of having ten or twenty feet of rubbish over all the surface, to be dug and cut about, every time a hole is made.

"I hear that Mariette most rascally blasted to pieces all the fallen parts of the granite temple by a large gang of soldiers, to clear it out instead of lifting the stones and replacing them by means of tackle. The savage indifference of the Arabs, who have even stripped the alabaster off the granite temple since Mariette uncovered it, and who are not at all watched here, is partly superseded by a most barbaric sort of regard for the monuments by those in power. Nothing seems to be done with any uniform and regular plan, work is begun and left unfinished; no regard is paid to future requirements of exploration, and no civilised or labour-saving appliances are used. It is sickening to see the rate at which everything is being destroyed, and the little regard paid to preservation."

Later, I saw excavations going on in front of the Sphinx. The men had dug down about fifteen feet to the bottom of a funnel pit of running sand. They filled baskets, with which children very slowly toiled up the sand slope, while more sand ran down from the top, to be carried up again. Not a twentieth of the labour was utilised.

A man was employed by Brugsch Bey to dig in the ruins of the Khafra temple for pieces of diorite statues; but the digger usually sold his finds to tourists, at about a halfpenny each. I heard, however, that almost enough pieces had been secured to build up a figure; no such restoration has appeared in the Museum. When inscribed stones were found in the Museum work, I copied them as soon as possible, as they soon vanished, being stolen for building; tomb after tomb and the small pyramids had fine stone linings—often carved—ripped out to build the Arab village.

All the winter I was in correspondence with Dr. Birch about matters which he desired. Visits from General Pitt-Rivers, Mr. Loftie, and Major Frazer, an Indian engineer, were useful for discussing detail of evidences and workmanship. General Stone, an old Confederate officer then in the Egyptian army, gave useful advice and backing. Above all there was Dr. Grant, who cared for my health, and sometimes came out for a night of work at the Great Pyramid. We went in and examined the chambers of construction, and I had a terrifying time when he fainted in the well; to raise a very heavy man, barely conscious, up a shaft of seventy feet with scanty foothold, when at any moment he might sweep me away down to the bottom, was a risk not to be forgotten. The pyramid theorists were a continual amusement to the Grants and myself; one of them tried to file down the granite boss in the ante-chamber to the size required for the theory.

By October 3, 1881, I was on the way again, getting a morning at the Louvre. "One is irritated by the great quantity of restorations; so frequent are they that nearly every label has a long list of them, which one needs to read through before one can begin to consider the statue. Everything—chronology, subject, and style —is made subservient to effect and appearance. It is all very fine to stare at, but for study it is spoilt. In the Egyptian department effect is everything, and figures of every period are all jumbled together, so that it is impossible to find what one wants."

On board I met Mahmud Bey, the astronomer, who was interested in the pyramid triangulation. Colonel Haig, of the Indian Survey, was also there and we had many talks over the theory of instruments. On reaching Cairo I had an interview with Maspero, who had succeeded Mariette earlier in the year. He was friendly to my survey and offered to put me nominally into his employ, so that I could work under his licence, but my permit was only made out for the first and second pyramids. "Saw Maspero, who was as polite and pleasant as before. I told him what had been done and found, and then asked to have my permission extended to the other pyramids here, which he immediately granted, saying, 'We thought it better to give an order for the two large pyramids first.' This showed, I think, that it was Brugsch's doing, for Maspero's written order to B. (as I saw) was to give me permit for *everything* in my letter, and keep my letter *as evidence of what was permitted*.

"I also mentioned about the Museum man being of no use, and Maspero did not even know who he was, but asked B. who falsely told him that he was a brother of the Sheykh (he is really a son of a *reis*) , and so then M. said, if that was the case, perhaps it would make too much ill-feeling to displace him now. Aly tells me that only a portion of the ten piastres a day goes to the man, and he has to hand over the lion's share to Brugsch or his people."

Some foolish remarks were published in England, and I wrote home thus: "As far as I have had to do with natives, I find that, though desperate beggars to strangers, if they once find you perfectly firm and yet kindly and jocular, they immediately settle down as good friends, and never bother you again. I am simply disgusted with the brutal tone I have seen adopted toward them by travellers. When they are troublesome, quiet obstinacy and a refusal to accept any proffered assistance, with—if possible—a joke against them, I have always found will carry the day.

"At Thebes, where I was not then known and had no connection with them, as here at Gizeh, I was not bothered by anyone twice; the second time they saw me, after a half-laughing attempt, they would leave off at the first refusal. Here there is not a man on the pyramid hill but what salutes me whenever he sees me, and many shake hands, though I have never given them a farthing. It is to the unmitigated European, who shows them that he despises everything about them, that they have a dislike; the smallest entering into their ways pleases them immensely; only sit squat, return the proper replies to the salutations, catch their tricks of manner, and imitate their voice, and they will laugh heartily and treat you as a friend."

The soldiery were getting out of hand in 1881, and while I was strolling round by the tombs of the Khalifehs a guard party arrested me on the ground that I was near a magazine. They searched me, and took forty sovereigns which I had in my pocket; a carriage was near by with a Greek and a Copt who saw the robbery. After long to and fro in Cairo with Consul and officials, they required me to identify the men; they ranked up thirty men in a row, with their backs to low windows so that it was difficult to see them, but I identified those who were at that post.

Then on trial I demanded to put questions, and framed such as turned on their false statements. After the first man had replied, the second came on and he contradicted the first, whereupon his officer leaned forward, hissed him down, and told him what to say. It being thus hopeless to get justice, I told the official interpreter to say that such conduct was not that of a court of justice, and it was useless to expect redress. There the case dropped, without restitution. There was much indignation among English residents, and two told me that they had been held up in lonely streets by soldiers demanding money.

All that winter of 1881-2 I used to hear, each time I went into Cairo, that people doubted if they would be there next week, a flight to Alexandria was expected. I reckoned that, if Cairo became too unsafe for transit, I could walk down to Alexandria in a week, going by night in the desert, and having Aly with me to get supplies from villages by day. However the crisis did not come on till three months after I had left. The real ferment of the military trouble was due to the *harim* left behind by Ismail; in order to be rid of them, Tewfik married them off to army officers; as he said one day, "I have had a long morning's work, marrying off eighty of my father's wives." These women, accustomed to intrigue and luxury, stirred up the officers to asserting their power.

The pyramid work of the second season was mainly in clearing pits through the chips which flanked the sides of the Great Pyramid, and tracing the trenches and pavement round it. For this, eighty-five holes were sunk and casing found on all sides, but not near the corners. These pits were risky, and in the deeper ones only negroes would agree to work. When casing or pavement was found, I had then to hang plumb-lines down the pit, go down and measure the distance of the line from the casing foot, and with theodolite fix the top of the plumb-line by my survey points. Just as I had finished one deep pit, making my way down, and up, very tenderly on the larger blocks, the whole caved in below my feet. It was always a chance of minutes or hours before a pit collapsed.

Around the Khafra pyramid and its walls, a hundred and eight holes were sunk in all, some clearing down to the casing and sockets; and others testing on the galleries of the workmen's barracks.

Round Menkaura's pyramid ninety-one holes were sunk, the corners being troublesome owing to deep sand with loose blocks. It was needful for me to arrange blocks in a ring round a hole so as to stay, and as the sand was removed they sank. All such work needed continual watching for safety, as no native could be trusted, being either frightened or rash, and not having the sense to see how to arrange for safety. With care, the five-inch theodolite, divided with vernier to one minute, was worked up to an average error of only four seconds, by estimating on several divisions, and it served for short distances instead of the ten-inch theodolite.

In the middle of the season, December 7 to January 18, I joined in a dahabiyeh with the Lofties, Sayce and various others. From January 18 to February 4 I was at Thebes, camping in the Ramesseum, partly with Tristram Ellis. Later, he stayed with me at Gizeh, and gave his engineering skill to help in the long levelling up and down the pyramid, and the raising of Khufu's sarcophagus so as to sight planes beneath it, for off-sets to fix the form. In all this, a skilled helper was essential as no native could hold a staff upright.

The only time I put my name on a monument, was when chalking on the bottom of the sarcophagus the date of raising it. Ellis put his name on the floor, before we let it down again; those may last a few thousand years. All work in the pyramid was unwholesome owing to the dust raised, which always produced feverish headache after a few hours of it. The inside of the Great Pyramid was also cleared, and the entrance passage opened down to the subterranean chamber, which was planned and levelled. It is a great example of rock-working, the ceiling being dressed flat and the walls begun, while the bulk of the rock was not touched, but only a pit sunk down to the intended floor level.

The pyramid Arabs are a colony of Tunisians who came in during the confusion of Napoleon's invasion, and they have always claimed the Bedawy exemption from conscription, which is hated by the fellah. Kitchener used this position when they came clamouring to be allowed to go and join the fight against the Italian occupation of Tunis. He at once agreed to their wish, adding "really you are such fine fellows for a fight that we must have you in the Egyptian army!" Not one left for Tunis. Another such case was when the Egyptian officers desired to join the Tunisians; Kitchener at once agreed, and asked how soon their regiments would be ready to start; the matter seemed completely settled, when he added, at the last, "of course we cannot leave Egypt unprotected, and your place will be taken here by British regiments." That was the end of Egyptian intervention.

The settlement of these Tunisians at the pyramids has been the destruction of countless tombs, as may be seen from the fine stone houses in the village, all built by ruining the ancient works. They present a united and organized front to the tourist, but after the last carriage had left in the late afternoon, there was a gathering at the north-east corner of the pyramid, in the shade, where the doings of the day and the proceeds of the plunder were discussed. Furious were the recriminations about getting extra bakhshish, and it used to take all the authority of old Abu Talib to repress the squabbles, which often amused me when measuring near there.

When in Cairo, one came in for curious news which never reached the papers. At one time a quantity of false Egyptian gold was put into circulation; it was made abroad, and imported under Consular seal, but so many and powerful were those who shared in the proceeds that I believe the matter was never prosecuted. A little later, two of the Khedivial princesses appeared at a masked ball *en garçon*, as pages; and two days after, I heard that the Khedive was enraged about the princesses, who were strictly immured, and an uncle who abetted them was imprisoned for five years in the citadel. Presumably he got out within five months, at the insurrection.

In those days there were still some archaic survivals. The P. & O. liner had all the passengers at one long Captain's table; not a course was removed till he rang his bell. The dining-saloon was lit with candles in glazed recesses along the sides; each candle backed into two cabins at the partition, and lit each cabin with one quarter of its light, quite enough to go to bed with.

When the time came for leaving, I took to Maspero everything of value which I had bought, for his choice, but he passed them all. He was not yet in train with the Customs authorities about allowing exportation, and told me of more than one instance in which things were sent to him that he did not in the least want for the Museum, and, on his saying so, he was rebuffed, and told that he was not to judge of that, but to keep everything. He recommended me to carry little things away in my pockets, and I asked about the relative safety of Alexandria and Suez Customs.

I was back in England by May 23, and settled down to preparing my material. The observations had been worked up day by day, or rather night by night, so as to check off any oversights of recording. The mean values of every angle of the triangulation were completed, and the task in England was to combine them in a final result. The reduction of Gill's survey in the transit of Venus expedition, I had done before leaving England. It was a matter of thirty-six simultaneous equations, which I worked in triplicate, one version with half values of co-efficients, the other with double values; by comparing these at each stage, any error was easily detected.

I was impressed by the blindness of the process; it was impossible to see whether the discrepancies were due to a single aberrant angle, or to the average error of all. I therefore carried out the reduction of my survey by a new graphic process. If an approximate triangulation is calculated, and all the differences of observations from it, around one point, are stated, then on plotting those differences of the actual lineal size on a reduced network plan, any small shift of the sheet of differences over the plan, either lineally or angularly, will correspond to a consistent shift of the whole of the observations around that point.

To carry this out simultaneously on a field of some twenty observation centres, twenty sheets of tracing paper would be too opaque. Sheets of ordinary paper were therefore pierced with a hole about two inches wide over each centre; over each hole a film of mica was fixed, and the traces drawn on it, so that the twenty sheets could be seen through at once. Then, by tags left on the edge of each sheet, it could be shifted lineally or in azimuth, and all its observed traces watched to see how they stood to all the traces on the other sheets, the tags of which were meanwhile pinned down.

Thus gradually, step by step, the sheets could be shifted about, one after another, until the traces were brought into the nearest coincidence. Each trace of observation was a band of the width of the probable error, so that the adjustment could take account of that, and give each trace its respective value in adjustment. When the best result was reached, then, laying this over the approximate network, the differences of the observations could be read off, and applied to correcting the places in the first net. That corrected net was then calculated, and the variation of the observations from it was finally stated. For the principal points, the resulting variations were drawn on pl. xvi of *Pyramids and Temples,* of the actual size that they were on the ground around the pyramid. It was then seen that there is seldom a tenth of an inch of uncertainty in the final results.

The principal result of the survey was to show that the casing did not slope down to the pavement above the corner sockets, but sloped down to the floors of the sockets, and the pavement was laid over it there. The base of the pyramid at the pavement was therefore much less than the distances between the outer sides of the rock sockets. Therefore instead of a pyramid measuring 9,140 inches, as was supposed, it measured only 9,069 inches.

Hence all theorizing about the days in the year being represented was entirely erroneous. The size of the pyramid was ruled by being 7 × 40 Egyptian cubits (20.6 inches) high and 11 × 40 cubits wide. This is strongly confirmed by the size of the pyramid of Meydum, which preceded it in date, being 7 × 25 cubits high, and 11 × 25 cubits wide; it shows the use of the same system of a large number of cubits, 25 or 40, as a unit, multiplied by 7 and 11 for the dimensions. The angle of the slope required for this 7 and 11 proportion is within the small uncertainty (two minutes) of the actual remains.

The theories as to the size of the pyramid are thus proved entirely impossible, and this is confirmed by later details of survey made by the Egyptian Govern-

ment. The fantastic theories, however, are still poured
out, and the theorists still assert that the facts correspond to their requirements. It is useless to state the
real truth of the matter, as it has no effect on those
who are subject to this type of hallucination. They can
but be left with the flat earth believers and other such
people to whom a theory is dearer than a fact.

Besides the survey, other subjects were examined,
such as the length of the cubit given by various monuments, the mechanical methods of sawing and tubular
drilling by hard stone points, the history of the destructions of the pyramids, and the nature of probable
error as a multiple of the quantity, not a term. Just as
I had finished the manuscript, I heard that the Royal
Society had made a grant of £100 for the expense of a
survey by the Royal Engineers. I wrote saying that the
survey was already done, and asked if it might be inspected. Francis Galton was directed to report on it; I
went up to show it to him. In due course I was told it
was considered sound work, and I should have a grant
of £100 to pay for the publication. Thus, I found by
the time I was thirty that my work would be accepted.
This brought about a friendship with Francis Galton
which lasted till his death; his stay at our excavation
camp at Abydos was a most charming time, which I
always remember with pleasure.

Beside all the work on the pyramid survey, I had
begun to collect and observe the small antiquities; as
I wrote: "I begin to suspect that the varieties of glazes
and fashions in Egyptian work changed rapidly and
clearly; and that by having sufficient examples we may
be able to pin down the changes, so that the mere look
of a thing may fix its age within a few reigns."

That summer I heard of the work of Naville for the

Egypt Exploration Fund, and inquired if there was an opening for me. All the management was against me, including Miss Edwards, as I heard later. But Erasmus Wilson, who was supporting the Fund, had seen my Pyramid book, and insisted that I should be given an opportunity. At last my working (gratis) for the Fund was settled, and I wrote to Miss Edwards, on October 27, 1883: "The prospect of excavating in Egypt is a most fascinating one to me, and I hope the results may justify my undertaking such a work. I believe the true line lies as much in the careful noting and comparison of small details, as in more wholesale and off-hand clearances."

## CHAPTER III

## IN THE DELTA

On November 6, 1883, I started with definite instructions to take a boat along the Wady Tumilat for examining sites, and then to begin excavations at Tanis. On the way, direction was to be gathered from Maspero in Paris and Naville at Geneva. I was also to see Lanzone at Turin. At Venice I had a morning and copied all the graffiti in the square of the palace, also noting "the two globes in the council chamber, which are about six feet in diameter, and were drawn in 1630. The terrestrial shows Central Africa all filled duly with the various rivers, not an unknown waste, and the equatorial lakes are put in. Australia is much out of shape, and not marked definitely, but it is separated from Tasmania . . . both globes are made of a mass of black-letter sheets, about one-sixth of an inch thick, being perhaps twenty or thirty leaves glued together. What were they? The globes are now worth more than the chance of discovery in such a heap of print.

"The trireme galleys, in the pictures which were contemporary with them, are all shown as having three oars coming out of one hole side by side. The great seated lion at the Arsenal, about eight feet high, with a long Runic inscription winding up and down his sides . . . is the most impressive thing, for nobility of original work, and for the strange added interest of the inscription, that I saw in Venice."

At Cairo, the smallest dahabiyeh that was to be had

was far too large for me, and I asked Corbett if he
would like a trip. He could not go, but put me in
touch with the Amos's who were seeking a change.
They came on with me through the Wady Tumilat to
Ismailiya; this made an intimacy which lasted through
their lives. He was a charming philosophic Radical,
and she an ardent fighter for causes—people with
whom one could completely enjoy a difference, and
each like the other the better for it.

Their house made a second home for me when in
Cairo, beside Dr. Grant's, and Mrs. Amos took care
of me, ill or well, with the greatest kindness. At their
house I met many interesting people, Cookson, Colonel Watson, Edgar Vincent, Scott-Moncrieff, and Captain Speedy. The last named had been long in Abys-
sinia, and was a marvellous talker—almost actor, in his
mimicry and detailed descriptions.

Beside prospecting on sites in the Wady Tumilat,
there was another search to be made on the west, for
the origin of an archaic Greek figure which I had
bought in Cairo. In spite of a feverish cold, some long
days' tramps by Desuk, Teh el Barud and Damanhur
at last brought me to a site where "the whole ground
is thick with early Greek pottery, and it seemed almost
a sacrilege to walk over the heaps with the fine lustrous
black ware crunching under one's boots. Pieces with
fret pattern, honeysuckle pattern, heads, arms, legs of
figures, horses, and such-like lovely things were soon
picked up. It seemed as if I were wandering in the
smashings of the Museum vase-rooms. Such a half hour
I never had before." Nothing more could be done that
season, with other engagements fixed. The next year,
on settling there, the first day brought to light a decree

ΗΠΟΛΙΣΗΝΑΥΚΡΑΤΙ˙
ΗΛΙΟΔΩΡΟΝΔΩΡΙΩΝΟΣΦΙΛΟ
ΤΟΝΙΕΡΕΑΤΗΣΑΘΗΝΑΣΔΙΑΒΙΟ
ΣΥΓΓΡΑΦΟΦΥΛΑΚΑΑΡΕΤΗΣΚΑΙ
ΕΝΕΚΑΤΗΣΕΙΣΑΥΤΗΝ

THE DISCOVERY OF NAUKRATIS

STATUETTE WHICH LED TO FINDING THE SITE
INSCRIPTION WHICH GAVE THE NAME

of the people of Naukratis, and a problem which had troubled scholars for half a century was settled.

I had, however, to pay for this tramp by a week's illness at the Amos's. The station-master at Teh el Barud was obliging, and let me sleep in the station; "he remarked that it was great trouble to go about in that way from place to place with all the things; and then asked if I were doing it for Government. No, for an English Society. And how much do you get? Nothing, I do it because I like it, and if I were rich, I should do it all the same for myself. But, do you expect to have anything afterwards, he asked, unable to believe in my motives. No; well then he dropped that.

"When I returned, he told me about a marvellous gold ring found at Naukratis, and a file which had on one side writing that was to draw fish out of the water. Also about Eshmuneyn, a very rich place for antiquities, and that a Copt there can get at the treasure, when he wishes, by going to the top of the hill at 12 noon, on Fridays (when all good believers are at mosque); that he calls, and a door is open for only about five minutes, and he goes in and takes as much gold coin as he can, large gold pieces, and that once the door shut quickly and cut his heel; yes, true, the station-master saw the wound, and he is now a very rich man by all this gold."

A private letter to Spurrell, the most intimate friend I ever had, came back into my hands after his death, and as an account of motives I may perhaps quote it. This was written when I had time to think over life, alone on a boat, "between Tell el Kebir and Zagazig, December 20, 1883. . . . Now pardon my noticing what you have not written to *me*, but as you seem to be under a misapprehension I must try to remove it.

You seem to take for granted that as I am not working for money [I received nothing from the Exploration Fund] I must therefore be working for fame: fame of some sort—present or future—miscellaneous or select. But would you be surprised to hear that this is not my mainspring? No, it is not. I work because I can do what I am doing, better than I can do anything else, in comparison with the way other people do things. I enjoy it because I know that my time produces more result in this way than in any other, and I am aware that such work is what I am best fitted for.

"The work ought to be done, and I may fairly say I believe that at present there is no one else who will do what I am now doing; hence I delight in doing it. If credit of any sort comes from such work (whether of this trip, of Pyramid work, or of any other that I have done) I have no objection of any sort to it, on the contrary it is very pleasant, but it is not what stirs me to work at all. I believe that I should do just the same in quantity and quality if all that I did was published in someone else's name. The only motive you mention that influences me at present is the idea that I may do more in an easier-going twenty years than in an active ten years; and this I had already before me, and but for it I should be far more extravagant of risks than I at present am. I consider that I am timorously careful in many ways, just because if I do not do the work myself it may have to wait before anyone else will have the time to take it in hand. . . . If *you* do not realise my motives, who will?"

Knowing Dr. Grant, who was physician to the Khedive, and to the railways, I heard many curious things about the days of Ismail. The Ezbekiyeh was a dusty waste, dotted with Greek drink-shops; Ismail designed to make the gardens, but the Greeks would not be bought out. One night a shop took fire, the next night four were burnt, so they all gave way next day and cleared off. Ismail was fond of driving furiously, and when tram lines were put down, he soon caught his wheel in the rail and was spilt. Next day all tram lines were taken up, and Cairo did without trams for years. There was a younger brother in the Khedivial family who was thought undesirable; so when he went to Alexandria, by secret order the rail bridge at Kafr-ez-Zayat was left open, and the train shot into the Nile; but the brother, an agile son of a Bedawy girl, slipped through the window and swam ashore. There was only the bill to pay, which never troubled the spendthrift.

An earlier edition of Arabi arose as an army agitator. He was flattered by Ismail, until asked to join in a drive one day; after going far along the river, the carriage stopped and Ismail remarked that his companion would find it cooler to return by water; a boat with two men lay handy, and the officer troubled Cairo no more.

When Arabi was beginning to move, he went to try for sympathy and help from the American Consul; the American said that if he followed his advice the Americans might materially and directly help him. "But what is the advice?" asked Arabi. "First, absolute religious equality and, secondly, universal free compulsory education," so Arabi did not try for American assistance.

About this time "two clergy and a layman were sent out by the Archbishop of Canterbury to inspect and examine the Coptic Church; but a Coptic priest and a monk got hold of them and began catechizing them about the English Church, and putting them through an elaborate explanation of the Athanasian Creed, and requiring their definition of individual will in the Trinity, with all the oriental love of metaphysics. This was like a sweet old Swedenborgian, Dr. Bayley, who went to enlighten and instruct the Theban Presbyterian Copts, and was kept up half the night discussing Free Will and the origin of evil. A man must be well up in scholastic theology, if he intends to talk with Copts."

The weather had been bad during my boating in the Wady Tumilat, days of rain and head wind when the only way to push on was to be out, along with the men at the tow-rope, through mud and wet. It continued bad at Tanis (San) where I had to pitch a little tent on a mud flat by the fishing village, in the age-long stenches of fish, amid the marshes. Before leaving England, it was planned to send out a stock of iron roofing in fit time for me; but Poole delayed it in order to hear if I got there, and when it reached Port Said it was not forwarded because it was thought that no one could be at San to want it. So for weeks I had to tent in storms, while building walls in faith on the top of the mounds, which I roofed with loose boards that let all the wet through. It was deemed needful to take a daily dose of quinine or strychnine in alternate weeks, to avoid fever.

As the work at Tanis was the first start of work on a large scale, the running of it may be noted. I had 170 employed, with perfectly free labour, and without any blackmail or intervention. Old Aly Gabry was with me, as he was sturdy and honest; through him, I gathered information about the people, and so knew better how to handle them. The sheykhs of the place of course tried to be intermediaries. Their plans failed

by my recruiting men from all sides, whom I housed
on the mound, so that any attempt to withhold labour
was only the worse for San. After frustrating and snub-
bing them, I sent to each of the five a little present,
three lbs. of coffee and ten lbs. of sugar, and they subsided.

"In fact I have the two ends of the chain, the people
themselves, who, so long as they are paid regularly,
defy anything short of open violence to stop them;
and, at the other end, the European authority of Cairo,
before which no one can oppose me openly. Hence all
the spongy links between find that they cannot absorb
as usual. The sheykh of the fishings, with whom I had
trouble about levying men, sent up in a confidential
way to know if I would allow him to send me some
milk every morning and some eggs; of course he wants
to be able to take men away, and make them pay him
to let them off.

"My reply was that I never accepted anything from
anyone here. I have so long groaned over this abomi-
nable system of blackmailing, which rots the country
all through, that it is one of the most delightful things
to me to be able in one little point to stamp on it. It is
this brood of sponges, which may be summed up as 'all
in authority over us,' that ruin everything, as much by
their irregularity and illegality as by direct extortion."

An old *reis* of Mariette's turned up and, as he knew
much of the place, I took him on. He was "a fine figure, with a commanding voice; always with a large
black wrapper over his head, falling around him; he
wears a pair of huge black goggles, which—with a nose
and grey beard—are all that I have seen between the
edges of his overall wrap; whether sitting, standing, or
walking, he always carries a long stick bolt upright,

ready to smite the wicked. The people were scared at seeing him come up to inspect, as they remembered his former doings under Mariette, but Aly assured them that he would not be allowed to go on in that way now.

"It is very well to have such a man here, he will serve as a ferocious sheep-dog who would bite if he dared, and the Arabs will appreciate mild treatment all the more. He cannot do harm so long as engagement, dismissal, and the money-bag are all in my hands and anyone can complain direct to me at once." I also took on the son of another old *reis*, who was very active, but whom I always distrusted, from his face, and was later justified in my impression.

The only test of anyone was the face; I have never known a dislike which was not justified sooner or later; a favourable view may be taken of a lazy man, but not of a false one. With children, it is more a question of working power, shown by broad jaws; narrow peaky faces are weak and hysterical. The old *reises* only knew "Mariette's way of working, which was to get a requisition for so many men from a village, and then send over a *reis* for them; the *reis* levied the richest men he could venture on, they bribed him to get off, then he tried the next, and so on until he had fleeced all but the poorest, and they were marched off to work. No wonder that dealing by free contract, without any *reis* or sheykh, is not identified as the Museum style of dealing, by these poor people.

"I have the satisfaction of knowing that each man or boy in the work expects to get exactly the pay he will receive, and that none of it sticks in any man's hands between theirs and mine. They are not angels by any means, but they are not at all bad according to their lights and way of life, and they do deserve honest treatment." Two wild looking lads and their sister came up out of the desert world, lean and large-eyed as young gazelles, quite alien to the Egyptians, each wearing nothing but a single thin smock. They took their silver gladly for two or three weeks, and then vanished back into the shimmering waste.

"An Arab's notion of digging is to sink a circular pit, and lay about him with his pick hither and thither, and I have some trouble to make them run straight narrow trenches. I have three different classes which I keep distinct according to their work, trenchers, shaft sinkers, and stone-cleaners. They are all in small gangs, generally two men with picks, and three or four children or women to carry, the largest parties being three men and six children. Thus I can see exactly what each does, and lazy men are left out in the cold. The number has steadily crept up from a dozen to eighty-nine [later it was a hundred and seventy]. Such numbers of men, women, boys and girls, all split into small parties, require a great deal of individual attention."

Incessant care was needed to prevent men getting into danger from letting stones slip upon them; "what between their stupidity in mechanical points, and their unreasoning fear, anything which requires engineering care or precision, in order to avoid accidents, I have to do with my own hands."

The most ticklish matter was turning over a pile of dozens of big granite blocks, from a fallen pylon, to search for inscribed or sculptured faces. A hole had to be dug to receive a block, and then I had to lever it loose on the pile, for it to roll over into the right position for inspection. Standing just below the stone, and loosening it over its supports with a crowbar, the sound of crushing granite was the signal for motion, and I had to look over my shoulder every few seconds to verify exactly where to step back among the blocks, so as to get out of the way instantly.

Then, in a second, down would roll a block of a few tons past me on to its bed, ready below. Of course no one could be allowed near at such work, owing to their getting in the way, and their speaking so that the sound of the moving block was not clear. For searching under large steles of ten or twenty tons, lying flat, one end was cleared and copied, then that was blocked up firmly, and the middle cleared, so that I could lie on my back and copy it, looking up.

Besides the boys who were employed in former times, we took on many girls, some full grown, and in Ramadan while the men fasted, the bigger girls did pick-work. "I split the work of two girls who were too much addicted to getting up a long bout of singing and clapping in the middle of work. One of them is rather a boisterous damsel, and how she paid out the old man she had to work with! she slanged him unlimitedly, and kept time to her tongue by banging him with her basket. I threatened, if she did not work well, I would set her with old Aly Basha far off in some out-of-the-way part; and as old Aly Basha is about the oldest and dullest old fellow on the premises, the threat was serious."

Then there was Bedawiyeh, "a poor girl here—an orphan—who has not quite all her wits about her; she was rather a nuisance, as she never stopped at the same work, but went shifting round exchanging with others, and was always getting into a row, and going off in hysterical sulks. However I tried generally to find some place that would do for poor Bedawiyeh, though she managed to squabble with old men and young, with girls and with boys. She began work in a garment, scanty and well worn, and it went from bad to worse and more full of splits.

"At last when it came to holding it together all day by hand, I, through Aly, made the munificent offer of an old pair of trousers (they came out of packing three years ago, and the moths had lived in them since). Then it appeared that her aunt, with whom she lived, was well off, and her cousins were among the best dressed girls in the place. Her wages were absorbed by the aunt. Aly turned the occasion to profit by saying that I should pay her in clothes and not in cash. So next day she came out resplendent in a new snowy white garment, from under the edges of which drooped down tails of the old blue rag. Soon after, she disappeared; I inquired, and Aly said that as she had a new dress she was married. I was surprised, but was told, 'Oh, she has been married many times, but they always divorce her because she is so quarrelsome.' "

When I returned to San next year, as I walked down towards the desolate marsh, a party of girls came up, laden with brushwood that they had been gathering. They passed me without the least sign of recognition, but then all put down their loads, tidied out their smocks, and all came after me to kiss my hand fervently in greeting—a nice instance of native manners. Another time, a girl trotted fifty yards behind me for miles over the marsh, rather than be left to stray company. When you have got the confidence of the shyest part of a community, you have won the whole.

The usual time-table in the longer days was to start at 5.30; after seeing all the workers in position and booking them, I went to breakfast at 8 or 9, watching the pits with a telescope from my hut door. The rest-time was from 11.30 to 2.30, and then we went on till 6.30. After dinner, there was all the recording, marking, and stowing away of pottery and other things, and writing journal and letters till 10 or 11 o'clock. Doing one's own cooking makes time pass quickly.

The weekly pay I soon learned to fit in to the last afternoon, so that there was no crush in the dark for it, and no one was kept from work except just for going over his own accounts. The difficulty lay in the currency. The standard was the piastre, equal to 2½d., which exchanged at 96½–101 to the sovereign, while the nominal piastre of account was half this value. Largely, it was forged, of brass silvered, but it was usually accepted unless very vile.

The unpassables I used to clean with ammonia, pickle all night in waste hyposulphite fixer which silvered them decently, and send them off quite respectable, adding sound silver to the currency. Another way was to keep a store of unpassables in one's purse; when a man objected to a coin, give him one a little worse; on refusal, then one yet worse, and he promptly asked for the first again. For larger money, there were pieces struck in Paris and called Parisis, of 10, 5, and 2½ piastres. After loading the country, the Government had decried them to 8½, 4¼, and 2⅛, but the 10 passed privately at 9 or 9½.

Then there was a dollar currency copied from that of Maria Theresa, of the previous century. This had been issued by the Government at 17 piastres, and decried to 14, barely silver value, but circulating at 15 or 16. Lastly, the sins of Egypt were capped by a copper currency of 1, ½ and ¼ piastre, decried to a tenth of the nominal value. All salaries were paid one-tenth in copper, and Dr. Grant used to get monthly some hundredweights of it. As this value was less than the cost of copper, 400 tons of it were shipped off to Swansea to be melted up at a profit. The coin circulated at a seventh of its face value, and these with Parisis, at 2⅛ and 4¼, made some awkward sums. Besides Egyptian money, of these four variable values, there were in circulation French francs, Spanish, Italian, English and occasional Swiss, Turkish, and Indian coins, each with three values like the Egyptian, for taxes, for town, and for country.

The dearth of small change made me keep a list of multiples of all the currencies at the end of my wages book, and then patch up any odd sum required, by adding one or two of each of several currencies together. As soon as a man agreed to his account, I put the coins in his hand, saying that if he wanted explanation he must come after the pay was over. Usually they puzzled out the addition before then.

At last the Egyptian Government tried getting silver coinage struck in Europe, undeterred by the false gold which had been sent in before. A Swiss firm contracted for it more cheaply than anyone else. The stock arrived, was duly tested, and passed into circulation with applause. After a time, false money was found about, and it was said that boxes of specie had arrived by the same ship as the true coinage, struck by the same dies but of lesser value, ready to pass all together. The Egyptians deserved it, for they had had it all stamped with a lie on every coin, "Struck in Cairo," to satisfy national feeling.

This is like the instance of the pattern Quran, photographed from the most perfect manuscript that the Ulemas could find, so that the schools should have a true text. Yet no one would use it; every kind of objection was raised. At last the head of the department asked the true believers what was the real difficulty. Turning to the last page, they pointed out the imprint of Vienna: "How can you expect us to use a Quran with that upon it?" They wanted a lie, like that of the currency; a nationalism fed on lies is a perilous pride.

Owing to sheer stupidity, the currency of later times, though sound, continued to be a mass of confusion. After striking nickel piastres and halves, the Government made another issue of coins with a central hole, the new half-piastre exactly the diameter of the old whole piastre, so that they could never be distinguished in rouleau but only by fingering every one; the new whole piastre was the size of the silver five piastre piece, so these also were easily confused. Then, to make it worse, a third currency, with the king's head, was issued of the size of the first series. Thus the three sets of piastres all in use together, needed the fingering over of every coin, a tedious matter when getting many pounds of change every week. The whole muddle was fatuous folly.

At the end of the season, I heard more from the old *reis* of how Mariette's work went on. "He only visited his excavation once in a few weeks and left everything to native *reises,* just ordering a particular area to be cleared out. The *reises* often did not go to the work all day, and the workers did no more than they could help. The *reises* used to make a handsome profit, having an order to levy perhaps two hundred men and drawing pay for them, and then excusing half of that number at a price, per month, of two Napoleons for men at a distance, and half that for those living near.

"They were much afraid of the work being stopped,

so when their digging did not produce enough results to be encouraging, they used to buy from dealers, in Cairo and elsewhere, sufficient miscellaneous *antikas* to keep up Mariette's interest in the place. Of course it goes without saying that a good find was kept back so far as was prudent, for Maspero himself later admitted that the Museum never expected to get more than half of what was due. Thus the great boast of Bulak (the Museum), that they are certain of the locality and genuineness of everything there, is rather dubious."

My work was closed down by the middle of June, after many dust storms, heat over 100°, and violent rain. One thunderstorm was of continuous discharge of a rushing, swishing sound without any clap, but continued for half an hour. It seemed to be a brush discharge through the raindrops, between earth and clouds. About two inches of rain fell.

The original prospect, on which I had been sent out, was to continue the clearance of the temple, reported by Naville to lie under the mounds. But, on first view, I saw that it ended at a great enclosure wall. That wall proved to be eighty feet thick, and every brick, up to the heart of it, was stamped by Pasebkhanu of the XXIst dynasty. I cleared about the temple area in various directions, but reached nothing except a great well with descending steps.

The close search and planning of the temple site produced the second part of the stele of Taharqa, but nothing more. The outskirts of the mound and a desert rise, at Zuweleyn, only produced late burials of the XXIIIrd dynasty to Roman times. One good stele of Ptolemy II was found, flanked by sphinxes. This gave the sacred name of the region, and was allowed to come to England. It was cemented against the wall in the British Museum, which treatment is fatal to any stone with salt in it. Soon it began to crumble, and I begged that it should be soaked to remove the salt, but was told that no such risks could be taken; so it was left to destruction, until too unsightly to remain.

Besides that, I cleared many burnt houses of Roman age, and found in one the statuette of the owner, and a large quantity of objects and pottery, mostly now in the British Museum. The most important part was a basket full of carbonised papyri, which could be separated with care, packed in soft paper, and put in tins. These, with some other baskets full (which had mostly gone to white ash) were all brought to London, opened up, and mounted between glass. Two of them were transcribed and published; one, copied by Griffith, was a unique school book of signs with their names; the other, copied by me, was a design for astronomical and geographical decoration of a temple.

Of demotic papyri there were 228, beside thirty-eight Greek. These were then sent to Revillout, whom Poole much admired. He never did anything with them, and though several times in the last forty years I have tried to get some of the Committee of the Exploration Fund to make inquiries and claim the papyri, no one would ever take the trouble. The greater part of my results of the year were therefore wasted.

At Cairo, Maspero was agreeable about the larger things that I produced, but he and Brugsch were greedy for small valuables; two good figures of apes, in sets of figures, were both taken, though I counted eighteen already in the Museum. A silver chain and various other nice things were also kept. The objects which I was allowed to retain I showed in London, at the first of a long series of annual exhibitions which has done much to educate the interest of the public.

I had written to Poole saying that a room should be obtained for exhibition; but all that was done was to agree on a shed at the back of a dealer's garden. This was utterly impossible, so I went to the Royal Archaeological Institute, then in Oxford Mansions, and got the loan of their room. This led to my continuing to exhibit in that building until I was housed at University College.

On the voyage back, there were two delightful old Scotch ladies, who went ashore with me at Malaga. There, a cheerful grub of a chorister showed us the choir of the cathedral and insisted on my staunch Presbyterian friend, in her white military helmet, sitting on the archiepiscopal throne in most Catholic Spain. An old Roman Catholic lady on board called her "that great Minherva of a whoman," and Minerva said of the old Irish lady, "Oh, she is an awfu' woman; her puir daughter-in-law in Cyprus, when she bid her good-bye, just said 'God speed ye' and that's a'."

In England, the copies of the inscriptions were drawn facsimile, for the time of dry-squeezing had not yet come; the account of the work was written up and finished on the way out to Egypt again. Just as, previously, it had been the wish of Erasmus Wilson alone that brought me in to the work, so now it was my turn to urge that a new young man should be given his chance, Frank Llewelyn Griffith, who was devoted to the interest of hieroglyphics. As I wrote to Miss Edwards on September 17, 1884: "Now here is an Egyptologist turned up, a genuine English one, or rather Welsh, and he tells me that he has written to you on the same lines that he has written to me for advice. I will do everything in my power to ensure such a chance. . . . I would rather give a quarter of my small income than lose such an opportunity." The tide turned in his favour, and thus was started the man who has proved to be, for a generation, the principal English scholar on the subject.

Miss Edwards was asking for journals from me, and writing up articles in *The Times*. I commented "I was amused with some touches in your article, but particularly with the 'camp furniture' which you evolved like the German's camel. I sit upon boxes, I stand upon boxes, I slept upon boxes until I took to the sand floor; I eat out of boxes, my very plate is a biscuit-tin lid, and all the little *antikas* are stowed away in boxes as they are brought in."

Spurrell reproached me with leaving all the publicity to be done by Miss Edwards; the reply, on October 23, '85, was: "As to A. B. E.'s letters I am only too glad if any one will relieve me of making anything public. I can turn up at least three times as much as I can publish in the year, and as long as it is done, that is all I care for. *Finding,* no one else will do, or scarcely anyone; *publishing,* many will do. Stick to what you can do more, or better, than other people."

The working up of the material occupied the summer, and after the selection for the British Museum the remaining objects were divided among other museums. By November 9 I started to Liverpool for the long-sea way, and at Malta visited Hagiar Kim. The writing up of Tanis I was done during the voyage, with Greville Chester as fellow passenger.

On December 1, 1884, I went down to the great Greek site and looked round for accommodation. An

LIMESTONE HEAD OF APOLLO

POTTERY HEAD OF HERAKLES IN LION'S SKIN

old house belonging to a pasha was only partly occupied by his *wakil,* and so I could have two rooms; later, we moved up into two more rooms above. It was a convenient place, except that all the dogs of the village barked all night under the windows, and hosts of sparrows invaded the rooms all day.

Labour was shy, only two or three men could be persuaded at first, but after delays by illness, the tide turned. As I went up to the mounds they were bristling with five hundred men who swarmed round me for work. The only way to handle them was to rush to the highest point, then look over the crowd and mark out man after man with a long measuring rod, make up gangs, and then tell them to go and wait at some spot out of the way. Those nearest to me urged that nearest should be first, to which the reply was that I never took anyone near to me, which made a clearance. After planting out as many as I could manage, the rest were dismissed, and I made rushes across the crater of ruins in various directions to see the selected groups, altogether 107 men, and thus broke up the huge tail that followed me. After setting each group a definite job, I went back to the house to let the tail clear away.

At the door of the house stood two mounting blocks and, on turning one of them round, I beheld a decree of the people of Naukratis, which left no doubt as to the place we were on. Both Griffith and myself were much hindered by feverish colds which needed rest, partly due to malaria as well as wet weather. By February 12, 1885, we found the first foundation deposit, the beginning of a succession of such historical tallies, which date buildings, or even the sites, after every stone has been removed.

The work went on till June 5. There were three

classes of things that seemed inexhaustible, the pieces of painted vases, the amphora stamps from many Greek sources, and the weights. Every day many came in, and not only did we get things from our own work, but a host of *sebakh* diggers were cutting away the mounds actively in the season and finding much. I used to go over them about noon, before they broke off for the day, with a sack on my shoulder to take in all they found.

The business increased so that I could not get enough change to pay them, and they asked me to book the amounts promised. Soon I had a list of eighty accounts with these men, and tapped our best supply of good things. All bargaining was done away with, for if the men would not take my price, I gave back the thing at once, and offered less if it came up again. Scarcely anything was missed thus, as the scale of local value was soon evident. These values served to regulate our *bakhshish* to our own men, so that there should be no temptation to sell to dealers.

From the *sebakh* diggers, I secured a lot of seventy-five Attic tetradrachms in perfect condition, which served to show the accuracy of the mint in Athens, for most of the coins would have passed our own mint standard. I always gave the value of the silver, and so two other lots of varied early Greek coins were also secured, all weighed against modern coins in the scales and a little extra allowed. For this purpose I tested all the currency silver and found that Austrian dollars were the cheapest, so a large stock of these was kept always ready to serve as weights, making payment in gold.

This business was delicate, as the owners were very shy of letting their finds be known. A find of gold was rumoured, and so I poked about the region for an hour or two, just showing in the distance. Presently a negro came up to me offering a silver mirror and some small things; seeing he did not recognise the metal, I got them for a couple of francs. Hurrying off and weighing them, I returned, found him and gave him full silver value, telling him why.

I waited, and presently half of the gold was brought to me, but the remainder had unfortunately been carried off already. What I secured was the gold headband of Tiberios Klaudios Artemidoros, with relief figures, and a delicate gold chain. The more important matter was that quantities of tools and small objects were secured at the place where found, and so they could be dated from the known strata of the site. Iron tools were frequent, and the dating of iron chisels and other forms to about 600 B.C. was a great step in the history of metals.

All the best were sent to the British Museum, and on my inquiring to see them, some years later, I was told that "Mr. Newton said they were ugly things and he did not want them, so they were thrown away." All the other examples were thrown away in a general smash-up of the objects which I had arranged for distribution. The perils of discoveries are by no means over when they reach a museum. Thing after thing has been spoilt, lost, or thrown away after it seemed safely housed.

On one occasion I was shown in a hut a beautiful Greek dedication of the Palaistra. After copying it, I laid two dollars on the stone and told the owner to keep which he liked, money or stone, so after a protest he brought up the stone. Whenever an offer is made, put the money by the object and present both as a choice. The sight of the money is irresistible; the vendor cannot bear to see it taken back.

The historical value of Naukratis consisted mainly in the mass of inscribed Greek vase fragments, specially from the waste trench of the Apollo temple. The marble temple, and even the earlier brick shrine, had been entirely cleared away in past years by the *sebakh* diggers, only the deep trench full of sherds remained, but they gave a great variety of the earliest Greek alphabets, and some fine dedications such as the Polemarkhos krater, and that of Phanes. The latter was probably the renegade described by Herodotos, and the fragments were found very widely scattered, as if in spite at his treachery.

The site of the small temple of the Dioscuri was also found, and several dedications to Hera and Aphrodite. The position of the latter temple I gleaned in the opening of the following year, from a dedication, and my new student of that year, Ernest Gardner, reaped a great store of inscriptions from it. The principal landmark for dating was given by a scarab factory, with hundreds of moulds, and soft paste scarabs. Many were of Psamtek I and II, but none of Aohmes, so it could be dated to about 590 B.C. The earliest depth of the site was probably of about 700 B.C.; a burnt stratum, early in the history, showed the end of a village of booths, before the erection of brick houses.

The town grew up from the time when Psamtek I planted troops here, in 660 B.C., until about the second or third century A.D., but it was entirely eclipsed by Alexandria before Byzantine times. The area of the middle had been dug out almost to the bottom by the *sebakh* workers, who must have destroyed much of the early architecture and provided a large supply of Greek coins and other things to dealers.

This crater of clearance went down about twenty feet under the level of the fields and canals, but remained quite dry, as infiltration was evaporated at the sides quicker than it soaked through. The mounds, still left, rose to ten or fifteen feet around the edges. It was well that we stepped in before it was all lost, as now the ground has been filled up with surface stuff and the whole is reduced to cultivation. The lines of the streets were clearly shown by the white limestone dust and chips which were thrown down to make dry paths. The diggers had destroyed the houses, but left the road stuff as unfit for putting on the land.

At the south side of the town was a large enclosure, and in it a block of brickwork rising some twenty or thirty feet, pierced with deep chambers, which were filled with dry stone and brick rubbish. The work next year at Defenneh gave us a similar block in an enclosure, and both are evidently camps containing the basis of a high fort.

On the Naukratis fort were many recent graves which obstructed our clearance, as we respected them. The *sebakh* diggers had no respect, and began demolishing fort and graves. The families concerned raised objections. I retorted that it was their own people who were destructive. "True, but would I remove the graves?" "Not by my men," I replied; "you may set men to move your graves, and I will pay the cost." So for twelve shillings the cemetery was emptied out into some new cenotaphs below, and the place was clear for our work. The Greek camp also contained an Egyptian temple, and in later times Ptolemy Philadelphus had built a large stone entrance and chambers in the camp wall  My men cleared down the corner of the gateway, where the stone had been removed, and left it on reaching the sand foundation. Some boys sheltered there from a storm and, grubbing in the sand, turned up little glazed vases and bronze models of tools. As I jumped to the idea of a foundation deposit, hitherto quite unknown in Egypt, we cleared the other corners and found three similar groups. A lazuli cartouche of Philadelphus dated the whole.

Since this accidental discovery, many other temples and forts have yielded their deposits, and much information has been obtained as to dating, and the nature of the tools and objects used in building. When 1 named the subject to Maspero, he said, "For the present, there are no foundation deposits in Upper Egypt," as he was much afraid of diggers wrecking temples by undermining. Much time was spent on the great fort, emptying out the deep pits, but only some sculptors' waste and trial-pieces were found. Evidently these were merely construction chambers, for supporting an upper platform on which the defensive works rested.

There was a good deal of trouble about dealers coming down from Gizeh for their usual supplies. One market day, the diggers' weekly holiday, some men got into our work and found a large group of bronzes, which were bought up by a dealer. After many chases, searches, and official worries at Naukratis and in Cairo: "the general result of my Cairo business is very unsatisfactory. It seems that all the stringent measures of the Bulak Museum rest on private decrees and regulations of Mariette or others, which cannot be enforced in law, and that consequently all the beatings, imprisonment, etc., were illegal, and only to be covered by the despotic authority of the Khedive or his agents.

Hence, since we have legalised the country to some extent, there is really no power left. Such at least is Brugsch's statement, when pressed; he evidently wishes to avoid my taking active steps. But he shows such great care to prove the smallest detail of his statement to me, that I cannot say my natural distrust is removed. I put the case to him; 'if a man chose to go into an excavation which the department is making, and there began to dig beside your men, and find things, what would you do?' 'I should beat him and turn him out,' was the reply; it is simply a case of *force majeure* and hold all you can.

"Next, Sheldon Amos found the articles of the Code bearing on it. Belig Bey, whom we saw, quite agreed, so that I have a clear case, and it seems plain that Brugsch tried to baulk me." As I was told that the things had been sold at the Museum, though only one was actually bought, it is probable that he had bought the objects himself. I had a long chase after a dealer, and noted—"Nothing like bounce; if fifty men chose to come and sit all over the *kom* all day I could not touch them, nor anyone else; and if they bought things I believe I could do nothing, unless they came into my workings." This state of affairs was variously handled in later years.

A main object of mine in working for the Fund was the hope of getting training and criticism to guide me. But I received little or none, and gradually it seemed that there was none to be had. It was in fact a case of breaking new ground in archaeology. I saw that I must learn from things and not from people. The head of the American school at Athens came over, and I had great hope of getting all the pottery and other things dated; but he could not tell me anything, and did not even know Greek coin types. Similarly in later years, Kisa's book on glass seemed to be a mine of material, but as soon as it came to dating there was nothing quoted but my old results of past years.

Some strange characters turned up in Egypt. An American boy "ran away from home in Detroit, got somehow to New York, stowed away for Liverpool, thence stowed away on a Moss boat for Alexandria; there was taken in and kept by the soldiers at Ramleh. Thence he was sent to Cairo. There he wishes to go to Khartum as a servant; failing that, to work in Cairo, learn Arabic, save money, and go to the American College at Beyrut, or else he would like to make his way to Lake Chad."

Another curious history came out at Benha: "I was in the waiting-room, lighted by one candle on end without any candlestick, and saw a native enjoying a nargileh; after a time he finished and began a few questions to me. I found that he spoke very fair English, and his story is characteristic of Egypt. A Tunisian by birth, he was educated at Brugsch Bey's hieroglyphic school as one of the Arabs who were to be learned; that however led to nothing. He was then secretary to George Kilgour, the engineer; this lasted for eighteen months; then he was Governor of Bedrasheyn district and had 120 villages under him; now, he is evidently left high and dry. Such is the history of Qassym."

By April 18, 1885, I was again over at San, the marsh village reeking with old fish, to pack the stones and pottery, having arranged that they would be examined and sealed at Port Said; this saved two long and difficult transports to Cairo and back. Some further search was made about the wells of Tanis, at this dry end of

the season, but it was evident that the land had sunk
so much that we could not reach the old bottom of the
wells. Griffith was left in charge at Naukratis meanwhile. My nickname was *Abu Baqusheh,* "father of
pots," and that of Griffith *Abu Shuqf,* "father of potsherds."

After sending off things from San, "I tried for a boat
and, after a lot of talk, got one to go to Abu Shekuk,
returning to Naukratis,—the canal being dry to Faqus
—and here I sit, in a swarm of flies, munching dry
Arab bread and chocolate paste, with some old Egyptian Gazettes for literature, reading the *menus* of the
restaurants. Such is 'bread and point' in the midst of
a little canal in the Delta flats."

All the winter we had feverish bouts, and our eyes
went wrong as the fly season came on; we were neither
of us fit, with stomach out of order, to do much more,
when we retreated in the middle of June. For the packing at Naukratis, I could not get a competent sawyer,
and had to be "making boxes and packing them every
day. But how to get through sawing when it is 85°
indoors, and 90° to 100° out, is a difficulty."

"We have a storeroom downstairs and, retreating
there, I work away much like Brady's Japanese carpenter, who had nothing on but a pair of spectacles,
except that I do not need the spectacles." Griffith
elected to go on with the workmen on the mound,
whilst I did the packing, which came to twenty-eight
cases, besides thirty-six cases from Tanis this year.

The principal results were that we had found
Naukratis, got its early history, the dating of early
Greek pottery, the varied inscriptions, the source of
the scarabs found all over the Greek world (at Rhodes
and up to Olbia) , obtained hundreds of weights, some

early tools and Greek coins, and for the first time reached the system of foundation deposits.

When travelling about in those days, the railway station was of general utility. In some out-of-the-way parts trains only ran twice a week. I could pitch my tent on the end of the platform, being dry ground with a guard at hand. Boys used to play games up and down the platform, with or without clothing. Everybody flocked up to the train, and brisk business went on in sugar-cane, bread, eggs, and other local produce.

After some years a German administrator, who signed all notices "Prompt," began to regularise matters; stations were fenced in, and no food could be bought, even on long journeys, except at the official buffet; there, it was difficult or impossible to get anything but liquors, and these station drink-shops have been a curse to a sober population, especially to the staff of the stations. It was often difficult to get a booking office clerk to come along to his office before the train arrived.

Though our work at Naukratis stopped on June 5, and the Cairo business was over by the 10th, I found at Alexandria that Griffith was laid up with ophthalmia, and it was a fortnight before we could leave. That summer was occupied with the exhibition, writing up results and drawing plates. The early Greek inscriptions were the main interest of the season, and were discussed by Ernest Gardner with enthusiasm, as opening a new page of the subject.

On November 23, 1885, this new student Ernest Gardner joined me at Charing Cross and we went by Venice to Cairo. Sayce and his friend Myers were in our cabin. By December 9 we were at Naukratis and Griffith joined us on December 11. On the first day we walked over, but our stores were delayed. We got some native bread. and each tried a mouthful, rich with Arab smells. We put it down, and sat with it between us all day, not venturing on another mouthful. After a day or two, the men accepted working by the cubic metre, and most of our digging was carried on thus, both to their advantage and our own.

Where there is much earth to move in block, and no tracking of dubious walls, the metre work is much the best; it saves attention to keeping men going, a few minutes of examination and measuring up once or twice a day being enough, and so leaves time for observation and recording. In place of the usual wage (at that time 2½ piastres (6d.) a day for men, and 5d. for boys) about ¾ piastre per cubic metre paid them about the same for equal work.

Practically I used to assess each day's work by measure and by time, and give the average: the weakest men should get day-pay rate, and the best up to double day-pay. If any grumbled, I paid them up and ended their work. Of course allowance has to be made for the nature of the ground, and for any extra depth or distance of throw. The ground varied from ½ piastre for loose sand to 1½ piastres for hard chips.

At Naukratis we began by dividing the work; while Gardner cleared as much as possible of the cemetery, which provided many terra cottas of Gorgon heads, from coffins, Griffith was on the Aphrodite site, and myself on the large metre work.

By January 4, Gardner was left in sole charge of Naukratis, and Griffith and I moved over to a site that I had seen when going to Tanis, between there and Faqus, known as Tell el Bedawy or Tell Nebesheh. A partly broken granite shrine stood up like a sentry box, and around it we found a temple site, which was dated by retrieving the foundation deposits of Aohmes, from the sand under water. There was also a small town, and a cemetery of the same period, from which various small objects were recovered.

At that time, nothing was known of dating, and sites were useful to us which would now be superfluous in our present knowledge. Some great basalt sarcophagi of the XXVIth dynasty, which we found, were later removed by d'Hulst for the Fund, and are now in the British Museum. The district was troublesome; it could only be reached by wading or swimming the canals, and exploring around was a messy business in the mud. The sandy rise on which the temple stood had been given over to old Sheykh Nebesheh; he had fought with Ibrahim Pasha in the Syrian war, was eighty-five when we met him, a most cheery and affectionate old fellow, credited with having had innumerable wives, but only one son remained to him.

He provided us with a rambling guest room and annexe riddled with rats and tunnelled by white ants. The rat-holes we plugged with broken ushabtis, and the ant-holes with insect powder. Griffith kept up an interest in biology, dissecting birds while at dinner, and skinning an ichneumon which hung for several days in his bedroom doorway. At the temple we found a sphinx, six feet long, with four erased inscriptions, and two surviving ones of Sety II and Setnekht. There was the site of a Ramesside temple traceable, apart from that of the XXVIth dynasty. Here we first found the spears with forked butt-ends, associated with Cypriote pottery, and as such spears are represented in Karia, the burials were probably of Karian mercenaries.

Having thus developed the work at Nebesheh, I left that to Griffith, and went, from February 13 to March 5, on a long search of the middle Delta, examining all the sites with a view to further work. The most interesting result was finding a new type of fortress, with high walls, rectangular, and no house ruins inside. From work in after years it seems that they might be late Hyksos, but excavation is needed to settle the date. These sites are Tell Tanbul, Hakleyh, and Tammud el Hagar. It was a wild region, and I was thought so suspicious a stranger that a sheykh sent miles for the police in the night to come and arrest me, but of course they made no difficulty with me.

There were various interests in such a trip. In the west, the women wore a long robe and no face veils; in the middle region they had a short tunic and very baggy blue or bright red trousers to the ankle, visible a mile away, and face veils varied; in the east the robe is like the west, but they all have yellow face veils. The hospitality of the sheykhs was not always convenient. "Nothing could be more polite, but the case stood thus —I had had breakfast at 7.30, only a scrap of bread and water since, and it was now 5.30 and I was just wanting a quiet feed. Instead of that I had, sleepy and hungry, to sit up talking till 8 before I got anything. Of all the worries in travel, this dining with sheykhs is the worst." I used to try to rush my dinner on, and say that I would come into the guest room when I had done.

Having searched over dozens of ruined sites, I came back to Nebesheh. Griffith had found a colossal statue of Ramessu II, and a kneeling figure of Merenptah overshadowed by a hawk, on the top of a clustered column; three large sarcophagi; and a figure of Isis of

the finest work, sixteen inches high (kept in Cairo).
Griffith had moved on to another temple site at Gem-
ayemi, finding there much inlaid glass-work of a great
shrine.

As no further historical results seemed likely, I
moved on to Tell Defenneh, the ancient Daphnae,
where Herodotos records the Greek settlement. "We
went off a string of men, girls and boys, about forty in
all, straggling along in groups, with two camels carrying my baggage in the rear." After going about fifteen
miles into the desert, we camped along a line of sand
heaps covered with tamarisk bushes bordering the
canal.

"As I write here in my tent there is the prattle and
babble of the Arabs, settled under the bushes around
me. I start here at once with forty, who know and trust
me, and shall have shortly many more, and thus we
make a considerable settlement, who all hold together,
and with whom there is no bother about the payments
or work.

"This place makes a strange sort of *fantasia* to live
in; here, on one side of my tent is a group acting as
derwishes all in the dark, howling and groaning in set
phrases . . . the combined noise sounding more like
a great engine puffing hoarsely. On the other side, a
party of girls are wildly singing snatches of songs half
in unison chorus, slapping each other a counted number of times; around are the clumps of tamarisk
bushes, with the gleam of the old canal on one hand,
and the dim mounds of the Qasr on the other, seen in
dark starlight, with the glimpse of a fire here and there
under the bushes. There is not another soul within ten
miles of us, nothing but sand, and tamarisk, and marsh,
and water, and desolation.

"But I like it all better than the more civilised places; one lives with the people more, and the ever fresh air and living in a tent doubles one's peace of mind and contentment at once. Neither Griffith nor Gardner would appreciate it, I fear. . . . To me all the by-play, the jokes, and songs, and wills and ways, give a colour and interest to life here, which one will never reach in staid, school-boarded England.

"Fine *nebbūt* play, like old English quarter-staff, goes on here, whenever the men feel fresh; fencing and foiling in the evening with long staves most gracefully, while another generally plays the double pipes. . . . It is now a case of every bush has its bird, pretty nearly; some have made an approach to huts, with walls of earth left between their holes, and branches over the top; others have made a sort of tent of branches, and some have only a scooped-out lair."

The figure-head was a graceful girl called Bukadadi (of a Baghdad family) who lived with a more robust Egyptian girl; they used to come round on market-day mornings to beg a piece of soap to wash out their hair. For market, some used to go off half a day before, and walk back next evening. The rest enjoyed themselves, especially in fishing. The men used to stand in a row across the canal, with their arms forming a palisade alternate with their legs. Boys stripped and ran a couple of miles up the canal, and then came down splashing all the way; the driven fish, as soon as they touched the palisade, were grabbed and thrown ashore. In the evening, every bush had its fire before it, every-one feasted on broiled fish, and they always brought me a few.

I never had a moment's trouble with any of them the whole six weeks I was there, nor heard a single squabble. Being near midsummer, our work began by starlight at 4 A.M., by 10 I returned to breakfast, and whistled men off at 11. Till 3 we all rested, then they went on, and I lay for an hour in the canal (about 85°), feeling the fishes wandering round, and by 4— well cooled—I worked on till starlight at 8. I went barefoot on the sand all this time, and wore but little.

It was difficult to keep up supplies, as the nearest station was twelve miles away, at Salahieh. I ordered money to be sent there, but as there was no money-order office, a dragoman was sent down from Cairo with it. He was much ruffled to find that the train only ran on alternate days, so that he was stranded for 48 hours. As he sat in his gold-laced jacket, there tramped in out of the desert in the burning heat a barefoot rag-a-muffin, asking for a hundred pounds, which infuriated his dignity. However, I proved who I was, and bolted with the money before the scanty population of Salahieh should see me go and follow me.

The Arab boy with me sat down in the shade of a telegraph pole when he could, in the sweltering desert, and was so knocked up with the twenty-four miles that I had to leave him to crawl in the last two miles of return. I never had a hotter day. The canal water was almost too brackish to drink; the people used to debate it daily. I had to rely on bottled water, and raw tomatoes were so enticing that use of them resulted in jaundice; it was well it was no worse, for when they were first brought into Egypt, many people died of eating too many raw tomatoes.

The first touch of history on reaching Defenneh (Daphnae) was the name of the mound of ruin, Qasr Bint el Yehudi, "the Palace of the Jew's daughter." Looking back at the history of Tahpanhes, one could

RESTORATION OF PHARAOH'S HOUSE, TAHPANHES

GREEK VASE FROM STORE-ROOM

not but recognize this as a tradition of the Jewish royal family taking refuge here. On digging out the plan of the place, there appeared a large platform of brickwork in front of the entrance, a peculiar feature which explained "the brickwork which is before the entry of Pharaoh's house in Tahpanhes," Jer. xliii, 9, R.V.; and Pharaoh's house this certainly was, by the large number of sealings of royal wine jars left in the pantry.

Materially, the prize here was the multitude of painted Greek vases, which could largely be restored, owing to the pieces being shot into a lumber room of the palace, and not widely scattered. The Greeks were removed from here by Amasis, as Herodotos describes, and jar sealings of Apries were found amid the vase fragments, so that the date of the vases was very closely fixed.

The plan of the central fort was like that of Naukratis, a square pile of brickwork, the cells of which were filled up with rubbish; and enough remained to show some of the doming over the top, for the dwelling platform. At one corner the fort was joined by a lower mass of chambers which was entered by a doorway at the top of a sloping approach. On the other side of the fort were lower buildings occupied with stores, and here the painted vases were chiefly found, such as the ninety-nine pieces of the great Triton vase in the British Museum.

Around this mass of high building was a quadrangular camp, with a wall forty feet thick, but so swept by high winds that I crossed it for weeks without suspecting it. The wall was even slightly lower than the desert, as the mud-brick had been scoured away more readily than the shard-strewn ground. The date of the place was not only seen by the sealings but proved by deposits. On sinking pits, I recovered the foundation deposit under each corner of the fort. There were plaques of gold, silver, copper, lead and faïence, all inscribed; with plain plaques of lazuli, jasper, green felspar, and a mud brick, at the bottom of a hole twenty feet deep. "I look forward to seeing a table case in B.M. full of series of foundation deposits, some day. Here is the fifth." But in the British Museum the plaques were stowed into the vases, and all skied on a shelf. The case of foundation deposits was realized instead at University College, with later discoveries.

In the surroundings of the fort at the south-east corner "beneath one room which was crowded with pots, was a hole in the sand, filled with various pottery, broken and whole, two fine large flat dishes, perfect, amongst it; the room seems to have been a kitchen or some such place, for benches or long recesses on two sides had more than a dozen jars lying on them, three small pokers of the hand type, such as those from Naukratis and Etruria, and quantities of pottery, perfect and broken, fine and coarse. Also the pair of rubber (corn grinder) stones, a large iron knife and weights." In many houses large jars, broken below, were sunk in the ground near a wall; in these were masses of potsherds on edge, and they seem to be sinks for washing plates, the water running down into the sand bed below.

The general area of the camp was also productive for, owing to denudation, the surface was rich in scraps. Old women and children came from scattered tents among the marsh bushes, to search the ground, and brought up to me every day scraps of gold work and silver from jewellers, weights, iron and bronze arrowheads, and scale armour. "I continually have to buy 5s. to 10s. worth of silver scraps from the Bedawin. Of course they are worth nothing to us, but there is always the chance of a coin or bits of jewellery among them; and, if I do not buy, they will take them to Kantara and sell them, and so I may lose getting the things I do want." The Bedawy trading went on so that it outran my change, and the people gladly took to having a booked account, like the *sebakh* diggers of Naukratis.

"I went over to a man who was put to clear along the side of an enclosure, where I had noticed iron and copper workers' remains; he had wandered from his line, and I took up his hoe to cut down some earth to retake the wall. I hacked some down, never expecting to find anything, when I saw pieces of a green bowl. I picked it out and thought it was very thin, and then saw a little chunk of metal in the earth, which I knew to be silver by the way it was cut. So I put it on one side, and grabbed for more; soon I had six and three-quarter pounds of crucible lots of silver . . . and then I saw my bowl was silver."

The greatest haul, however, was on the last evening. As I was finally paying off, a man produced a lump of melted silver. I weighed it and paid; then his boy had a bit, so I thought of a group; next, seeing his reward the man produced many pounds of silver, which I also weighed and paid for. When all this was settled, he gave up a gold handle of a tray, weighing fourteen and a half sovereigns, and that he also was paid. It would never have done to break faith about it as the whole tray might have been in the background. Another charming find was a little silver amulet case with sliding lid, in which was a gold figure of Horus finely worked.

The most out-of-the-way corner of the Delta was visited, Tell esh Sherig, or Tell Belim as it is known there, nine miles due north of Defenneh. "I first crossed our canal, and then sundry more wide stretches of water on the way. But the wading was the pleasantest part of it, the other ground being (1) dust so hot that one could not stand still on it, but had to scrape a hole into the cool ground, if stopping for a couple of seconds; or (2) ground strewn with crystals of sulphate of lime which cut through the skin occasionally, boots being impossible in the deep mud; or (3) hot black mud which could not be crossed more than a few yards, or (4) best of all, mud and water with a crust of white salt on the top which kept it fairly cool. At last I reached Tell esh Sherig, a low mound about a third of a mile long, half as wide, and twenty or thirty feet high, a mass of dust with pottery and brick scattered over its surface. Around lay either water or salt flats almost as far as one could see, with scattered desert bushes on the landward horizon. The mound is all late Roman or Cufic on the surface."

After long packing up, at 90° to 100° without shelter, I got all our things to Salahieh, weighed, paid for, and into the train, when the station-master rushed up with peremptory orders, just received, that nothing was to travel without a permit from the Museum. This foolish regulation was issued by some official to worry me, although all the boxes were going to the Museum, and later it caused incessant trouble. The number of boxes must exactly tally with the permit, and it was impossible to say, when writing a week in advance, how many would be required. It resulted in applying for too many, and sending empties to make up the number, or else in putting two or more smaller cases into one old broken case to reduce the number. As a safeguard the Museum only needed to rule that all antiquities sent by train must go to the Museum *en route*.

"At Cairo, Maspero asked if I had brought anything important; I told him of the best, and he at once said, 'Don't bring them here to be seen, put them in a box ready and leave them, and we will seal them.' I had been much interested in many remarks of his about not *showing* things at Bulak; he does not want anyone *else* there to see all I have, and he actually asked me not to show two of our best things.

"He remarked to me also on the 'large eyes my second made' (Brugsch) on seeing one fine piece, when the said second was out of the way, and even said of a headless inscribed statue, 'If it is seen here, I shall be always asked afterwards why I did not take it; but if I propose to exhibit any of the headless statues we have already, there is an outcry at once.' Brugsch took care to be present at nearly all of our examination; in fact I am amused at the general interest taken in our boxes; I should have thought they would have been looked on as a nuisance, but on the contrary Maspero, Brugsch and Bouriant all sit or stand round, and many things pass round them all."

The main value of the season lay in fixing the history of Tahpanhes, the Greek details of the camp at Daphnae, the foundation deposits, and identification of Am with Nebesheh. The long tours in the Delta showed several lines of work worth trying but none of it has borne fruit, owing to the various restrictions on exploratory work. I came back to London by June 9.

In England there was the working out of surveys and results. By August 7 the boxes had arrived and

unpacking began; a great deal of mending had to be
done before the pottery could be exhibited. At last the
show opened on September 2 and was well attended.
The weights discovered in the last two years amounted
to fifty times the number known before. The weighing
and classifying of them was a long business; but they
formed the first step to a metrology in original material, instead of resting on the inaccurate and confused
statements of literary sources.

The constant mismanagement of affairs in London
made the conditions of work too impossible. Poole and
Newton cut out the founder, Miss Edwards, deciding
on work without her or the Committee; yet without
the advantages of autocracy in promptitude and fore-
sight. When reform was decided on by a meeting of
the Committee, it was quashed by Newton ordering
that the resolutions passed should be suppressed. After
this there was no hope of securing tolerable management, and I felt it necessary to resign. At the Fund
annual meeting the reason was concealed, by Poole
stating falsely that my health had suffered, that it was
necessary for me to retire, and that he had arranged
lighter work for me. In reality Galton heard that I was
retiring and asked me to undertake the photography
of all the heads of foreign peoples on the monuments
of Egypt.

## CHAPTER IV

## UP THE NILE

THE work for the Fund having now ceased, I was left to my own resources, and it was needful to plan accordingly. From my great-aunt, and supplemented by a small share of family property, I had £110 a year; of that about £40 was due at home for my living while in England, leaving £70 in all to face work in Egypt, and I had no more fixed income till I was forty. For the coming year my expenses were safe because the pyramid book had almost paid its way.

I consulted Francis Galton about returning the Royal Society publishing grant; but such a step was unheard of, and he counselled my spending it on similar work, which I did at Dahshur. He had also promoted a small grant for taking Racial Portraits in Egypt, which aided my expenses.

So I set off on November 29, 1886, from Liverpool, and joined Griffith in hiring a little boat at Minieh to go up the Nile. There was nothing for us to do below that place, and at Minieh we found a boat with a cabin twelve feet long and four and a half to seven feet wide; just enough for two to sleep on the side benches, and hang a box-lid by strings to serve as a table by day. Our bargain was to have it anywhere below the cataract, with a man and two boys for ten francs a day. We walked most of the way up the shore, looking into every tomb and quarry, and copying inscriptions, especially at Aswan.

In many places, by removal of dirt and mud plaster,

we succeeded in reading much more than was known before. At Eshmuneyn, "The place is being ransacked by an Arab dealer, in the interests of the Bulak Museum." At Ekhmim there had been great expectations, two or three years before, of results from a large and undisturbed cemetery of all periods; but a French Consul was put there (without any subjects to represent), and he raided and stripped the place under Consular seal, which could not be interfered with.

"We stopped at the pyramid of El Kula, about four miles north of El Kab on the west bank. It has been barbarously mangled in order to open it, just as Maspero wrecked the brick pyramids of Dahshur, and by him likewise, so far as I can learn. All one side is torn out in a great gash from top to base, right in to the middle, and quite needlessly, as the chamber is below the base: the cut is made on the wrong side, west instead of north. There has been no attempt just to clear the base, and find the proper entrance. The deeds of the Bulak department in Egypt remind me of that blackbird who used to pick off all the finest bunches of currants, eat one, and leave the rest to rot."

At Elephantine, I found the block with kings' names from the Vth to the XIIth dynasty. When De Morgan, later, started the great corpus of inscriptions (which never went north of Aswan) he listed a large number of our copies as not found by his party; the list curiously skips a great deal near the end, as the printer cut it short to fit the page.

"I am in excellent condition now I am glad to say; work from 7.30 to 6, without a break and scarcely ever a feed. The ferry boy inquired how it was we did not come back to lunch, and cast up his eyes at the notion of not having any." The subject now to be attended to here is to copy all the Cufic gravestones; I roughly estimated 2,000 of these early Arab inscriptions, ranging from A.D. 800 to 1200, overthrown in the old cemetery. There is nothing like such a mass of monuments of Arab time anywhere else in the country, and they are fast being destroyed. They still remain uncopied.

Having dismissed our boat at Aswan, we went down by the steamer; there was no room in first class, the second was unbearably smelly, and we went third on deck; but "the Government uses the Post boats for transports, and it so happened that sixty Egyptian soldiers were to go down with us; they had filled up the third class with their baggage, and we had a hard fight morally, if not physically, to get room. We had just space to stretch ourselves on the top of our baggage, Griffith and I sharing an area two and a half feet wide by six and a half.

On going down from Luqsor, "we could get no place except on the gangway along the side; it was crowded with soldiers again, and not only decent folk, but our immediate neighbours were a dozen malefactors going down to prison. . . . At one stage something even worse came on, a line of half a dozen criminals each wearing a heavy iron collar, and linked by a heavy chain to his fellow. These were dumped down on the small remainder of the gangway. . . . For the second night I watched one available space on the top of the paddle-box, and when its occupants moved I squatted on it at once, and triumphantly held it."

The principal business was to get the Racial Portraits at Thebes. It was obvious that it would be impossible to place a camera twenty feet up opposite a wall; so I concluded to take squeezes of all the heads, and then in England to cast, and photograph the casts.

To reach many of the sculptures, it was needful to hang a rope ladder down from the top of a wall, then to go up with sheets of wet paper rolled round a spoke-brush full of water. Hooking the left arm through the ladder, the paper was unrolled, the wall wetted by the brush, and then the paper beaten on, into all the hollows, and left to dry on the wall.

Thus paper casts were taken; the plaster casts from the paper were all photographed, and copies issued to order. The casts, after being exhibited at South Kensington, were accepted by the British Museum. There they were put on a wall high above the staircase, in bad light, and painted dark to insure their invisibility. They have since, under Dr. Hall's direction, been brought down into accessible use.

Before leaving Aswan, I had a telegram from Chester saying that he had important news for me at Luqsor. This was "that an anonymous friend in England had placed a considerable sum at my disposal for excavating. . . . On calling on Grébaut, I found him pleasant . . . but when at last I suggested that just for two or three weeks while here, I should like to dig a little, he at once came out dogmatic. . . . I was told that we (the English) had plenty of space in the Delta and that was enough for us . . . yet the fellahin are allowed to dig here, giving half to the Museum. No, it is an Englishman, and particularly one who may make discoveries, that is forbidden." The Delta being appriated to the Fund, and Aswan to Dr. Budge, there seemed no room for me. Next year, however, I found room. I took complete squeezes of the chamber of foreign plants at Karnak, and lent them to an Egyptologist, but have never been able to recover them.

After a month at Thebes, I went down to Dahshur

and pitched tent under some palms, in order to survey the pyramids there. Although the sites of the temples were obvious, I must not touch them, and it was only when almost too late that I got permission to find the pyramid-casing edge and pavement. The condition of the northern pyramid was such that the delay prevented finishing the survey there.

While waiting, and scouring the desert, I found the ancient road to the Fayum marked by stones at 1,000 cubits apart (a little over a kilometre), and surveyed it for about eight miles. There was also a road swept clear of stones, leading toward Siwah. The time there was diversified by long proceedings about some murdered men whose bodies I found. There were often men driving cattle across from the Fayum while I was surveying, but I prudently took no notice, as it was a regular thieves' road.

Finally, "As far as I can trace, the men had murdered somebody; and for some other offence a brother of theirs was lately hung in the Fayum. Of course that somebody's relation had a blood feud with them. Knowing they were passing here, the relatives came . . . and waylaid them on the way back (to the Fayum) at the pyramid, and catching them asleep they finished them with revolvers and pickaxe. The whole of the parties seem to be thieves on all sides."

The police, who were over about the affair, were up in the desert, when a convoy of stolen cattle came across, so five buffaloes were brought back in triumph by the police that evening—somebody else's in the Fayum, who probably never recovered them.

A long-standing bother occurred owing to a Mr. Cowan and Dr. Riamo being sent out by the Fund with no credentials; but they appropriated all the private boxes of Griffith and myself, in order to do something. It would seem impossible to pack more absurd mismanagement into an affair than occurred with these people.

Early in the season, I heard that Brugsch had represented to Grébaut, who was new to the place, that I had been smuggling antiquities. I wrote to him a strong denial, which he fully accepted, saying that the accusations were made by an employé of the Museum. Brugsch later said to me that the climate affected him so much during the summer that he "sometimes spoke against his best friends." The remark seemed to prove the need he felt for an explanation. Grébaut's habit of not answering letters or telegrams, however urgent, made it very difficult to do business, but personally we were on friendly terms when we met. He said that the railway regulations, issued by the Museum, which gave us so much trouble, were only enforced against us because we and Naville did not give bakhshish as everyone else did.

Altogether some permanent work was done that season on Racial Portraits, and the Dahshur pyramid, and Griffith and I learned a good deal of the country, but the restrictions wasted a large part of our time. Yet beside the Racial Portraits series we published over 700 inscriptions and a large series of cones and weights, in *A Season in Egypt*.

While in England, I heard that the offer of help in excavating came from Jesse Haworth of Manchester, through the kind intervention of Miss Edwards. Just at the same time I had an offer of assistance from Martyn Kennard, who had a family interest in Egypt. Nevertheless I did not wish to pledge my time to be entirely at the service of anyone. The plan which worked very smoothly was that I drew on my two friends for all costs of workmen and transport, while I paid all my own expenses. In return, we equally divided all that came to England. Thus it was my interest to find as much as I could.

The whole proceeds I divided into three lots as equally as possible, made a list of each, sealed the lists, and sent them to one friend, who sent on two lists to the other, who returned one list to me. Then we agreed on exchanges, if desired. A good deal of my share went to Philadelphia, and this paid for publishing the results. The Haworth share went almost entirely to Manchester University Museum; unfortunately the Kennard share was mostly sold by auction on his death, but a good deal was given to the Ashmolean Museum. The great flood of the prehistoric material from Naqada I proposed we should all present to the Ashmolean, before we divided the duplicates. The joint arrangement with these friends lasted for eight years.

## CHAPTER V

## IN THE FAYUM

I LEFT England, December 16, 1887, by long sea, and in Cairo found Grébaut amiable, and offering to name me as his agent to work in the Fayum; a satisfaction somewhat chastened by knowing that "one of the most active Arab dealers has been turned loose in the Fayum with a permission to work, and is getting large quantities of Arab things." "I went to see Sir Colin Scott-Moncrieff; he was as friendly—I may almost say affectionate—as ever. He took me over to the surveying office to see new plans, and told me to look in and see Major Ross."

Dr. Grant, in those years, had an excellent gathering on Wednesday evenings, where the more intelligent Europeans and natives met and had a short discourse on some matter of history or antiquities, looked over the Grant collection, and exchanged ideas; one met Chester, Corbett, Waller Bey, Scott-Moncrieff, and other officials, "and Cope Whitehouse, who fussed about and button-holed various people, and to whom, at the end, I imparted pretty plainly my views on his accusation of forgery against Naville or Jaillon, saying to him that by no possibility could it be supposed that the Roman milestone (at Pithom) was forged." This American was for some years stirring in Cairo, with the idea of flooding the Wady Rayan, and held many strange and impossible views. His name was usually shortened to "Copious."

The temple site of Medinet el Fayum was my first

objective. It was much encumbered with house ruins and rubbish, twelve to fifteen feet deep, and in one instance twenty-one feet down to native Nile mud. "There have been four periods of building here, which I believe to be XIIth, XVIIIth, XXVIth and Ptolemaic or Roman, but I have not seen a fragment of sculpture which I can fix to any one period to date it." The pieces of granite of the XIIth dynasty had been moved out of position, and they proved nothing as to levels. Since then, it has all been cultivated, and work now is impossible.

"I daresay many folks think it is a very pleasant and easy sort of life in a tent; and so it would be if room were unlimited. Imagine being limited to a space six and a half feet long, and about as wide as the length, and you have the ground plan of my square tent, sloping up to nothing, at less than standing height. Besides bed I have nine boxes in it, stores of all kinds, basin, cooking stove and crockery, tripod stand (serving for clothes) and bag and portmanteau, and some antiques; and in this I have to live, to sleep, to wash, and to receive visitors. I tried to get a rather larger tent, but in all the bazar there was none, unless I had one of ninety pounds' weight, instead of thirty, and that was too cumbrous." Important mummies were put under my bed.

From Medineh I went over daily to Biahmu. In a week's work, the meaning of the two piles of masonry was cleared up. They were not pyramids but, as Herodotos said, two colossal seated figures of Amenemhat III. The nose of one colossus and various other pieces proved that the figures were about thirty-six feet high, monoliths of highly polished quartzite, with a row of nome figures around the bases. The best pieces are now in Oxford. I found the name of Amenemhat III on part of the granite jamb of the gateway to the enclosure.

Having in three weeks drilled a good body of workmen, I moved over to my main objective, the pyramid of Hawara, with as many men as I cared to have, and had a corps on the spot, independent of distant villages. Here I was joined for a short time by Mr. Kennard, with tents, dragoman, cook, two donkey boys, two attendants, and a valet. The disgust of the valet at living among a crowd of mummies was the cream of the entertainment; he could not share his master's pleasure in getting into dirty pits. However, I had my workmen to console me of an evening: "They seem to like the place very well, as there is a constant tootling of pipes, singing, clapping, shouting, and general jollity going on."

Though I came for the pyramid, I soon found a mine of interest in the portraits on the mummies. These portraits, painted with coloured wax on thin wooden panels, had been found at Rubaiyat, but were not dated, and gave rise to wild hypotheses. Here at Hawara were all the stages from plainly wrapped mummies, next with coloured head cartonnage, with gilt modelled portrait busts, and finally with panel portraits. These panels were hung in the house during life—in one instance an Oxford frame was found. After death they were bound on to the mummies Each mummy was kept in the atrium of the house for perhaps a generation, until a cartload of ancestors was cleared away and all put into a pit in the cemetery.

From the pottery and occasionally dated papyri, also a Flavian name on a head cover, the dating of all these portraits was pretty well fixed to A.D. 100-250, agreeing

PORTRAITS IN WAX ON WOOD PANELS, 2ND CENTURY

with my first impression from the style alone. Sometimes we found portraits on alternate days, but occasional rushes poured in, of five in twenty-four hours. "A boy came with report of a portrait, and, before I could reach it, a party arrived. Schliemann, short, round-headed, round-faced, round-hatted, great round-goggle-eyed, spectacled, cheeriest of beings; dogmatic, but always ready for facts. Virchow, a calm, sweet-faced man, with a beautiful grey beard, who nevertheless tried to make mischief in Cairo about my work. Schweinfurth, a bronzed, bony, powerful fellow of uncertain age, an infatuated botanist. They were all three much interested in the work in different ways—the Iliad papyrus, for Schliemann; the plant wreaths for Schweinfurth, and the skulls for Virchow. . . .

"Then a report of another mummy, and by the time they have lunched a procession of three gilt mummies is seen coming across the mounds, glittering in the sun. Painted portraits, but the body covered with bright red-brown varnish, and scenes in relief gilt all over. The name of each mummy across the breast, Artemidoros (now in the British Museum), and Thermoutharin, also another portrait, but a poor one."

Many of the portraits were injured by damp but, by putting a coat of fresh beeswax over them, the old colour was revived and safely fixed, so that it would not drop away. In later years, paraffin wax was used for this purpose. One pay-day a man insisted on leaving at noon because he had found nothing, so reluctantly I paid him up; while doing so, two boys crowded up to see the money pass, and slipped down by the crumbling edge of the trench; I observed they lay still. So soon as the man took his money, they began grubbing in the dust, and disclosed a fine portrait mummy, which they had felt as they fell in. The man was vehement that it was his, but as he had refused to go on there it was clearly due to the boys, and they got the bakhshish.

The native longing to see money was also shown one dreary wet evening at Naukratis. A girl was wet through, her single garment clinging tight to her, and I paid her off as soon as I could, then I turned to pay a man; but the girl stayed on, and walked into a pool of water, just to see the man's money in the dusk, instead of running home.

Besides the portrait mummies there were many earlier things. Beneath late burials we found a large massive wooden sarcophagus, with finely drawn scenes inside and out, and of much interest in the mythology and local references of the inscriptions; it was the finest thing of the kind anywhere, and when the drawing was shown in London, Poole said that that alone was worth a season's work.

I had a long business re-waxing the stucco on to the wood, for indeed I first got the idea of waxing from seeing that the painting had been waxed over, anciently. It travelled safely to Bulak, and was taken for the Museum. There it was set on edge, along the side of a path, where the sun baked it on one side, and water splashed it on the other in watering the path.

After two or three years it disappeared; I asked about it, and was told it had dropped to pieces, because there was no room for it in the magazine; I asked why it was not placed upright in the magazine—oh, they had never thought of that. One more first-class object sacrificed to the folly of the administration!

The ideas of museum management are a serious

danger. In one of our larger English museums, a great number of necklaces were all hung up in pretty festoons, and the labels neatly stacked in a corner of the glass case. After some years I was asked to sort them out, and settle which was which. In another museum they imitated the British Museum and the Louvre, in plastering up stone tablets against the walls, where the damp works through and brings all the salt out on the face, and the sculpture perishes in powder. Sculpture has also had scant treatment at the hands of the Treasury. Franks applied for many years for a grant to glaze over the Indian sculptures on the staircase, but was always refused. At last he paid for the glazing himself, at a cost of £500. Such an interference with fiscal authority was not to be tolerated, and he received a severe letter, winding up with the desire that such irregularity should not occur again. I had this from Read. But this is by the way.

The main quest of the survey of the Hawara pyramid, and the entrance to it, went on all the season. The plan was recovered by clearing the corners, but the north side proved entirely blank, in spite of great ravages made on it in the past. As the sides were heavily encumbered by the rain washing down the mud-brick of the pyramid, it seemed the most practicable course to tunnel to the middle. The bricks were all laid in sand, which ran out from between them so soon as a hole was made.

The tunnel required boarding up all along the roof, hitching the boards into the joint on each side. On reaching the middle of the pyramid without finding anything, I searched the floor, and discovered that the surface dipped down, so we lowered the floor, putting in two false roofs to hold up the sides. At last I noted that one side was of brick laid in mud, which suggested a wall. Searching the floor, it was found to slope down away from the wall, and, pushing in that direction, I saw that we cut through a great relieving arch of five courses of brick in mud. "At half-past one this morning (for we had a night gang on the work), April 5, two of the boys on the night work came running down to the tent crying 'the stone appears, the room is come' . . . it was the roofstone of the chamber."

I feared that there might be three layers of roof beams, as in the pyramid of Pepy, so I made a cut further back in our tunnel, to try to find the end wall which might be thinner. After some days it appeared that the end was buttressed up with gigantic blocks set on edge against it. Further, the chamber was built so close to the sides of the rock pit that there was no room to get at the side wall. After trying to get masons to quarry down through the roof, and not succeeding, I reluctantly had to leave the place for next season.

There was a flow of small objects from the Hawara cemetery, for besides the burials there were chapels or family enclosures, like a modern *hōsh*, where the relations had funeral feasts and left baskets, papyri, pottery, and many little things. One piece of papyrus had an official block stamp in red, the beginning of block printing with ink. Two plano-convex lenses were found, scarcely intended for ornament as the glass was quite colourless, and though too conical to magnify well they would serve as condensers. A fine roll of the second book of the Iliad was lying beneath the head of a woman.

One grave of a girl had a great variety of toys, all now in University College. Elsewhere was a pottery model sedan chair with porters, and a separate figure of a lady which could be taken out. Knitted woollen socks occurred with separate great toes, in order to allow of a sandal strap: these anticipate the rise of knitted stockings in the sixteenth century. Dummy mummies were made; "One coffin that I opened contained a tiny child's figure; I wished to preserve the painted cartonnage, but on pulling away the dummy's sandals, I found no infantile toes, but a man's knee joint. It seems that the undertaker had not troubled to mummify the little brat at all, but had picked up three old leg bones, and an old skull full of mud, and the rascal had done them up tidily to satisfy the parental feelings, and put on a little gilt headpiece and sandals to look proper."

Elsewhere "there were two little girls, quite too splendaciously got up; all head, bust, and arms and feet of moulded stucco, gilt all over; all sorts of jewellery moulded in relief on neck and arms and hands, and inlaid with actual stones, on one of them three good-sized onyxes, two agates, and a large polished green glass (now in Cairo Museum). . . . The girls are really superior beings, as good work as one could have in such a style. Then with them—most interesting of all—was a woman with painted portrait on canvas, and a boy also painted on canvas. These are evidently the first stages of the system of portrait painting." Large amounts of fine coloured textiles were also found of the later centuries, but mostly fragmentary. Some jars full of minimi of the Vth century were left here, and one lot of plain blanks of copper, to such a state had currency fallen.

Though in the winter my tent was always 34° in the morning, if the sky were clear, by the end of March the heat came on. To get money I walked eight miles into Medineh, and then back, before 10.30, while a gale at 105° was blowing. Several of our men were laid low with the sun, and took long to recover. The effect of being surrounded with so much organic dust from the mummies, with a walk at 105°, was to give me a bad infection in the breathing passages. "I can hardly do any packing. By the time I have stood out for a couple of hours over the men, I am fagged out, and can only sit or sleep in shelter. This has lasted now for about three weeks."

It was well that I had kept up box-making and packing all the season, sending each week a load of boxes in to the kind care of Mr. Hewat at Medineh, and having out a load of wood to go on with; thus there was a manageable amount left to wind up. The cargo to Cairo was sixty cases. At the Museum, Grébaut as usual delayed, the cases were laid out in the garden, without any cover, a violent storm came on, and next morning I found them standing in three inches of water. To wet such perishable organic material was almost fatal, yet to take out wet mummies to dry was impossible, as there was no shelter.

The charges imposed by the Museum in a single year would have paid for a shelter, yet, so far as I know, antiquities taken to the department for examination have never been protected from the storms frequent about May, nor put under lock for the night. I went back by long sea with the cases, and had several out on deck and dried the mummies in the sun.

"When passing the things, Grébaut appreciated the portraits immensely, insomuch that he bagged all the finest female portraits and two of the best men. He took a dozen in all, and we have not one left which could compare with the best half dozen of his." When he had apparently done, I asked if he was now content; he hesitated, and then said that he "once knew a young lady like that," and therefore took one more of the best. He also took the whole of the finest textiles.

For the exhibition in London I had written to Martyn Kennard to secure a fitting place, and he hired the large square room at the Egyptian Hall in Piccadilly. An aged visitor said he remembered Belzoni exhibiting in that hall. I had written to my father to get forty plain broad oak frames suitable for the portraits. In a fortnight I managed with Spurrell and Riley to get all unpacked, and to mount and hang the portraits. With three colours of card at hand, I laid each portrait on the cards to see which harmonized best, and then quickly ripped out a mount with a penknife and framed it, little thinking that those mounts would be retained for over forty years at the National Gallery.

There was much public interest in the exhibition. Sir Frederic Burton had his choice for that gallery, and the visitors brought me friendships with Holman Hunt, Richmond, and many others. Sidney Colvin asked if he could come before ten one morning; I gladly appointed nine, as I was usually there by then. But he never appeared. Some time later he reproached me about it, and it seemed that he stood for long outside the baize door but never pushed it to see if he could come in. It was Varennes over again.

To Miss Edwards, on June 15, I wrote: "If you had seen the scramble I have been living in, going to bed at 12 and up at 6 mending portraits and writing letters, and in London from 8 to 8 every day, you would pardon my not sooner writing, or sending you the notes on the exhibition . . . the only time I could get to do them was writing from memory in the train.

. . . Now I really must go to bed; I am too dog-tired to sit up and direct cards to-night."

On October 24, 1888, I was on the way overland to Egypt. "It is very striking all down the Rhone valley to see the enormous mass of rolled stone and sand which forms the bed of the valley. In many places are hills sixty or eighty feet high, formed of nothing but river detritus, and how deeply the same stuff fills the valley can only be guessed—perhaps a 100 feet or more. It is not so impressive as the vast detritus of the Lombard plain, into which the Alps plunge down as into a sea, and which may be hundreds or thousands of feet thick. We want now to know the depth of such valleys filled with detritus, to find the maximum elevation of the land above the sea.

'On reaching Cairo I found Dr. Grant was in trouble about a native servant robbing his antiquities, and firing the house to hide the theft. Grébaut repudiates all idea of the Museum inspection having gone on at my work, but cannot deny that old Farag, the Arab dealer, was allowed to work at Hawara. He was there for two and a half months, but he only got four or five portraits it is said, beside a lot of the common gilt masks. . . .

"I then saw Scott-Moncrieff, who is annoyed and indignant at Grébaut setting an Arab to ransack the places I was working." The matter was really still worse. "The German—Kruger—who came into the Fayum simply to plunder, has not found Medinet Madi a success, as he has got no silver or gold, and only some statuettes which he knows nothing about, and does not think they are worth much. It does not say much for Grébaut's regard for antiquities, to let

so completely ignorant a man enter a district solely for
pillage.

"However here he is, with apparently just the same
powers for work that I have, and he has been here
ever since last spring, poking about. . . Hewat (the
irrigation inspector) finding that he was unsettled,
asked where he was going to work next, and Kruger
told him the Illahun pyramid and then Gurob! Now
these are just my main objects for work this year. . . .
I decided that I must run no risk of being forestalled
by Kruger; so on Monday morning (November 26) I
walked over with Mohammed (*reis*) and four men
with boys, and set two on to the tombs at the pyramid,
and two others on Gurob." This holding of the
ground involved my walking over seventeen miles
twice a week to direct, and was very unsatisfactory,
but the only course possible for safety. The policy of
turning dealers on to plunder sites and destroy all the
history, was carried far, as Suleyman was turned on to
Defenneh.

The main purpose of my work was to open the
Hawara pyramid first, and during most of the season
I had the pleasure of help from Maurice Amos, who
was taking a holiday before going to college. As a further search round the base of the pyramid was fruitless, masons were got from Medineh, but they were
afraid.

Then two good masons were brought from Cairo
and began December 8; they would only work by the
day, so after keeping a close watch on them for a week,
I measured up their hole in the enormous roof block,
and thus estimated how much longer it would take to
get through. Then, telling them that they would still
have day pay, I promised them a lump sum on getting

through, less the day pay for every day till then. They could not object to this, as it was a possibility of getting more if the work ended sooner. This stimulated their rate of work, as was required, in order to close the matter and get on to Illahun. What this tunnelling involved will be best stated in an account which I sent over to Miss Edwards:

"Thinking that I would go into the pyramid, and see what the masons had done in stone-cutting the day before, I went up there first of all, on going out. Horrid to say, there was what we euphemistically call 'a brick and a half' in the passage; a piece of the side wall had fallen in the night, there were roofing boards lying about, props straying at all angles, and the floor choked with pieces, from the size of a whole brick weighing about half a hundredweight, down to scraps and heaps of sand from the joints.

"Now the masons would soon be up from Medineh, and there might be an end of all the work if they saw it. So with the boy—whose face and intelligence gained him the name of 'Caliban's brother,' and who is libellously but briefly called Caliban—I hastily set about clearing up the place; soon a man joined us and we trotted in and out, embracing staggering weights of bricks to such good purpose that it was all tidied up and dis-catastrophized just in time before the two sententious Cairenes appeared.

"Nothing further 'occurred' while they were at work; but when they left in the evening Caliban and a man went in to clear out their chips, and came back with the hideous news that the pyramid had just caved again. This time a long length of the side of the passage had all come down; the props were struck over in all directions, and the ground piled up with stuff for twenty or thirty feet along.

"The first thing to be done was to take down tenderly some more that threatened to fall, which would have swept away still more of the supports. Now, given a pile of loose bricks just ready to topple, and all held up by some slight jamming at one point or another, it is no easy matter to lift them away one by one without letting them all down with a run. They have to be looked over in all directions, their cracks and dislocation observed, and then lifted away as lightly and delicately as possible, though weighing enough to tip a man over if not well in hand; further they must be abstracted from behind supports without the least jolting, and if possible without letting a scrap fall against the woodwork.

"The whole time the operator must be expecting the chance of a further fall from his meddling, and be ready to bolt with half a second's warning, the path clear for retreat, and the notion of how to retreat all ready in the mind and only waiting the touch of the trigger to go off. At last brick after brick has been taken down, and all that threatens instant collapse is removed; now begins the longer affair of reconstruction, and setting up such a support as will prevent any stray and isolated falls. The roof looks ugly enough; five or six bricks wide all staying up by mere sticking with loose sand. First, fresh holes must be cut at the side, and cross bars put in; and then, if the sides are not sound, uprights must be added.

"Three long hours after dinner in the evening, while my men slept the sleep of the fed, I was taken up in securing the bad places. To have a man with one in such work is worse than useless; if a brick falls and more may follow, he will either heroically rush forward to help and so block the retreat, or else tumble up against something in his own flight; while the whole time his whistling and involuntary noises—even of breathing—distract the constant attention of the ears, which take note of every scrap of sand that drops far or near.

"Next morning the men cleared the passage once more, and I went in to put a few nails in the timbering. Not that any such operation as nailing in a nail with a hammer could be thought of for an instant; the first blow would bring down showers of sand from all the joints, and before one nail was in the wood the whole place would be about your ears. Holes must be bored with a twist gimlet, and the nails put in and squeezed home with pliers. While doing this I heard a fearful thud, and then many more, and showers of sand came pouring down at the end of the passage. Here was the third fall seen in twenty-four hours, owing to the soft brick of the pyramid yielding to pressure.

"Luckily I had a double roof there, and this caught the stuff, for there would have been no time to clear it before the masons came. When they left I cleared it out, and looking up saw my upper roof, as loose boards jammed by loose bricks, hanging by some mysterious jamming in the passage. There it may hang till it falls; if I took it down there is no saying where I should stop. The whole of the sides were split and caving throughout; if only they will last till we get into the chambers then the deluge may come. . . ."

By January 6, we got through into the upper chamber. There I wriggled head down into a forced hole which opened into the actual burial, and saw two sarcophagi in the water; I had to be dragged out by the heels. After enlarging the hole a little, I could enter. The chamber was one solid block of quartzite, twenty-two feet long, eight feet wide, and six feet deep inside, polished, and cut so clean at the corners that I did not realize that it was not built, until I searched for a joint and found none. The water was up to one's waist, so the chips could only be searched by pushing them with the feet on to the blade of a hoe, and so lifting them up. I promised half a piastre for every hieroglyph found, and a dollar for a cartouche. This ensured a thorough search. The next day the name appeared, Amenemhat III, as was expected; the surface being half decayed by the water, there could not be any doubt of its age.

I had the sarcophagi emptied of chips first, and I verified by trampling that they were cleared, and then had all the chips in the chamber turned over into the sarcophagi. Thus nothing could escape notice. After pulling down a mass of displaced blocks, I got through into the passages, which were nearly full of mud washed in, on which one had to lie down and slide, stripped, with barely head room, through the various trap doors and complications until the entrance was reached. Then measuring back to the chamber, and through my tunnel, the position to search on the outside was found. There we opened up the original doorway and the descending steps.

As there might be important things under the mud, it was needful to empty out the whole of the passages. This was done by starting a gang of men and boys on metre-work at the entrance, and giving them an additional boy at every few yards, on day pay. The metre men thus kept the day boys going, each boy at a given station taking a basket and passing it on. The combined plan was effective, and needed hardly any inspection. The main prize was the unique alabaster altar for Ptahnefru, daughter of Amenemhat, with figures of more than a hundred offerings each inscribed with its name—the most valuable list for explaining the names found elsewhere.

There were also dishes inscribed for the princess, in the form of half a goose. Her name explained the purpose of the second sarcophagus, which was constructed by adding a base and end blocks between the king's sarcophagus and the side of the chamber. The finding of a long stairway at this period led to amusing dogmatism. Borchardt asserted that there were no stairways till later times; I quoted the pyramid; he said the stair was inserted later; I replied that was impossible, as the bricks were laid in sand, and would fall in before an insertion could be made; very well, then the pyramid had been taken down and rebuilt in order to place the stairway. Everything gives way to a German theory. As we found later, stairways are the regular feature of tombs as far back as the IInd dynasty.

While working at the pyramid, I cleared a large tomb-chamber forty feet deep. We had begun it the year before, finding eight splendid canopic jars. The sarcophagi were unopened, but waist-deep in water, the whole walls pitch black from some growth. One waded amid rotten wood and skulls, and the water was so salt that a drop in the eye half blinded one. We opened the sarcophagi, and got the sets of amulets of the XXVIth dynasty in position, duly recorded in the plates of *Amulets*. Then I suspected that an inequality in the side of the tomb might hide another burial; so that was quarried out for some time, till one afternoon a boy ran up to fetch me down because there were "images as large as candles."

There I found a sort of box hollow in the blocks with 203 large ushabtis of Horuza standing on end packed in sand. They were of the finest work of the XXVIth dynasty, and many retained their colour, though others were faded. The clearance of blocks went on, and in a few days I was called again to another deposit, of 199 more figures. These were in a difficult position to reach, and I had to lie in the water, and clear them with my feet. The brine made it impossible to dive. After seeing the two deposits, it seemed plain that an immense block between them was the lid of the sarcophagus. It was of very hard limestone, and only just the upper surface above the water. So I promised the lads there a good sum by the time they had cut across it and raised one half, enough to get inside.

I had to leave Hawara to take up Lahun and Gurob, in order to keep the dealer out; but the Horuza work went on laboriously, and I was fetched across when required. After some weeks, the half of the lid was raised, and two canopic jars found in the sarcophagus, but it proved impossible to loosen the head end of the coffin. A fortnight later the lid of this coffin could be moved, but not the body coffin, which was packed round with sand. A week later, having felt that there was no inscription on the inner coffin, I bored holes with a centre-bit at arms' reach under the water, put in stout bolts, and tied ropes on, so as to get several men to haul on it. I excavated all the sand I could with my feet, lying in the water up to my nose, and at last the coffin moved, and was hauled up looking "like a buffalo" as the men said.

We towed it along to the light of the shaft, and then opened it, and I removed the richest set of private amulets known, recording the position of each. That set was, of course, kept at Cairo (see *Amulets*) ; there were gold finger cases and sheath also. By giving proper rewards to the workmen, it was possible to let this valuable tomb be opened, with the certainty that I should be fetched whenever attention was needed. An unexpected piece of gold was found later, and immediately brought over to me. Among other stray finds were two large and perfect land deeds of Byzantine time. I lent them to Sayce to publish, he deposited them for safety in the Bodleian Library, and since then they have not been found.

The work having been divided, and my reis apart from me, a weakness was revealed, by a lad asking if it were true that the reis was to share in the bakhshish, even when not at the work. This, of course, undercut all the value of the bakhshish, and could not be allowed. I collected evidence by calling up one man after another, questioning him, and then making him sit silent while another came up. The evidence was clear, between one-quarter and one-third of the bakhshish had been extorted by the reis. That was the end of my ever having any reis in the work.

I sent over to the reis, by Maurice Amos, the wages due to date, and also several men to try to recover what had been levied on them, which they partly extracted. I heard afterwards that all the reises employed by Naville levied a share of the wages, as he did not give any bakhshish, so they found it almost as profitable as did Mariette's reises. I was very sorry to lose my man, as he was very intelligent. I had known him to be faithful, and he had been about me for eight years, but the work could not be allowed to suffer by his greed.

When settled at Illahun, or Lahun, for the pyramid and the town of Gurob, I also noticed another town on the desert edge; the only name I could find for it was from one old man who was told in his youth that it was Medinet Kahun. Gradually I reached the evidence that Gurob was entirely of the XVIIIth and XIXth dynasties, and Kahun was entirely built in the XIIth, though slightly occupied later. Thus these two towns gave for the first time a full and clear series of the products of these great periods, and provided an archaeological basis which had hitherto been lacking. At the Lahun pyramid, I searched by trenches and tunnels all over the rock surfaces without finding any entrance—that was disclosed after I left. But many fragments of the temple adjoining the pyramid, and of the lower temple near the cultivation, were recovered, giving the name of Senusert II. I had not at that time the means sufficient for the thorough clearance which I did a quarter of a century later (1914, 1920-1).

In the cemetery of the XXIInd and XXVIth dynasties we found many burials, though none gave us dates or history. The finest was a beautifully draped figure coffin, covered over with a perfect false sarcophagus with corner posts. It was taken at Cairo and, though the coffin remains, the rare covering has been lost, probably destroyed because it was in separate pieces to be built up.

When a fine example of a beadwork scarab and wings was found, I fetched the petroleum stove down to the tomb and, pouring spoonfuls of scarcely melted paraffin over the beads, secured them completely; on lifting and reversing the sheet of paraffin, the clear under-surface of the beads was exposed, and doing this while the wax was soft it could be flattened out, and then set in a shallow wooden tray. Long after, Clermont-Ganneau lamented to me that the beautiful bead coverings of the sacred rams at Elephantine which he found, could not be preserved. He had never heard of paraffin wax, and ought never to have been allowed to destroy beautiful things by such ignorance.

Fortunately for me, the administrative province of the Fayum included the Nile frontage of Kahun and Gurob, and thus I could dig these sites. Just beyond the border was the Coptic Deir, where I was asked to work by some Copts. I began, in the rubbish mounds, but as soon as I found papyri the priests stopped me, as being over the border of my permit. They then dug over the place themselves, but I did not hear of anything being published.

At the temple of Lahun we found three wooden pegs together, two pierced, one plain, exactly confirming the explanation of a scene of masons dressing stone, published by Wilkinson. Since then other examples of drafting pegs have been found. A portion of a large sledge for dragging stones was lying in the pyramid rubbish, made from old ship's timber. Among the fragments of the pyramid temple was a graffito of Ramessu II and the destruction was proved to be by him when I walked over to Ehnasya, and found three blocks of Senusert II reworked by Ramessu.

In the lower temple there was a square stone inserted in the middle of the site; on removing that, another was seen; below that was sand, and then smashed pottery mixed with copper models of tools of all kinds, sandstone corn grinders in pairs, and as much as 13½ feet length of globular carnelian beads. This is the earliest deposit yet known, and the difference of having beads instead of models of food is notable. In the early scenes of marketing, strings of beads are used as exchange, and their value as currency for buying food seems the motive of placing them here.

The town of Kahun had been laid out in the XIIth dynasty for the workmen who built the pyramid. A portion of it was turned over, reserving the rest for the next season. We found copper tools, stone figures for lamp stands, scarabs and sealings, burials of babies in boxes, pottery, flint tools, pieces of wooden furniture, flint sickles, game boards, mud toys, and—above all—papyri. These objects gave us a wide view of the daily life and habits of the XIIth dynasty, and made this the standard type of that age for comparison.

The inspection house at the bridge of Hawaret el Makta, near the modern town of Lahun, had kindly been lent to me by the Irrigation Inspector, Mr. Hewat; it was about a mile and a half from Gurob on one side, and on the other side two and a half from Kahun. So I could not give more than half a day to either site, which hindered detailed work, yet the impending German pillager made it needful to occupy both.

At Gurob, the foreign connections were the special interest. For the first time, Mykenaean pottery was found in place in Egypt, and so completely mixed up with remains of the end of the XVIIIth dynasty as to date it decisively. Efforts to confuse the issue by the Enkomi publication, or a dealer's made-up group bought for the British Museum and favoured by Cecil Torr, were quite useless, and the date has been abundantly confirmed at Amarna and many other places since.

While looking at a piece of ground, I suddenly saw a bit of Mykenaean ware; by the middle of March I noted finding "more pieces of proto-Greek pottery," and by the middle of May 1889 the correct term was started. "Another piece of distinctly Aegean pottery (I cannot call it *Greek* at this age) . . . was found on the floor in a deep small chamber." The term was also used in the *Ten Years' Digging,* yet Reinach and Evans debated which of them had started the name Aegean some years later.

Besides the Aegean pottery there was a burial for foreigners—Anen-tursha, with a foreign determinative, and another of Qa-shedi-amia. Many alphabetic signs were noted on the pottery, which pass on, along with those at Yehudiyeh, in unbroken sequence into the Mediterranean alphabets (see *Formation of the Alphabet*). A foreigner was found with yellow hair and a black wig, the colour of the wig proving that the hair was not altered by burial; with him was Aegean pottery.

All over the enclosed town there were buried in the floors of houses groups of personal objects, toilet, and clothes, burnt in a pit and covered with a layer of sherds before being earthed over, a custom quite unknown in Egyptian houses. The large walled enclosure, side by side with the Egyptian temple enclosure, seemed to have been the ground of the foreigners. After getting Naukratis and Daphnae, to be able now to step back to 1400 B.C. and firmly link Aegean archaeology, was a decisive gain, as hitherto there had been no definite fixture, and dating varied from 800 B.C. backward.

Of normal Egyptian things, there were some fine examples—many bronze knives, two wooden statuettes,

WOODEN STATUETTES, 18TH DYNASTY

IVORY BABOON AND SCARABS, 17TH DYNASTY

one of which is the finest of that age, two polished bronze pans with lotus handles, and inscribed for high officials. Besides important pieces, there was a great flow of beads and amulets coming in. As at Defenneh, the wind had blown away the loose dust, and the whole site was dotted with small objects. At one time I counted eighty girls and women crawling on hands and knees to get their eyes close to the ground for seeing the beads; all of these beads I bought up, and so learned the range of varieties of this period.

Some large groups were also found, such as a body with dozens of strings of beads of very various kinds (Univ. Coll.). The burnt groups found in the floors of houses gave excellent dating by scarabs and amulets, for the glazed work, glass, and Aegean pottery. A new measure was found of twenty-six inches, which I recognised as double of the Drusian foot; since then, this has been found in two other examples in Egypt, and was also identified as the standard measure of northern Europe.

Later periods were also important here, such as the Ptolemaic burials and cartonnage composed of papyri. By damping and opening these, large pieces of documents were obtained, including many wills of the Macedonian and Thracian soldiers settled in the Fayum, and very early MSS. of Plato and other writers, since published by Mahaffy. Still later were the Coptic textiles which the natives found in the district, dated in one instance by a coin of Heraclius.

The people were fairly well in hand; but a large slab of four hundredweight was stolen from a tomb at Lahun and brought up to the bridge by night to be shipped. The bridge-keeper was firm, and would not allow this. Next morning I got hold of the men and told them to hand it over to me; a threat of fetching the police enabled me to make them show the stone and deliver it at my house. Thus I got it raised from the pit and brought in some miles for nothing. The distance from Medineh was troublesome, as I had to walk twenty-seven miles, there and back, to get a supply of money. The only ailment here was ophthalmia, after a very dusty day. Zinc would not cure it, and after nine days I tried quinine solution which put the eyes into excellent condition at once. Since then the mixed sulphates of zinc and quinine have been commonly used.

One day at Lahun I heard a disturbance, and, looking into the official room, I saw a man getting the bastinado on the soles of his feet. It was for stealing rope and timber, put out for the safety of the great dam during high Nile, thus imperilling the whole province. An anxious message came to me to excuse such illegality, to which I replied that I was very glad to see justice done.

A curious link with old times was reported, the death of the last of the Janizaries at the age of 125, born, therefore, in 1764; as he had been doorkeeper in a military college since Mehemet Aly's massacre, there would be no question of his identity. It may not be on record elsewhere that "the collection at Miramar was a hoard of Mariette's, hidden by him at the end of a season; it was raked out, under compulsion, by his *reises,* under order of Ismail, who wanted a fine present for the French protégé Maximilian. Mariette returned, and gnashed."

Another matter to record is the finding of grains of wheat in the sarcophagi presented to the Prince of Wales (Edward VII), by the Khedive. These were planted, and grew; but I was told that the coffin had lain in the Khedivial stables covered under a heap of corn, hence the intrusion. It was like the raspberry seeds from the Laurium mines growing. Sir Joseph Hooker told me that when these were exhibited, with modern seeds for comparison, he saw visitors taking some of each in the hand to examine, and throwing all together back in the tray from Laurium.

At Hawara I tried experiments on seed under the most favourable conditions possible. I had found a large quantity—some bushels—of Roman corn. From the middle of the heap (least oxidized) I picked out the fattest grains, and planted rows of them immediately in a sheltered canal bank at three stages of moisture; at the same time, I planted Roman grape stones. None of them showed any sign of germinating. This test was the most favourable, as not a day elapsed between finding and planting; also there was no chance of substitution.

A curious example of kinds of intelligence occurred with a very bright little boy, who looked after my premises, and who had a marvellous memory. I was marking some pottery with two letters, while he looked on; as there was much to be done, I told him to help. "But I cannot." I put a pen in his hand, and encouraged him to begin; with great tension he drew the upright of E, then tried to make a cross stroke, but broke down crying, completely paralyzed by the effort. Every fellah in my work who has been taught to read and write has lost his wits, and is the butt of all his comrades for his stupidity. It needs generations of habit to enable English children to pick up reading without being taught.

In a letter to Miss Edwards, December 24, 1885, is

the remark: "I well know how hard it is to do correspondence when ordinarily visiting. It is a melancholy
fact that the influence of one's fellow-creatures is always to a diminution of work, both in quantity and
quality. I never do anything so well as when quite
alone. Now I will mention a notion that struck me
strongly on reading Stanley's *Eastern Church*. It is to
a Western mind astonishing to see on what recondite
point the phraseology of the Arian controversy turned.
Their expression was 'There was when He was not.'
Not *there was a time,* but there *was* something *before*
time. In short it was all a question of the Divine Nature before the existence of time and matter. Now this
was a purely Egyptian question in origin and in development. Started in the Alexandrian Church, it was
fought almost entirely, as far as dogmatic reasoning
went, by Arius and Athanasius, two Copts. . . . Depend upon it, there is good scope for a lecture on the
influence of Egyptian thought on Christian dogma.
But an awfully thorny subject."

To Spurrell I wrote at the end of the season, "Out
of sight out of mind, and I never expect to bulk so
much in the public mind when silent in Egypt as
when playing showman in London. But I am not
working for that end. So far as my own credit is concerned I look mostly to the production of a series of
volumes, each of which shall be incapable of being
altogether superseded, and which will remain for dec-
ades to come—perhaps centuries—as the sources of
facts and references on their subject, as much as Le-
land and Dugdale and Camden on British monuments. . . .

"In so many cases I have worked out and exhausted
unique sites that it is impossible for the record to lose

its value. I might occasionally do without a chapter by
a specialist, but the result would be less safe and
would occupy time which would be far better spent
on my own specialities. There are five subjects which
I consider my own specialities and they are enough
for any one man. (1) The fine art of collecting, of securing all the requisite information, of realising the
importance of everything found and avoiding oversights, of proving and testing hypotheses constantly,
as work goes on, of securing everything of interest not
only to myself but to others. (2) The weaving a history out of scattered evidence using all materials of inscriptions, objects, positions and probabilities. . . .
(3) All details of material, colour, fabric and mechanical questions of tools. . . . (4) Archaeological surveying. . . . (5) Weights."

By the middle of June, 1889, I left the Fayum, my
friend George Fraser being willing to spend the summer at Lahun in charge of the sites. There were 101
cases, which I had myself made and packed, to be examined at Cairo. "After wasting two days in waiting
for Grébaut I went by appointment at 8.30; Grébaut
appeared at 9; and then talked and maundered inter-
minably over the list of cases, and proposed, as there
were so many and I was leaving next day, to do nothing then, but let it all stand over to be examined
with Grenfell as my representative (who knew nothing of the objects).

"By talking further, and then making a sudden
move, I got him out about 10, and started on looking
at things. I had about a third of his time, during which
he would maunder and go off the business, and could
scarcely be got to settle about taking anything. By
pegging away I got some things done, secured all the

bronze implements except the best two knives and a chisel. But after stuffing G. with the Horuza amulets, the altar and ducks from the pyramid, the finest coffin and sarcophagus and a portrait, at the last he bolted the whole lot of fine things, proposing to take them all, in consideration of leaving the whole of the remaining cases of pottery and stones untouched and unexamined, and giving up all claims on papyri.

"It was a fearful swoop to lose all the finest things, but I doubted if I should get better results by haggling over a quantity of the other boxes, and losing some days more in this wretched unbusinesslike way. So I had to grin and bear it. Thus the two bronze pans, the three wooden statuettes, the best block of Usertesen's temple, and the best stele of XIXth were all kept."

Fraser employed a few men, including two old plunderers. While digging along the pyramid they found a shaft on the south side, forty feet deep, and on cleaning it they got in to the pyramid before Fraser. The alabaster altar of Senusert was secured, and there was no rumour of anything else being found by them in the pyramid. When we made the exhaustive clearance a quarter of a century later, we got the gold uraeus and a tall lampstand.

In England I was back by June 28, and there was the work of plotting out the plans, drawing objects, helped by Spurrell, and writing up the account; as the unpacking could not be finished till August, the exhibition was held over till the middle of September. It was very important for me to get back to hold Lahun when Fraser was to leave, and Spurrell came to my rescue and undertook to distribute and pack the collection in London.

When I returned to Egypt I wrote to him, "I cannot

thank you enough for such a great lift. It was also important for health, as I was getting near the end of my tether before I left, and much doubt if something would not have gone wrong had I stuck to fourteen hours' work a day for another month. As it was, when I got to Illahun I slept nearly—or quite—twelve hours a day for the first two or three weeks. . . . I am now fairly right again and getting a proper work-hunger. The only salve to my conscience in leaving you such a job, was that I did not see it possible for me to have done more than I did in the time in England."

I went off to Egypt again on September 26, 1889, reaching Lahun in seven and a quarter days. A great find of sealings had come in, 717 legible, including 143 varieties. They were nearly all from jars of resin, tied down with leather and cord, or with cloth. I went down into the pyramid for a careful measuring of the sarcophagus, alone and undisturbed; the heat was such I soon shed clothing, and went on at work till, when I came out for breakfast, it was 4 p.m. The average error from true planes was one four-hundredth of an inch, and the worst errors from true vertical planes were only one-eightieth of an inch on the side, and one-fortieth on the ends; the difference of lengths of the side is only one-sixtieth, and in the length of the ends one-hundred and sixtieth of an inch.

The way to detect such errors was by putting a horn of wax on each corner, stretching a thread all round on the horns, and measuring the distances of the parallel threads. Then, hanging plumb lines down at intervals, taking off-sets from the planes to the plumb lines, and from the lines to the threads. Thus nothing but measuring-scales, thread, and wax was requisite, along with a magnifier to read thousandths of an inch. The same method gave me similar results on other sarcophagi there in 1914.

The clearance of Kahun went on till the end of the year 1889, by which time I had over 1,800 rooms emptied and planned, the first and still the only time that a complete lay-out of an Egyptian town has been obtained. The most important result was finding painted Aegean pottery of a different style from that of the XVIIIth dynasty, and mixed up with pottery which was unquestionably of the XIIth. This was disputed in England for years after, and authorities declared that it was like the Naukratite ware, which I totally denied.

No one sided with my fixing it to Aegean civilization of the XIIth dynasty, until suddenly the Kamares painted pottery turned up in Crete, the Middle Minoan period was defined, and Crete fell into line with the Egyptian facts. Thus the contacts of Greece with Egypt, which six years earlier were not in hand before Alexander, had been carried back over two thousand years. Many more alphabetic marks were found, and that these had reached the stage of use for writing, was proved by a name of five signs being put on a tool handle. Even after thirty years there is still a stubborn disregard of these facts by philo-Semites; the history of thousands of years can afford, however, to wait a century to overcome prejudices.

A fine seated figure of Sa-sebek in basalt was found (Cairo) ; parts of wooden columns with palm-branch capitals; another flint sickle; a second cubit of twenty-six inches; a torque now recognised as being of Caucasian type. There was a female figure wearing the Bes mask, also part of the actual mask of cloth and stucco; unhappily at a provincial museum the figure was in a case left open during some rearrangement, and it was stolen. Once lost to sight, things may vanish entirely; in the same museum, a charwoman was away, and at 8 a.m., when the night guard went off duty, a substitute charwoman appeared, a case was forced open and many scarabs were taken, some of which were found in the drains—the rest may still be there.

Among the things of Kahun there was a very fine carving of a baboon in ivory; this was taken by Grébaut, and when Dr. Grant went to see it next day at the Museum it could not be found, nor has it ever appeared since in that museum.

Kyticas was the principal dealer for fine things in Cairo, and his antiquities were at the back of his shop. One day a friend of mine was there when a keeper of the Museum came in at the back door with his arms full of paper parcels. I went rather quickly to the back of the shop one day, and found Kyticas and this keeper sitting there, with about five hundred sovereigns on the table between them. The Museum had curious ways of doing business without cheques. The keeper had fortified his position by relieving a prime minister (Cherif) of a discarded favourite, and by assisting the peccadilloes of young royalties whom he conducted up the Nile. While the country folk are fairly decent, within the limits of Islam, many a tourist is a moral pestilence wherever he goes.

Passing now to the XVIIIth dynasty, there was some settlement then at Kahun, which left a fine lion-hunt scarab; some perfect shirts neatly folded up and stowed on a mummy; above all, the Maket tomb. One evening a boy found a pit in the rock, and was rather afraid of the darkness; I stopped him, and next day, putting on a good worker as second, we tackled it. A large rock cellar was filled with coffins which were partly crushed by weight and age; the mummy wrappings were all black and powdery. I had to sweat away all day lifting down coffin after coffin, black as a sweep and shirtless for the heat, searching each coffin as it came to hand.

There was also a heap of small pottery, decayed baskets, part of a chair, and much else lying in a corner of the chamber. The only name recovered was that of the lady Maket; the date was given by scarabs of Tehutmes III, though at the time our ignorance of bead-dating made me suppose it later. There was much foreign pottery, and one good Aegean vase with ivy leaf design. The bulk of the group was given by Kennard to the Ashmolean Museum; but unfortunately he clung to the gold scarab and silver ring of Maket, the jasper prism of Tehutmes II, and the reed pipes, which were all sold at the sale after his death. Oxford tried to recover these important parts, but French dealers and Berlin could afford to outbid for these, and it was only by a final bid that I got back the prism for Oxford.

For work at Gurob, which I could not combine with the care of Kahun, I had the help of a new volunteer (Hughes-Hughes), which was better than leaving it to the natives. He came in an unhappy state of irritation with everything, which compelled me to leave him entirely unchecked, merely registering what came in, and only when he had done could I go to make a plan. Shortly after his return to England he vanished. Hence the detail of discovery was neglected. I might have done more after he left, but on going to Cairo I caught influenza, and lay helpless and medi-

cine-less in bed for nearly a fortnight, eighteen miles
from any advice. When I could move again, I had
scarcely strength to finish box-making and packing. As
I was pledged to go to work in Palestine, I could not
extend my time. The place really required a sound
guarding of the site for a future year's work; but with
two dealers, Arab and German, hovering to ransack
it, I could not hope to hold it over for the future. Such
are the difficulties of getting archaeological records in
the face of official indifference.

Our principal results from Gurob were dated
groups of burnt pottery buried in houses, a lintel of
Tehutmes III from his temple, a cubit inscribed for
Tut-ankh-amen, an altar dedicated by Queen Thyi for
"her brother," Amenhetep III, and several good blue
glazed vases. At the end of this work, "I have now
really outlined the greater part of the long blank of
hitherto undefined history of domestic and personal
objects of the XVIIIth and XIIth dynasties, which had
been such an attractive unknown region. If I can now
do the VIth, IVth and possibly earlier times, in as
complete a way in future, I shall accomplish what has
been my particular aim in Egypt."

At Cairo "having had the four days, which I had
arranged to attend to the examination of the antiquities, entirely swallowed up by Grébaut's delays; and
being informed by him, after he had seen all he wished
of the things, that nothing could be decided until
some of the Committee inspected these things at some
uncertain time hence, I did not think it well to put
off all my Syrian arrangements by indefinitely staying
on in Cairo. So I left open four of the cases which
Grébaut had inspected, beside leaving the altar of
Senusert, the XIIth dynasty stele, and the great

wooden door (of Usarkon I); and deposited the money with Brugsch for forwarding the cases, and so just managed to leave Cairo in time for the steamer. . . . When I saw Moncrieff a little before, he said he really could not tell how the inspection was going to be arranged, evidently very much annoyed with the whole business; and I think he will be still more provoked at Grébaut's clumsiness."

## CHAPTER VI

## PALESTINE AND MEYDUM

We are but snowflakes on the stream of Time
  No sooner fallen than we melt away;
So thinks weak man when he has passed his prime,
  So dreams the idle puppet of a day.

Yet man does not thus vanish without trace
  But, like in some vast pyramid a stone,
Helps to build up the glory of his race,
  Or seen, or hidden in the mass alone.

LEAVING Egypt on March 7, 1890, I was in Jerusalem by the 11th. There I found that my firman to work for the Palestine Exploration Fund had not arrived from Stambul. At the hotel I fell in with Hayter Lewis the architect, and Dr. Chaplin, who had been so many years there and was back on a holiday. These friends gave me the best possible opening to the conditions and archaeology of the country, and as I was held up for nearly three weeks for the firman I could make good use of the time in such society.

By April 4, I camped at Bureyr to examine the site called Um Lakis, but three days there proved that it was only a shallow village of Roman age. After testing various sites, I went over to Gaza for supplies, and made friends with Dr. Elliott, the medical missionary, who was most helpful in dealings with officials.

The kaimakam was a man of European experience who made no difficulties. The block was that the effendi who was to represent the Government on my work never came, although he was drawing a large

121

allowance. When he appeared, the kaimakam took my part and speeded him along. He demanded tent and various things, for which he already had the allowance of £15 a month; he dismissed his cook and made my guard work for him, and squeezed, in every possible way, up to the last. I had to keep him in good temper, in his solitude, by going to dine with him often and used to work up, from *Whitaker's Almanac,* the salaries and staff of our Government departments, to amuse him with the only subjects that he could understand, effendis and cash.

At Bureyr there was a small recess between two houses, grown over with weeds; in it was a stone shelf, and on that a conical Roman millstone—the venerated fetish of Syria continued. Later, when travelling, my donkey man turned out another conical millstone from his saddle-bag, saying he could not carry it any further. I asked why he had carried it for several days, and could only get the reply that it was "a good stone"—so persistent is the primitive idea, continued through the ages of Christianity and Islam.

It reminds one of Joseph Wolff, the missionary, who was instructed by his English wife that he must put on a clean shirt every day when he stayed in society. After a week he returned and, tapping himself, said triumphantly, "I have got dem all on." Thus religions are overlaid, the last is the one that is seen, but the first is still next to the skin all the time.

On April 17 I moved a few miles on, to Tell Hesy, so called from the "gravelly valley," Wady Hesy. This was an early city, repeatedly fortified, and from its nearness to Um Lakis it doubtless was the ancient Lachish. "This is the entirely Arab country, and they are considered to have a certain right to the ground, simply because no Turkish governor is strong enough to reduce them to obedience. There is not a house in sight all round the country, only straggling groups of low brown tents. . . .

"The effendi would not hear of my saying anything to the Arabs because of their rapacious expectations, but *he* would attend to all that by asserting his official authority. . . . So as he took all the responsibility I left the matter entirely to him, and he had to attend to it with a vengeance. For two whole days he was in constant parley with interminable sheykhs of all the neighbourhood, some decent and friendly, some demanding money, some threatening, and all feeling their way. . . .

"Only the other day a big effendi of Gaza, and some others were stopped and stripped of everything within a few miles of the town. . . . I dined at the biggest sheykh's, the other night . . . (with small-pox the other side of the curtain) but the utter ignorance and lack of all ideas outside of their daily life, and impossibility of talking on any matter but what they had already talked of, hundreds of times, was crushing. I urged on the sheykh that if they would only dam the watercourses, and hold up the winter rains, they would have good water and cultivate as they liked. He only said that no one had a head to do that. . . .

"There was a skirmish between the Terrabin and the Azizin down at Nejileh, where I went last Sunday, with the result of eight killed, five of one and three of the other, only leaving a blood balance of two to be wiped out. . . . The other day I saw dozens of sheykhs riding past to go and see the pasha at Gaza; they fell out by the way, and at Beit Hanūn two were killed."

This state of society is worth record, now that one

may walk alone over all that country, and not a single raid occurs in a whole year. Ten years of unselfish rule has cured the miseries of the land, and by 1928 not a single British soldier was needed in all that country, and only a few police officers, over the native police. Yet the Arabs have since preferred a disturbance.

At Tell Hesy "we are badly off for water, our three sources being springs here, clear but brackish; ponds of rain water at Bureyr (six miles away) contaminated; a deep well at Bureyr, stagnant, very green, and rather salt. This is what we trust to, and though I boil it well, yet the colour and taste is almost too much for me. When boiled it is three courses in one: soup, fish, and greens." To get cash, I had to go to Gaza, covering the thirty-six miles by riding a donkey halfway, leaving him and walking on, and picking him up as I returned; one had to take great care to avoid the Arab tents as we came in the dark.

For labour, I got people over from Bureyr, six miles to the work, the men sleeping on the spot, the women and girls mostly going to and fro; the pay was 1s. a day for man and girl together; thirty-six years later it was 2s. 6d. "But they are poor workers after the Egyptians, not doing more than one-half or two-thirds of what my old hands in Egypt would have done. At first they were all over the place, talking and smoking, anything but work." During Ramadan fast I made a short noon rest, and then stopped at three, which they appreciated. After that, I gave a couple of hours at noon, and said they must go on till sunset; but I found them all slipping away at three. I hurried back to the tent, looked out my small change, and then called up the most unfit man in the place, and paid

him up, as he did not want to work my hours. After
him the next worst; then the third, and by this time
all the people were buzzing round and calling on the
effendi to intervene. I paid off a fourth, and then gra-
ciously listened to the prayers of the effendi, and said
that the remainder might be allowed to continue. I
got rid of four troublesome fellows and the rest would
work on into the dusk, if I were occupied in some hole
at sunset. Later experience, in 1928, of the agricultural
Arabs, not villagers, was much more favourable; the
same plan of short noon rest and early stoppage in
Ramadan was also satisfactory, and there was no trouble after it.

The currency question was as bad as in Egypt.
"Every place has its own valuation of all the coins in
an arbitrary standard which does not exist. There is no
such thing as the nominal piastre in actual coin, and
the coins are reckoned in piastres as 6, 3, 1⅕, ⅗, ⅙,
1/12."

The site was ideal for gaining a first outline of the
archaeology. The stream had cut away one side of a
mound of ruin sixty feet thick, and I could begin by
terracing along each level and getting out its pottery.
Subsequent discovery has dated the beginning stages
rather earlier than I then supposed, and the mound
ranged from before 2000 to 500 B.C. The successive
walls could be distinguished, and the outline of the
great early fortification round the hill.

In the Jewish level, about 900 B.C., we found a good
building, with carved limestone door reveals, re-used
from an earlier building; but it could not be followed
out to the end, though I tunnelled at thirty feet depth
in the mound for it. The working out of the pottery
of this site continued to be of use for reference, until

superseded by the much wider results, better dated, from Gerar in 1927. The work was closed by all the labourers going off for harvest, and as we had, before that, much hot weather, up to 106° in the shade, it was not desirable to renew work in June.

Then, with the dating of pottery that had been obtained, I went over southern Judaea, estimating the age and prospects of each of the ancient sites. The decisive fact was that in the hill country there were no potsherds on sites, though, by the names, it was certain that the places had been occupied in Jewish times or before. The explanation of this must be that the people had the nomadic habit of using skins and wooden platters, and ignoring breakable pottery.

When I was approaching Dhaheriyeh, my camel going in front was pulled down by four men, with faces tied in clouts, and two of them ran up to me, but I backed up a slope, revolver in hand, and dropped my purse and gold bag in the long grass. Then there was nothing much to lose, so when all four armed men closed on me, and grabbed my windpipe, breaking its top ring, I went limp and let them rummage. There were a few silver coins in my pocket for them; my watch, I remarked, had a number on it, which saved it; my notebook was returned to me, they got my little revolver, and the affair was over. I dropped in the grass and bewailed my losses, while I grubbed about for my purse and gold, put them in my pocket and we went on.

"Altogether I think the business was conducted quite as pleasantly as such affairs ever are. I had some difficulty in making Muhammed collect his mind to the needful business of roping up the camel again, and tying the cut ropes." A jacket that they took from the baggage was later found by the police left in a tree, and was sent to Jerusalem, but I never had it. A friend there said that probably all the Council tried it on, to see whom it would fit.

We went on to Dhaheriyeh, and there the people resented strangers. If one went a few fields away, men picked up large stones for heaving at the foreigner. I got hold of a little derwish, a mouse-like man who would go as guide all over the country, knowing how to avoid meeting people. One large village he reckoned would be deserted, as everyone was out at harvest; so we went boldly through it, all stone-built houses of Roman age.

Once my guide was suddenly met by men on two camels taking kegs of water up to the harvesters. He talked amicably to them, but gently diverged as they were going up hill; at last, when about fifty feet from them, he twirled his eyes away. I caught the look, and we both bolted off at right angles from the track. For the men to get down, to secure the camels, and then to overtake us, was impossible.

The coins brought up to my tent were of Trajan, dating the period of settlement here. As people were too inquisitive about our leaving, I had to do it suddenly, to avoid being again waylaid. One evening I heard that a pedlar was going to Hebron, and wanted escort. Next morning we packed up everything inside the tent ready, sent for the sheykh and demanded guards, and then set off with them and the pedlar, driving the camels hard to Hebron, and later went on to Jaffa.

The variants of curses were curious, the usual Syrian "may your house be ruined," became "may the house of your father be ruined to bits." The usual

Egyptian "son of a dog," which a father will affectionately apply to his son, became "son of sixteen dogs," back to the fourth generation.

It was noticeable how short the natives were as to thirst; they needed water every hour, though only half-a-pint; I went happily for four or five hours till a quart in arrear, at two quarts short I felt bad, at three quarts short I had to lie down on my back, often, to ease the heart.

"I saw a very interesting sight at Jaffa. On a bit of waste ground, almost out of the town, were five miserable tents, and in them, or rather under their shadow, were some of the wandering iron-workers, descendants of the primitive smiths who went from place to place. They were not at all of the Arab or Syrian types. Most of the men were away looking for jobs, but I noticed one with a close, thick, short beard. The women varied much in type, one was of a sallow complexion with very rounded features, another was of a European type, with fairish skin, a handsome intelligent face, and an enormous luxuriant head of black hair; she was blowing double bellows of goat skins."

I was back in London June 28, 1890. The destruction of monuments in Egypt had roused much feeling in England as to the official neglect and incompetence of the French management. I wrote to Miss Edwards: "The whole administration is left to go to the dogs, after Baring just used the threat of (appointing) an English official to serve as a pawn in negotiating the conversion of the debt."

A society for the preservation of monuments was formed: Henry Wallis was a main mover, Sir Colin Scott-Moncrieff joined it. There was a proposal to appoint an independent inspector from England, but it was quashed by the French in Egypt. The only action which took effect was that the society paid for erecting a house at Tell el Amarna, over the painted pavement which I found.

The writing up of the work in Egypt and Palestine for publication, and the exhibiting and distribution of all the things fully occupied me till leaving England again on November 6, 1890. The Kahun plan, alone, took some weeks of plotting.

When I reached Cairo, it appeared that Grébaut was not yet coming out. The idea of getting in English inspectors I talked over with General Grenfell, Col. Ross, who was over Public Works, Baker Pasha, of the police, and Sir Chas. Cookson, our consul. Then Sir Evelyn Baring wished to talk over the inspectorate with me; thus was started the idea of putting in local inspectors to prevent the scandalous destructions which were going on under the French.

My own application for excavating was for Meydum, but nothing could be done, not even copying, without Grébaut, as the Antiquities Committee could not act without him. At last Baring agreed that if Grébaut delayed further I might proceed. However, after my dawdling in Cairo for a fortnight, Grébaut came, and I got my order for Meydum. I had brought some colours out with me for tomb copying, but when I was staying along with Henry Wallis, he was so inspiring that I took to copying antiquities, and a copy of a blue bowl which I sent to Griffith, his friends at the British Museum declared must be by Wallis.

The tombs at Meydum—the earliest then known—had been entirely neglected. Vassali had hacked away much fresco to get out the celebrated group of geese; after removing the figures of Rahetep and Nefert, the

tombs had been re-opened, and visited by the boys of
the place, who bashed the faces with stones. Mariette
had taken wet squeezes off the painted sculpture, and
left it pretty bare of colour.

To copy the whole, full size, was my immediate
duty. For the first time, dry squeezes were used; that
is to say an impression of the outline was made in
paper by finger pressure, sufficient as a guide for drawing, while the minute details of face and hands could
be drawn in by free-hand. I banked the tombs up carefully when I left, but they were not guarded, the dealers attacked them, and wrecked much. So when, in
1909-10, I worked there again, Maspero desired me
to remove all the wretched remains of these sculptures,
which ought to have been put in safety fifty years before, when they were perfect.

From copying them, I was led on to the discussion
of the original nature of the various signs, many of
which had been quite misunderstood from only knowing the later forms. This was the beginning of Egyptian epigraphy, which has been usually neglected
owing to grammarians being satisfied with written
copies and printed texts; facsimile copies are the only
satisfactory rendering, but when I started such copying, a plate was actually cancelled by Poole as being
of incorrect forms, and was redrawn in a pretty and
orthodox way by Madame Naville. The copies of Meydum published by Mariette in the *Monuments Divers*
were full of errors, with figures omitted or misunderstood. The previous work for Mariette had not disclosed any of the tomb shafts of the mastabas, so our
digging was mainly directed to that.

In the midst of this, Grébaut started new terms
which would be very hard on the excavator, but not

bar the way to dealers. There was much to and fro, which I summed up in a private letter. "The real state of things was this. The Committee and officials none of them knew anything whatever about excavating, so far as results and expenses are concerned, except Sir F. Grenfell. The Armenians—Tigran and Artin—wanted to stop me, and Grébaut was not unwilling, I expect. So they passed the impossible regulations, against the votes of Ross and Grenfell. Then Wallis wrote to Baring, saying that I was stopped, the fat was in the fire, and letters, howlings and questions in Parliament were all coming thick, if the business was not righted.

"Now Baring was already in hot water about the monuments. So he would do all he could to keep this affair quiet. He wrote and telegraphed several times to me about it. Wallis urged me to come to Cairo, but I held off, as it would seem pressing. At last, as they could not tell in Cairo what would suffice, Baring asked me to come up and settle it. This put me in the right place, an invited party to the business, and I stayed in Cairo at their request till it was settled, not hanging on as a worrier. Then I stated what was needful as safeguard if the Government took more than the *sans pareil;* and this looked so troublesome to them, that they started to take only *sans pareil* objects, and waive all their claims. I saw that, this once started, I must stick to it tightly and keep the position.

"So when the *sans pareil* and one-third more (for the Museum) was offered I refused, as it would entail an average loss on us, and a great extra loss to me in working up materials before Government took one-third. Palmer hesitated much about dealers getting an unfair advantage, and so then I worked in my previous proposal of obligatory publication, and added the compulsory presentation of half to Museums. This safeguarded the position. I gently suggested that, if not passed, we should make a warm row in England 'to strengthen the hands of Baring and Palmer in urging terms.'

"And so, after a struggle in the Council, we got it through, Riaz having been squared on it by Baring. The net result is that all the essential points—*sans pareil* definition (of things taken for Museum), compulsory presentation to Museums, publication, and an alternative for dealers of giving half to Government— are all my own proposals without any modification. We should never have got anything practicable without my being there. I have scored on other points also. I have cleared up matters to Baring and Palmer, been on the most pleasant and friendly terms with them all through, shown myself desirous to be as reasonable as possible, but yet named my own terms, asked for nothing more than was fair, and got all I asked for, exactly as I named it.

"Meanwhile the Museum Committee, and the troublesome Armenians on it, are all shelved. Applications go to Public Works, even Grébaut has no necessary voice about them. Division is ruled by Public Works also, if Grébaut is unreasonable; and the Committee is utterly ignored, and never named in the Regulations. . . . We have definitely pushed archaeology into the political situation as a thing to be guarded, and not to be thrown away. All this has been much influenced by the recent outcry in England; and has been done without the slightest personal disagreement with any of the English officials. The whole discredit rests on the Committee who raised the difficulties."

"This done I rushed back, and began to take on men as quickly as I can expand the work . . . so I start work next week with sixty men and boys."

The result of the Council of Ministers taking up the question of inspection was the appointment of D'Hulst (who had worked with Naville) as inspector of Upper Egypt. "I hear that the French are furious at the idea of D'Hulst being appointed inspector. Not only must it not be an Englishman, but no independent party, for fear of exposing the scandals of the French administration. The French Consul has bullied Riaz, so that R. has gone to his country house; and the consul actually had the indecency to write to Naville to *withdraw* N.'s testimonial to Count D'Hulst's abilities!

"Meanwhile Grébaut has not rendered any accounts for three years, and nothing like an explanation of how the money has gone can be got from him. Artin was appointed to overhaul those awful accounts, but Grébaut quietly carried off all his accounts and official papers with him, or locked them up in his house, and nothing can be done. He demands pay for seventy new guards, and cannot name more than eight; so he was told that if he could not give a list of his employés, no more salaries would be paid them. He went on to Aswan and took not the least notice. An accountant was appointed, Basil, brother-in-law of Maspero, but he cannot make out any accounts, and says the Augean stable is such that he can do nothing to clear it.

"No wonder that, with such muddle and mess, the French want to prevent anyone getting a nose into it. Grébaut telegraphed from Aswan that he *could not recognise* any such decision as that of the Council of Ministers on antiquities and digging. Pretty, for an official to refuse to obey a ministry! I have all this on good authority. . . . The French Consul will go any lengths to keep things in French hands."

This arrogant claim to be above the law was again started, and carried through by the French, when Lacau, in 1924, put out his own impossible terms for excavation, and stated that he would block any applicants who would not first sign his demands irrespective of the law. *Francia semper eadem.*

Now to get back to the tranquil toils of desert life. I wrote to Spurrell, December 11, 1890, "Here I am once more in peace in this land, and the relief of getting back here I never felt so much before. The real tranquillity and room for quiet thought in this sort of life is refreshing. I here *live,* and do not scramble to fit myself to the requirements of others. In a narrow tomb, with the figure of Nefermaat standing on each side of me—as he has stood through all that we know as human history—I have just room for my bed, and a row of good reading in which I can take my pleasure when I retire to the blankets after dinner. Behind me is that Great Peace, the Desert. It is an entity—a power—just as much as the sea is. No wonder men fled to it from the turmoil of the ancient world.

"It would do many a modern more good than anything else, both for mind and body, just to come and live in a cave, and cultivate a little bean plot like an ancient eremite, for half a year, and then return to the jangle of Europe. Every time I come back to England I am more and more disgusted with the merciless rush, and the turmoil of strife for money, and the pauseless scheming and ousting of one struggler by another. . . . The writhing and wriggling of this maggoty world is loathsome. . . . It is delightful to have

done with the degradation of having always a lac-
quey—or still worse, a woman—helping you when you
don't need it; degradation to you, because a degradation to them. When I see an obsequious waiter, I can
hardly help begging his pardon for being accessory to
a condition which so unmans him.

"Life here is on the really happy lines of give and
take, without formalities. I have a picked lot of cheerful merry fellows, who are always ready for their work,
and wholesomely anxious to do what is expected of
them, while at the same time they are straightforward
fellow-men, who give or receive help with equal frank-
ness. I already have the usual train of sore eyes, sore
heads and grazed fingers to look after."

At the Meydum pyramid we found all the corners,
and I surveyed them, and also the corners of the inner
layers exposed above. The result was of great historical
importance, as it showed that the Meydum pyramid
was directly imitated by Khufu in the Great Pyramid,
and proved what was the real objective of the size of
Khufu's pyramid, thus undercutting all the elaborate
theories. The angle was the same in both pyramids;
Sneferu at Meydum set out his pyramid at seven units
high and eleven units base, on a unit of twenty-five
cubits; Khufu followed with seven units high and
eleven units base, on a unit of forty cubits.

I cleared the interior of the Meydum pyramid, finding fragments of wooden canopics, but nothing else.
Then, in search of a false door façade, I planned to cut
away the great stack of chips on the east face. To begin
rashly would have made such a mass an impossible
encumbrance: it was needful to spend some hours in
imagining where that amount of chip should lie at the
close of the work, so as to leave the face clear.

For this, I set out on the sloping rubbish horizontal paths to each side at several levels, and all the upper stuff was run out sideways at its own level and dumped on the flanks. Only just the lowest part was carried backward and left on the ground level. Instead of a façade, I found a small temple, absolutely perfect, to this day the oldest perfect building in the land. Its two chambers, altar, and two monolithic pillars, were as the builders had left them. Only on the walls were many graffiti, some of them long ones as late as the XVIIIth dynasty, ascribing the pyramid to Sneferu.

This belief of the Egyptians we must accept, as agreeing with the data of the neighbouring tombs, but no contemporary statement of the builder remains. The causeway was also found, and the gangway up which the great blocks had been brought, as well as traces of the lower temple and its foundation deposits of pottery.

"It is satisfactory to find that I am paying less than anyone else for labour. The Fund paid Jaillon at the rate of ninety-five paras per cubic metre, Government contracts used to be sixty, now (1889) they are fifty to forty, and I pay from thirty to twenty according to the hardness, or three-halfpence to one penny per cubic yard. Col. Ross who was over here yesterday, was astonished at the amount done *per* man, and chuckled over cutting down the Government terms. As one para on the metre means £10,000 a year to Government, a minute change of rate is very important. Notwithstanding the low rate, my men are, many of them, earning double the ordinary day wages, they work so hard."

The saving was due to letting the men get individual measurement and payment, so that zeal had its reward, also to there being no profit or remuneration to the manager; every man was dealt with by myself, unpaid, without intermediary, a system then—and still—scarcely used elsewhere.

Though the tombs at Meydum produced hardly anything but pottery, they were an indispensable link between earlier ages and the pyramid times. The system of successive coats explained the structure of later tomb chapels; the mummy of Ra-nefer, with its modelling of the body in resin, gave the first elaborate form of mummifying in the end of the IIIrd dynasty. The geometrical and perfect method of setting out a mastaba with sloping sides, on a very uneven base, let me into the clear structural ideas of the pyramid builders. The groups of flint flakes found in tombs enabled Spurrell to reconstruct the original block, showing how the flaking was done. The pottery of bright polished red ware is the beginning of the style of the pyramid builders.

For saving the early skeletons which were found, and which had much salt in the bones, I first devised the jelly process, melting a lot of size in which the bones were placed, and left to set for some weeks: thus the salt dialyzed out into the jelly, and on re-melting it the bones can be taken out unsalted. This is the method which I later applied to ivories, with good result, setting them in very stiff gelatine. Many burials of late times were found in the pyramid rubbish, giving good sets of dated beads.

I also bought up large quantities of beads in sets, brought over by dealers from the Fayum. "My object is now to make up a great standard collection of dated beads; type specimens, and strings of all the more usual varieties." A generation later, I carried this out at University College, with more than a thousand strings of beads, beside lesser specimens extending back to three prehistoric ages, undreamt of when I was at Meydum.

For some weeks I had the society of Bliss, who was learning to excavate, in view of continuing work at Tell Hesy for the Palestine Fund. "Among visitors I had Lieut. Lyons, R.E., an active young geologist and antiquarian, who makes expeditions and surveys on his own account. To-day I had F. F. Tuckett, of Dolomite fame, with Mr. Hudd, an antiquary."

I left Egypt, April 23, for Athens, in order to apply the dating which had been found at Gurob to the Mykenaean discoveries there, helped in all ways by my former companion, Ernest Gardner, who had become head of the British School there.

After drawing and examining the early material, "The general outline of my results are these. The Mykenaean civilisation was widespread, the objects imitated from Egyptian sources are *not* made in Egypt, but made in Greece, showing evidence of a high civilisation there, capable of inlaying metals in several colours, and of glazing pottery with elaborate patterns. From the cat and lotus on this native work, the makers must have been familiar with Egypt itself. Then the silver elk or reindeer, and the Baltic amber show a northern intercourse; and the evident origin of Celtic ornament in the Mykenaean, and the Scandinavian custom of draping tumulus-chambers, point to a continuity with the northern European civilisation. We deal, therefore, with a great widespread civilisation, and not a local culture. This agrees with the Egyptian inscriptions which show the power of the Libyo-Aegean league which attacked them.

"As to dates, many of the things came from Egypt in 1450 B.C., and the designs even from 1650, which is what we might expect if the Aegean civilisation was already rising as early as 2500 B.C." (referring to Kamares ware at Kahun). "The epoch of grand tombs, such as the great treasuries, would be about 1400 to 1200 B.C.; the splendid cups of gold from Vapheio, which show such high art, being about 1200. Then decadence set in, and is markedly shown in the great finds of Schliemann of the graves in the circle of the acropolis; those I date about 1150 by various points, mainly the colours of some green glazed things.

"Then, about 1000 B.C., came in the impressed glass ornaments, as they are nearly always along with ribbed Egyptian beads of 1000-800 B.C. The tombs of Menidi, Spata, Nauplia, and those lately found at Mykenae, all belong to this age. The Doric migration broke up this civilisation there, and a date has just turned up for the 'dipylon vases' from two glazed lions in a recent find which cannot be earlier than 650 B.C. As the vases cannot be later, this fixes their date very closely. All this was at first called my 'heresy' by Gardner."

When at last I put down all I had to say in order, and he read it, he said that he could not but agree with me throughout, and he considered that I had "done more in a week than the Germans had done in ten years to clear up the matter from an Egyptian basis." It may be worth recording how far matters had advanced in 1891, before the swamping effect of all the Cretan discoveries. There seems little to alter in the outline reached then, though forty years have since passed.

From Athens I had the benefit of going to the Peloponnesos sites with Walter Leaf. There I found examples of tube drilling, and sawing with a bronze saw set with emery teeth, on stones at Tiryns; it appears as if the methods had been carried down from the age of the pyramid builders. In the great treasury dome I noticed the plug holes at irregular distances in lower stones, proving that these were not for bronze rosettes, but for fixing a lining; and as the distance apart would be too great for a metal lining, they must have been for a woven lining, such as is indicated by the glazed imitations of tied-up linings.

"The so-called museum at Mykenae is melancholy; a shanty piled up with heaps of fine things, invisible in their confusion: forty large baskets of pieces of painted pottery, pieces of frieze, large leaden and bronze vessels." Is it any better now? "One morning, quite unexpectedly, up drove Prof. Blackie to stay with the Gardners; a genial hyper-borean of immense age and signal authoritativeness, with whom it is impossible to do aught but agree in silence to his harangues, as his mind does not readily conceive of any different point of view from his own. He argued on Greek accent all day with all comers, and sang Scotch songs with but small provocation."

I travelled home through Italy, with Pickard the American archaeologist, from whom I gathered the orthodox points of view on ancient art. "And I went to Ravenna. It is the Roman world still living. . . . Every other place, almost, has died; Pompeii is dead and only stands a skeleton; Egyptian temples are dead; even the Pantheon is in a new guise. But here are the churches as Honorius and Theodoric built them, brick for brick; here are the mosaics with which they encrusted them exactly as they were put up while

Rome was the world's power, as bright, as fresh, as clear, as when the Emperor passed his approval on them. . . .

"And they are still living buildings, cared for, used, and have never been a day out of human hands and attention since Rome was, and all northern Europe a wilderness. . . . As the mosaics are all of fractured glass not ground or polished, the surfaces retain their brilliancy. . . . Ravenna, from its vitality and its perfection, is a far more moving sight than Rome—perhaps the most impressive place that I have ever seen. It strikes on one as if an ichthyosaurus and plesiosaurus had kept house together in some unworldly nook since Mesozoic times, and offered to show off for a trifling consideration."

On June 15 I was back in London and took a small house for three months for unpacking and work at Bromley, near our own. The produce from Meydum was not of sufficient public interest to warrant having rooms in London. Each of the town exhibitions cost me sixty to eighty pounds for rent and door-keeping, and I had to recoup that by shilling entrances—if I could do so. A large part of the work was the joining up and inking the full-sized copies of the tombs of Nefermaat and Rahetep, eleven feet high. Large pieces of fresco had been found fallen down from the façade of Nefermaat; these, on cakes of mud plaster, a couple of inches thick, I had packed in straw, but I had now to arrange for their permanence. The fresco was laid face down on a table. Little by little I cut away the mud from the back, and as soon as a couple of square inches of the back of the stucco face was bare, I closed up the cracks by shifting the chips into place, and then put on a cream of fresh plaster on the back. When done, the whole stucco face lay with a backing skin of plaster. I then cut a slate to the over-all size of the fresco, laid on the fresco a pudding of very thin plaster and pressed the slate down on it as closely as I could. When hard, the fresco was then safely fixed on slate.

Beside writing up *Meydum*, I had also to do a small general account of excavations, brought out as *Ten Years' Digging*.

The publishing of all my work was a struggle, having only £110 of fixed income for living and travelling, and precarious additions from museums in return for some things in my share of antiquities. In August, 1891, I wrote to Miss Edwards: "I am so accustomed to shelling out to printers that it seems to me the course of human nature. I have about £100 sunk in publications already, beside a quantity due to me from those publishers who won't cash up; I write and ask for accounts and am put off, so that I have had no receipts, except through Riley, for two years. One is thus much more than a whole year's income in arrears, by the honour and glory of paying one's own printers; and I am going to launch into about £150 more of publishing this year, perhaps before I can get any receipts from the Barabbases.

"Even through Riley it is bad enough when there are five or six defaulters on one book alone, dignitaries of Church and State who have got a copy and calmly ignore all claims—even a request to return it.

"Even for antikas I have my troubles; only the other day I got £50 due to me for three years ago, and Murray (Brit. Mus.) owes nearly £20 and won't pay for a year or two more, as he is bled by this great purchase of gold" (from Aegina). I could but say in another letter, "It has been a bitter sight to me, everything being so split up in England that no really representative collection of my results could be kept together."

## CHAPTER VII

## TELL EL AMARNA

ON October 22, 1891, I left London. In Cairo Gré-baut had "got the native members of Committee, while the English were on holiday, to appoint two tools of his as curators of the museum, and two natives —who were not even guards before—as inspectors of the guards. I called on Sir Colin Scott-Moncrieff, who was as amiable as possible. He has written twice already to Grébaut about my fresh application—but no answer. Then to Sir Evelyn Baring, who was quite open and pleasant on the subject, but is evidently not free to take a strong course. . . . Baring had seen Reverseaux, the French Consul, about the affair, to tell him that he must make Grébaut reasonable, and Reverseaux had sent for Grébaut this morning. So when G. does come, he will be fully primed for diplomatic resistance. I expect we shall have a tussle, and I want to settle matters in Moncrieff's presence and not alone."

(Two days later.) "Again to Moncrieff's and had an hour with Grébaut. First M. took the question of place. I let out to him just before that I was not solely needing Saqqareh, but that it was G.'s weakest point—about Farag digging there—and so I could work best on him with that. M. took up my line excellently, and pressed and cross-questioned G. most diligently about it for a long time. At last, as G. stuck to its being reserved for the Museum and its agents, M. turned and asked me if there was any other place I could take.

G. had already barred Abydos—like Saqqareh—so I alluded to that, to let him negative it again, and then named Tell el Amarna. He said that they were working there and had been excavating the tombs for some time. I pressed for the town, and to that he acceded, and Moncrieff nailed him clearly to it.

"But as to terms he was out of all reason. M. asked him to name what terms he wished, to see at least if I agreed and so it could be settled. G. declined to discuss the question in relation to any private person. It was a general affair to come before a General Committee. I was to go at 10 on Saturday to consider new terms. I went, and found that G. had proposed almost exactly what they had fully discussed and negatived last year.

"I waited half an hour, and Grébaut never came. So then I forwarded my old contract (with an amendment which G. had proposed) and pressed that that should be used direct for this year, taking my stand on the existing law. . . . G. claims that all they decreed last year was invalid without his signature, which is preposterous, and not tolerated by Baring or Moncrieff. So I copied off my old contract modified, and left that, and M. promised to push it through if possible. . . . Even Artin, who backed G., called him openly *un imbécile* at the French Institute. . . .

"The Committee was held on the 10th . . . and Sir F. Grenfell began by saying (to me), 'We had a desperate struggle over your body for two and a half hours yesterday. . . . Grébaut was perfectly obstinate . . . and nothing could be done. Tigran Pasha moved that under the existing law you should be allowed to go on with work, until the two years of that law were expired. . . . But G., as President of the Committee, had drawn up his orders of the day, and refused to listen to anything else except his proposals, or to put any other question to the Committee. After wasting two and a half hours with him, we—Moncrieff, Palmer and myself—all left the room in a body and declared that we should not sit on any Committee in future of which Grébaut was President. . . . He came running after us with explanations, but we refused to hear anything further.' "

At Amarna I "was glad to find my contract come. It is amusing to see that—rather than be left out— Grébaut had signed it. As it is a contract between the Minister of Public Works and me, Grébaut has no official voice in it, and had refused to recognise the contract last year. But when he finds that it will be granted in any case, he comes round to putting his name to a precisely similar contract."

A few days later I hear that Grébaut had got passed a new set of regulations about excavating which were fatuously absurd. The affair had ended in a political bargain with Baring, and he wrote to me "that he does not see any reason to interfere with the regulations. As they are purely Grébaut's proposals, without modification, it is evident that B. has again sold us entirely (in a political bargain) with regard to voluntary work, as well as the appointments. So there is nothing further to be hoped for, except from a public agitation in England, or going over to some foreign Government. . . . The Fund is only working because Naville has weakly given in, and assented that he will not remove anything except small objects (which he never finds) ."

Two months later, Milner "had not heard about the new terms, but at once said they were preposterous when I named them." A day or two later came the news "Grébaut is out! and a mining engineer put in who is absolutely unknown, M. Jacques de Morgan, French, of course." Really he was the son of Jack Morgan, a Welsh mining engineer, and brother of a Parisian dealer in antiquities. He knew nothing whatever about Egypt but, as a capable business man, made the most reputable head that the French could find.

Now for the work. I went down to Medinet-el-Fayum and walked over to Lahun, soon having dozens of my old workers round me, who were most eager to join; one man for no more than he was getting in easy work as a guard, another who was lately married held my hand and was only kept back by his father; all were ready to go off anywhere. I picked half a dozen most suitable, and promised them 10d. instead of 7½d. a day, to pay for food away. "More willing or kindly fellows no one could find. No doubt they might be spoilt by a few months' carelessness; and in such a case, I consider, woe to the man by whom offences come." The bad master is more to blame than the bad servant.

At Amarna we settled against an outer wall of the village, resisted all the bluster and blandishments of the people, and built ourselves huts. The dogs were very noisy, but the worst I told them to tie up (as thus they are quite quiet), or bring me the carcase for which I would pay 5d., or I would shoot the dog next night.

When the sheykh tried to get between me and the people, to levy toll, I said I should move over to the rival village if he interfered. The sheykh ordered his people to bring my finds to him, so I wrote about him to Cairo. He guessed my subject, followed the messenger, and destroyed my letter. Then he came bullying to know why I was annoyed with him. So I told him the whole affair, and said I should write again; he tried to beg off, but I said I should write to my friends, the judges, whatever I chose. I got a good reprimand sent to him.

Soon after beginning on the site of Akhenaten's palace we found large painted pavements, one whole, and two portions, about 250 square feet in all. I wrote to Cairo asking that the Public Works should build to protect them. This was at last arranged, leaving the direction to me, and getting the English Society for Preservation to pay for the building. I had to plan it to allow of putting gangways resting on the blanks where there had been pillars, to adjust it so as to make a single walk through for visitors without reversal, and then to carpenter all the gangways and rails myself, 270 feet run, as no native could be trusted not to drag wood over the painting.

When the safe-guarding of the frescoes was complete, I drew the whole 1/10 in outline, and several of the best parts in colour on a larger scale. These drawings appear in *Tell el Amarna*. Visitors were greatly interested with the largest known examples of Egyptian painting, and its link to Mykenaean art: in later years tourists stopped regularly to see it. The department provided no path for them, and the fields were trampled; so one night a man went and hacked it all to pieces to prevent visitors coming. Such was the mismanaged end of a unique find. I was never even informed and allowed to pick up the pieces.

Another painting was more fortunate. On a wall there was the lower part of a royal group with two seated figures of little princesses. It was painted on a sort of whitewash on a mud plaster, which was riddled mostly into dust by white ants. On a still day, with a

THE ART OF AMARNA

PRINCESSES SEATED AT COURT
SCENES ON THE PALACE PAVEMENT

carpenter's chisel, I cut to pieces, without any vibration, little by little, the mud bricks of the wall, until I had the facing of mud, 30 × 16 inches, standing on edge, free in the air. Having previously cut through where it should part, I brought up a box lid against the face with newspaper padding on it, grasped the sheet of mud against the lid, and turned it down. On getting it to my hut I brushed the dust off the back, made a grid of wooden bars an inch square, and as much apart, put a layer of mud on each bar and then pressed it down on the back of the mud, and put more mud as keying between all the bars. On reversal, there was the fresco unhurt resting on the grid.

For transport, I cut a skin of thin wood just to the size of the fresco, laid it on with a layer of cotton wool between, and then lashed that tight to the bars. Thus it travelled perfectly. I did half a dozen pieces in this way; De Morgan took one of the best, and told a Museum servant to carry it off; he promptly put his finger between the bars, and it ran through the fresco, and came out on the face. The princesses went to Oxford, with all the best of the Amarna finds; then, after some years, a coat of varnish was mistakenly put on the face to preserve the paint, sadly darkening and yellowing it, besides destroying the most interesting dusting with powdered orpiment which indicated the high lights reflected.

If anything was needful, thin tapioca would have been best, as not darkening the surface: such a coat was well known, as I had coated the whole of the painted floor with tapioca. I took daily with me bottles of thick and of thin tapioca water over to the pavement, tried on each part of the paving what thickness would just sink in without leaving any glair, and then spread that over the surface, entirely with the side of my forefinger. Any brush would have swept up the loose blue frit paint, but the finger could just glide or roll over the tender parts without shifting anything. There were 250 square feet to do, but it could not be done every day, or the skin wore away too quickly for renewal.

While I did all this, my most skilful boy was plastering on a necking all round the broken edges, to prevent their being caught in sweeping. All the windows I had set in with mud, not opening, so as to keep out the sand. For the few minutes of visits, ventilation was not needed. However, all the care was thrown away by mismanagement and destruction a few years later.

Sayce came over, and was told by Alexander Barsanti, the Museum man, that he had been lately clearing Akhenaten's tomb. This is what Grébaut referred to as their work. "The tomb was found some years ago by the Arabs, and has been rifled by them of all that they thought saleable (such as the gold sold in 1881 to Loftie). Then they sold the secret of it to the Government; but it is hard to get to the bottom of the matter, as accounts vary.

"Alexander professes to have discovered the tomb by his unaided abilities on December 30, 1891, while some days before that an official said he knew all about it, that it had been known for two years to them, and that he could show the place. Then Alexander told me that Daressy had come here on January 1, to see it, and D. seemed to know all about the place as I went up with him; yet Sayce was told that D. had only seen it first the day we were there. Then one of the workmen muttered to me that they had been clearing it for four months past.

"The truth of the matter will probably never be set down, and certainly not if Grébaut has his way, for he has telegraphed to Alexander to stop clearing it till he comes, so that he may pick up something and say he discovered it. The work has gone on as slatternly as Museum business generally does. Alexander began it, certainly by January 1, and when I went with him on January 20, he said he had been to the tomb six times, so two days out of three, the men were left to rake about without supervision." The whole staff seemed, like the Irishman, to "have too much respect for the truth to be dragging it in on every occasion."

Barsanti was an Italian plaster-worker for casts; he became the salesman in the Museum shop, and then, without any training or skill except what may be native to him, he was left to rake over one of the most important matters in the country, without any idea of the historical questions to be ascertained. I observed what seemed to me clearly to be three unopened tombs in the hills, but as I was forbidden to touch that part, they remain unopened still, after forty years.

The ruins of the palace provided much of the sculpture, the naturalistic plant designs, the inlaid stone hieroglyphs, the glazed faïence columns, and an inlaid faïence capital. By the palace some boys picked up the plaster death-mask of Akhenaten, which apparently had been made as a model for the sculptors, because close by were the unfinished granite ushabtis. After Barsanti had finished the tomb, and left the place, the workmen brought me pieces of the ushabtis from there.

It was surprising to see the Aegean pottery, so abundant here, entirely different from that of the same age at Gurob. It seems that two different sources and routes must have been in use at once. All the distinctive fragments from Amarna I copied in colour, and left them at the British School in Athens as the best dated material for comparison.

The large waste ground of the palace, and of the glaze workers, we turned over, securing a great quantity of glaze and glass (now in University College), which showed the products and methods of that age. Hundreds of pottery moulds, for making the glazed ornaments, were found. The jar inscriptions were valuable for the dates; the highest year of Akhenaten was the 17th. Though so much has been written and done about that strange man and place, scarcely anything has been added to the scanty history that was traced out in my work of 1891, which covered almost all that we yet know.

One evening there was a curious instance of the insensibility of the Egyptian to natural beauty. I was walking with Aly Suefy, the most intelligent fellah that I ever met, and I remarked on the gorgeous sky of crimson dapple on a full blue ground, the most brilliant that I remember; but Aly could not see anything out of the way, and seemed surprised that I noticed it.

In the beginning of 1891, Howard Carter came, as a lad of seventeen, to join me in order to do some excavating for Mr. Tyssen Amherst. His interest then was entirely in painting and natural history, and I little thought how much he would be enabled to do. To keep his work distinct, I left to him the clearing on the temple site. There he found the broken statues of the queen, torsos and masses of chips from them. We carefully gathered up all the flakes in order to reconstitute the statues.

The torsos and the fragments of the queen's face were—after Lord Amherst's death—sold for hundreds of pounds at Sotheby's, while the boxes full of flakes which should have completed them were thrown away as stone waste. Thus perished the chance of reconstituting the priceless figures of that age.

During that season my whole prospects greatly changed, and a new order of affairs began. On March 5 my mother died, and my link to Bromley was much less. On April 15, Miss Amelia Betham Edwards died, and in the summer her will was carried out, by inviting me to take up the foundation which she had bequeathed for Egyptology to University College, London. My own health had been doubtful in the previous year, and the long heat (up to 112°) at Amarna brought forward a severe gastric ulceration, which crippled me in the autumn. In every way I had to rearrange my life, and it was two or three years before I was free of dangerous internal troubles.

In the first half of May I finished packing at Amarna, and sent off 125 cases, did the survey later, and came to Cairo on 29th. I was much surprised there at receiving a telegram asking me to accept the honorary degree of D.C.L. at Oxford on June 22. De Morgan proved very business-like and quick in settling things, and I left on the 4th, to London on 11th. I had to go to Miss Edwards' house and see after the removal of her antiquities bequeathed to University College. There was much to do in plotting out the Amarna plans, unpacking, and preparing exhibition by September 19. After that I was seriously ill, and unfit to move for some weeks, during which I listed all the Egyptian titles within reach in books.

So soon as I could get about, I had to come up to

lodgings in London, and see after the packing and distribution of the Amarna collection. Also to begin arrangements at University College, where the preliminaries of a new chair had to be discussed. A committee was appointed to interview me, and I drew up an outline of what seemed feasible; when I began to state the course, the Chairman reddened; it looked serious; I was deprecatory; he got redder; I went on to the end, thinking all was lost, and his face was flaming. A dead silence—at last broken by a gentle voice: "I do not see why we should not agree to all this." Such was my first experience of the shyness of the gentlest of men, Professor Ker.

At last the exhibition was all cleared and done by the new year, and on January 6, I moved, in a hard frost, to be near the College. Weakened as I was, it was a struggle day by day to get through a pile of business while feeling that I was hardly alive in the world; everything seemed unreal and strange. I arranged Miss Edwards' books, looked up book catalogues to buy needful additions, and gave an introductory lecture on January 14, and a six weeks' course after that on the history. Then at the end of February I went off, with an old friend, John Borrowman, to Naples, and rested in Pompeii, baked through in sunshine.

After two or three weeks we moved up north to all the Museums in which I had permission to photograph, and I brought back nearly 500 negatives of the Egyptian objects, and copies of all the ushabtis. I was scarcely over internal difficulties yet, but got through a good deal before I was back in London by May 1. In Rome there was an interesting company just then, Mahaffy, Stillman, Lumbroso, Lanciani and Dennis: one day, after seeing several places, Mahaffy suddenly grasped my arm saying: "My dear choild, we're seeing a ghreat dheal too much!" Dennis was a delightful old fellow with bushy white hair, saying he felt as much a boy as ever.

Back in London, Griffith lodged along with me, as he was then in the British Museum, and we worked up the English translation of Egyptian Tales; Griffith roughed out a literal version, I smoothed it into uniform shape, and then he reviled and revised it if the sense was not true enough. There was another course of lectures, and attending to new students at the College. In the summer, there was the working up the plates of Amarna and the text.

On May 17, a young man turned up who had graduated on Greek and chemistry, to inquire if there would be an opening for him in Egypt. This was J. E. Quibell, later on the Curator of Cairo Museum. By August 15 he was coming every day to learn things in the unpacking and arranging of Miss Edwards' collection and of my own things, at the College. Next, I had to begin working up a textbook of Egyptian History, in order to give students all the facts, and the references to the original works. This served for my autumn lectures.

It may be thought that my personal cares were over, when landed in a Professorship. The whole income of that, however, was only £140, and a share of fees, which I had put as low as was allowed. Out of that, I engaged Griffith for language classes. So I had little over £100 a year, on which to find lodging and living in London. Moreover, the lawyers who did the transfer of Miss Edwards' property to the College, and drew up deeds, "thought it would be better to pay all the costs out of interest," and left me with nothing for a year.

The College was then much in debt, and could not be expected to support an outside subject, although the staff always gave kindly interest to the new venture. It was only many years after that there was any aid from College funds, which gradually raised me to my supposed status of a half-time post. This limit was due to my only appearing in two terms, and spending my winter in excavating. Work in Egypt was not College business, though it gave vitality to the College in the public view.

As an open window on private motives then, a letter written to Spurrell, February 23, 1893, may be cited. "People do look at money so differently. I wish they did not. I have a little, but want less, therefore I am rich. When I want money to dig with, I have no scruple in asking for it. Perhaps I may ask you for £50 some day to excavate with; till then I want none. And as to money matters at the College, if I had my way there would be no fees. That is impossible by their custom. Hence I ask the minimum allowed, and make that include whatever I can do. Money and knowledge do not seem to me to have any common measure, any more than money and affection. A money-making professor seems to my feelings about as indecent a spectacle as a toadying heir or a venal beauty. I regard the saving of a sixpence as a sacred duty, when there is no good reason for spending it; and the spending of it as a still more imperative affair when there is a reason."

## CHAPTER VIII

## KOPTOS, NAQADA, AND THEBES

THE need of bringing on new students led to my starting a Research Account to collect enough for a student's expenses, my good friend Hilton Price being treasurer, and A. L. Lewis, accountant. On that basis I took Quibell out with me to Egypt on November 15, 1893, visited Maspero in Paris, and reached Cairo on the 23rd. The new management under De Morgan was pleasant, "but from other things I have heard, he is finding himself under the political thumb (of Paris), whether he will or no, and he has to trim his course accordingly."

I applied for Koptos (Quft), for by then it seemed likely that the dynastic people had come up the Red Sea from Punt, and across the desert to reach the Nile at Koptos. This supposition was justified by our results, and discovery since then has always confirmed this view. While we were in the midst of the work, De Morgan arrived on his voyage of inspection. He saw all we had found, and ceding to us two of the three prehistoric figures of Min, he settled to take the other large monuments, and left all smaller objects to us; further, he would remove his large things to Cairo.

These terms were the most convenient for me, but he was frank enough to say that if I found any very important site he would take it over himself. He said that it was inconvenient to have applications sent in at the November Committee, on such short notice, and that I had better apply in the previous May. I did so, and when I went out in November I heard that a Museum *reis* had been all the summer picking over my site. This happened again, and after that I never let out where I wanted to work till November. It was strangely short-sighted to think that the Museum would secure things better through an ignorant and corrupt *reis* rather than by taking what was desirable from me. Perhaps Paris was behind the business.

Picking up some of my old hands from the Fayum and Amarna, Quibell and I landed from the post boat at Quft, and after delays got settled into huts built under the shelter of the Roman fortifications. Having half a dozen fellows in a hut, all good friends together, some curious points of native habit came out. Every market day each of them would cook a separate little pot of lentils alone; I laughed at them, and tried to get the reason why one should not cook for all. They fenced for some time, till one blurted out: "If two people eat together, each of them thinks the other gets more than himself." Yet lentils were absurdly cheap then, but the innate feeling kept them apart.

One night I had to look in late about sending a letter, and all the six were lying exactly like mummies, side by side, full length on their backs, each with a shawl tucked in at the feet and drawn tight over the head, with arms at sides. Evidently the mummy attitude was the natural one for the historic Egyptian.

Grenfell was with us for seven weeks, getting accustomed to work in Egypt. Our first business was to clear the temple site; the built remains proved all Ptolemaic, but just as other Ptolemaic temples had stowed earlier work out of the way, so I hoped to get the primitive remains buried below. We found, in many places, pits in the yellow clay on which the place was built, cut to contain large blocks which could not be re-used. Thus the three colossi of Min, the vulture of Amen-emhat III, and the triad of Ramessu II were all sunk out of the way.

Further, the foundations of Tehutmes III were found to contain the sculptures of the Antef and Senusert temples; while, below all, we got a mass of potsherds and pieces of pottery figures, which we later knew to be prehistoric, back to s.d. 32. A Ptolemaic temple site is therefore a mine of history, even after the temple has disappeared. Many foundation deposits of Tehutmes III were found.

Altogether, we got remains of thirty-six Kings of Egypt, from Khufu to Quietus. Being so near Thebes, it was one of the most lively places for dealers, "as a public road runs through the temple site we cannot keep people out entirely, and there are frequent rows. At first a Copt dealer and his son were constant watch-ers, but we hustled them out of the way. Then dealers came riding in and prying about. When, to cover their position, they offered me forgeries, I threw them away.

"Both Q. and I have had regular tussles with men who would not move off, quickly seconded by our own men, who mauled the loafers considerably each time. Altogether we have educated the spy party into fleeing at once whenever they see us coming in the distance." One man Quibell held down while I walloped him. He swore he would go to the Consul; that I had broken his leg; I let him crawl off on hands and knees some way, and then, giving a shout, ran at him, when he made off like a hare. A week later, while I was going through a village a couple of miles away, looking for stones, this man came out of a house and followed me, soon joined by another. I walked on, and listened for their talk. The beaten man remarked: "Yes, he is a good man, he is strong." I knew then that I had made a friend by firmness; this being a rare quality in Egypt, it is valued.

As it was useless to arrest a man and take him to the sheykh—for no one ever knew their neighbours under arrest—I then took to grabbing at the head shawl in the fray, and winding it on to my arm; thus I secured half a dozen shawls, always with the promise of sending them to the man's sheykh if he would give the name. It was a great disgrace, to go back bareheaded, and shawls were worth a dollar each; so by this method the spy business was cured.

There was not only the danger of the spy buying from our men, but the worse risk of night raids. When we found the Antef slabs in the foundations, I said after supper that I did not like leaving them unguarded all night, and moved over a tent and some men on to the spot. At once we had dogs barking at us in the dark, on all sides, proving that villagers were out on the place, and it was only our guard which saved the sculptures.

I have never found it needful to chastise a workman, the eye and the power of the purse suffice; nor will I let the native use the familiar strap or lash on the children. The art of keeping the pot boiling lies in being surprisingly about. A private approach to the view of the work is so arranged that my coming up cannot be signalled along to the main body. On getting in sight of the work, it is best to stand quite still for five or ten minutes, watching everyone in turn, and looking for men or children who are not active. Then it is needful to trace out quietly what the cause may be,—usually the men waiting for the return of the basket boys. Look out the lines of discharge of the earth, and see if they can be shortened; make out the causes of delay and then rearrange matters, always pointing out the change as a favour and help to the workers, so that they feel it not as a reproach but an assistance. Usually the lines of work once started are continued blindly, running on the same course like ants, though the working face may have passed into quite a different position, and the discharge line may be shortened to half or less of the distance.

Of course sheer laziness without a cause means immediate dismissal; but the break of ten minutes in the midst of the morning and afternoon seems desirable all round. If the whole work needs tuning up, then "the devil take the hindmost," and whoever does least is cleared out; the same may be applied to keeping up punctuality in the morning. At San, working near the village, the people used to loiter over the dinner hour, and not heed the whistle; so one day, when they were worse than usual, I went to meet them as they tardily came up, and dismissed them all for the half day. After that they all came as soon as they had their food, and sat round my huts waiting for the time.

The essential spur is the quiet eye; let the workers see that you are watching and assessing them without any bluster, and never calling attention till you have examined what is going on; then everyone feels the need of keeping up to the mark, as they cannot tell when a fatal dismissal may suddenly fall on them. The same way applies in London; when a carman lashes a horse in a temper, to stand quite still watching—or take out a note-book and pencil—checks the passion, for fear of being reported, and the fellow will stop, and, turning to you, say: "There, is that all right now?"

while it does not leave an excitement to be vented on the horse afterwards.

At Koptos we tried hard to find the cemetery on the desert, but could not get a single grave. Yet by the Customs tariff it was proved that the funerals went up to the desert. The only conclusion was that the cemetery had lain on the neck of land between the clay rise of the town and the higher desert, and had been entirely covered, since, by the rise of Nile deposits, now cultivated fields.

An interesting character called on us, Bishara Nakaleh, a Coptic landowner, who carried on much the same life as the old feudal chiefs of the early times. He had thousands of acres, and was buying up still more. He regularly bought up crops at harvest, when the improvident would sell cheaply, and then retailed them later. He thus mopped up the loose money of the district, and then gave it out as required. He had the greatest reputation for generosity and kindness, and fulfilled the old Egyptian ideal of a good magnate.

He looked at our bread, tasted, and disapproved of it; then said if we would send over twice a week he would supply us, as he had the best bread-maker in the country. We gladly accepted it. His house had all the business of the district going on in it, by his servants: the old scribe sat crooning over ancient airs as he cast up the accounts; it was the XIIth dynasty still alive.

By the end of February I left, as there was much to be done in London, and Quibell stayed till early in May, carrying on the work and packing. The excavation here was the founding of a tribe of workers who have been sought for by every excavator since; a "Qufti" came to be almost the name for a good digger. There were many substantial old families here, entirely unspoiled by tourist ways, and they formed a fine stock; even their grandsons are still in my work.

There was also a mixture of Ababdeh desert folk; one of the mixed lot was Erfai, then a little lad of beautiful proportions, who grew up into our finest workman, six feet high and of immense strength. There was a second strong man rather shorter, and in Sinai I saw Erfai take the other by his upper arms, lift him up in the air, turn him heels over head above his own head, and let him down gently behind. Erfai would carry a block of four hundredweight over rough ground, down hill and up. Unhappily he insisted on going back to his village while there was an epidemic, took it, and died.

The drilling which we gave our Quftis about water supply proved its value. One summer, cholera was virulent in Egypt, and though five hundred died in Quft, not one of our men or their families were ill. They said that, as soon as illness came about, they all went far into the fields and dug new wells, and, using only the fresh water, so escaped. The country, of course, regarded this as a piece of *baraka,* good fortune, due to our work.

In London the first business was to open a thick roll of papyrus which I had bought, seeing it was on the affairs of the country. This was the now celebrated Revenue Papyrus, edited by Grenfell. It had been sufficiently rotted to make the two layers liable to part and fall to pieces, so it could not be damped, to unroll it. Then it had been crushed while rolled, so that it could not unroll dry. It was needful to cut through every bend, and so take each turn into about a dozen pieces, and then mount all the bits in right position.

Warned by the injury done in pasting papyri down

on card, as so usual in museums, I tried a new method. Very thin paper was taken as a backing, so that it could, if needful, be torn up, liberating the papyrus. Each fragment was stuck down by minute touches of paste around its edges. Thus no expansion or warping could affect it. When card is mounted under glass, it warps, falls back, and.lets air in, which is most injurious. So I used thin picture back-board for the backing, picked for even grain, and baked dry in an oven. Then the edges were secured to the glass with glued strips of linen, air-tight. Thus it is now in the Bodleian. The management of this took a fortnight.

The statues of Min, which were the most important examples of prehistoric work, certainly older than the dynasties, I much wished to send to the British Museum. As it was not probable that the Egyptian department would accept them, I went to the Prehistoric department, had a long talk about it with Read, and went so far as to agree what would be the best position and lighting for them. The matter had to wait till Franks came back from holiday.

On return he wrote to me that he was "advised that the figures are unhistoric rather than prehistoric," and therefore declined them. The comment was absolute nonsense, as applied to figures of gods from an Egyptian temple, and it is not difficult to guess the source of advice. Much followed in consequence; the Museum's refusal made us immediately offer the figures to the Ashmolean, where they were at once accepted. Those figures being there led next year to the offer of the whole of the great type collection of the prehistoric Egyptian civilisation from Naqada going also to Oxford, and making that the standard place for the early Egyptian art. That in turn led to the Hierakonpolis

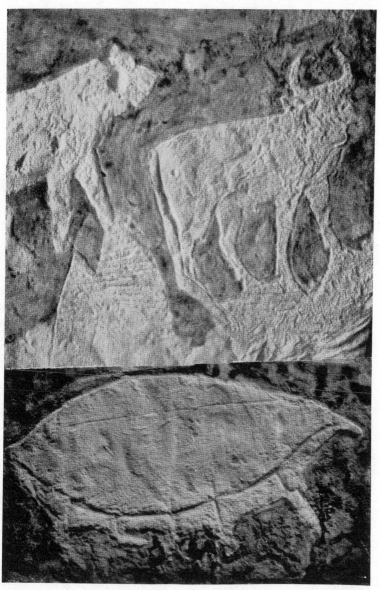

RELIEFS OF PREHISTORIC STATUES OF MIN
HYAENA CHASING COW ON THE HILLS
PTEROCERAS SHELL OF RED SEA

sculptures following there. Thus the folly of a bit of spiteful advice put Oxford for all time ahead of London in early Egyptian history. Such chances never recurred, nor are likely to arise again.

The summer passed in preparation for the exhibition, opened on July 23, and in getting ready the volume on Koptos, though I was partly laid by with old troubles at this time. I was working up the History, and lecturing on Decorative Art. There was much stir about the drowning of Philae by a great dam. A petition to the Foreign Office (in which I was concerned), was signed by nearly all who understood the questions, and for the time the dam was not raised high enough to ruin the temples. Though as historic or artistic works they were not of great consequence, yet as the only Egyptian temples which retained the colouring they were unique, and should have been preserved.

The delay was only temporary, and after a few years the dam was raised to full height, and the temples ruined, amid a strange lot of false statements and inspired comments. I went to Sir William Garstin and pleaded hard that at least Sir John Aird's offer should be accepted, to level down one of the higher islands, and transfer the temples block by block (with wire rope haulage) across to a site above the flood.

Garstin replied to me that the archaeologists had that offer before, and they refused it, therefore they should not have the chance again. In short, Philae was sacrificed to Garstin's personal pique. The real reason for the strong drive made officially to put up the high dam has never been stated. But stray details that came out later revealed the political force. The benefit to Egypt was only a good cover. When I was up the Nile in 1887 I saw a long tract of old Nile bed, of rich mud, above the present level on the east side; it was obviously of great value if it could be irrigated. Sir Ernest Cassel bought this piece of desert for a nominal sum. Then he wanted the water.

As the Marquis de Soveral remarked to Edward VII, he "saw the great importance of being Sir Ernest Cassel," who could get what he wished as a boon companion. Thus influence bore on the British Government to push through the high water scheme in order to convert Cassel's barren acres into land worth millions. Later, there appeared varied accounts of the high dam, a jubilation about the valuable estates which it had created in an extinct Nile bed. Hence all the tuning of English wire-pullers and toadies, and the manner in which officials, who were at first zealous to protect the temples, dropped the subject like a hot coal.

While at Koptos I had eyed the hills on the opposite side of the Nile, and heard of things being found there; so I applied for the district on the western side. Leaving London on November 15, 1894, I settled business with De Morgan in Cairo and, accompanied by Quibell, went to Naqada on December 3. There we were joined by Quibell's sister, who needed to be out in Egypt for health, and they took up work at the north end near Ballas. Grenfell and an invalid named Price came and joined in my work, and on January 24 Garrow Duncan also came to our camp. As visitors, Hogarth and Carter both spent some days.

Our obvious first task was on a temple site, beside which we built. This was of Tehutmes III, but contained work of other kings of that dynasty, especially a colossal *uas* sceptre of blue glaze, five feet high; this is the largest piece of ancient glazing, and was presented to South Kensington Museum. The site was identified, by inscriptions, as Nubt, a place of the worship of Set; it was thus a second Ombos, and explains how the feud between the people of Tentyra and Ombos was possible. A very fine lintel of Tehutmes I with Set and Horus was found and, as it was difficult to move, I reburied it and reported it to the Museum. It was neglected, taken by dealers down to Cairo, and there the Museum had to pay £40 to secure it.

The great surprise of the place was the immense prehistoric cemetery, from which that age is commonly called in France the Naqada period. Gradually we extended our work until we had cleared nearly two thousand graves. As the pottery and other products were different from what we knew in Egypt, they were provisionally referred to a "New Race," and some indications here and at Ballas suggested that these people were invaders in the dark period after the VIth dynasty. De Morgan, who found similar graves, put them to predynastic times, though by a happy guess without any evidence. By the evidence of the royal tomb at Naqada, later cleared by De Morgan, it was proved that the latest of our new pottery linked with the earliest dynasty, and so the prehistoric age of Naqada was fixed.

We developed here the most thorough system of cemetery work. Boys were set to hunt for soft places in the gravel; so soon as they had cleared round the edge of a tomb pit they were moved on. Then ordinary men were put on to clear the pit until they should touch pottery in position. Next first-class men were put in to clear round the pottery and skeleton, but not to move anything. Lastly the skill of Aly Suefy came in to remove every scrap of earth and leave the pits, bones and beads, all bare and exposed; any group of beads was covered with a potsherd, and a pebble put on that to show that it was a cover. Thus the skill of the men was not wasted on any work that others could do, and when we came to register the group everything was clear and visible, even the cage of ribs would be left standing up in the air, unshifted.

The clearing of this place occupied Grenfell, Duncan, Price and myself fully for three months, after which Quibell came on to finish it. The varieties of pottery, the ivory work, stone vases, flint knives, copper tools, the beads, combs, ornaments and toys, all showed an active and vigorous civilisation. As more came in, it began to be possible to distinguish the early and late forms, and when more material was found in other sites, the whole could be divided into two civilisations, followed by the dawn period of dynastic ages.

The drawings of the pottery constituted a *corpus* of the forms, arranged in a consecutive order of shapes. Thus was begun, from sheer necessity, the *corpus* system of denoting forms of all kinds of objects, and hence registering discoveries by *corpus* numbers—a system which revolutionises all archaeological work, and gives brief definitions in place of repeated drawings or long-winded descriptions.

De Morgan, of course, took specimens for the Cairo Museum, but we had three hundred cases for London, and a large exhibition, which surprised all those who knew the usual things from Egypt. Seeing the great importance of such a series, I proposed to my partners, Haworth and Kennard, that we should agree jointly to present the most complete series to the Ashmolean Museum. Among other Museums, a considerable amount remained for University College; in later

PREHISTORIC FLINT KNIVES AND LANCES

years our discoveries added to that, and I bought in Egypt all that I could of fresh types and objects. Thus the College collection is the most complete for varieties of form and purpose, and it is all published in the catalogue volume *Prehistoric Egypt*.

After my return to London at the end of March, an invitation came to accept the honorary degree of LL.D. at Edinburgh on April 17. The continuation of the History occupied me, and the second volume was finished by May 21, when I started on the Palestine geography of the Amarna letters. I was also writing articles for the Dictionary of the Bible. To my deep regret, my faithful friend Riley was too ill to join in the year's work, and died soon after.

In September I had to go to Ipswich, as being president of the Anthropological Section of the British Association. At that time harm was being done by the views of people who were ignorant of the real condition of less civilised races. The subject for my address therefore was our relations with races whom we controlled, and I invited some colonial administrators to come and state their knowledge. Several amateurs of policy were bursting to join in at the meeting, so I said we should welcome all accounts of experience, only that a speaker must hand up his name and state in what country his experience had been gained. This put a stop to all the theorists. As Cromer said to me one day: "I do not know which is the greatest nuisance, the man-and-a-brother or the damned nigger."

While at Ipswich I heard of a fine retort. A party of East End girls were down at the sea for the day, and soon went in to bathe. A defender of propriety reproved them; whereupon an Aphrodite arose in her wrath, saying: "I'll eat my 'at if there is anything here as God Almighty didn't make." Presumably they had to finish like Pharaoh's daughter in the Irish ballad, who "ran upon the sthrand to dry her shkin."

The autumn was occupied by beginning the third volume of the History, with the complication of the hundreds of monuments of Ramessu II to be indexed, and the duplications worked out, especially in the repeated names of private persons. This is the most wearisome period.

By November 26, 1895, I left for Egypt; Quibell came out and his sister, also two College students, Miss Paget and Miss Pirie (Mrs. Quibell), who settled in at Saqqareh to copy tombs, and later came on to the work at Thebes. I asked for the temple ground on the west of Thebes, from Medinet Habu then being cleared by Daressy, up to the temple of Tehutmes III, reserved for the Museum. De Morgan's terms for such important ground were reasonable, all royal monuments to the Museum, and half of the remainder.

As this was so important a site, he required me to have a *reis* from the Museum. Before long I saw the *reis* bowing low in the road and kissing the hand of one of the notorious dealers; as the work was so critical, I demanded the immediate withdrawal of the Museum man, and I was left to my own security. We settled in, to live in some of the brick store galleries of the Ramesseum, clearing a deep trench all round to prevent anyone prowling in. Stray visitors glared at us, and one day while at lunch, a gaunt figure looked in, and turned to cry out in Americanese: "I say, come here, there are people living here!"

On December 16 we began on the temple sites, piles of stone chips and dust, with some broken brick walls. First we found that of Tehutmes IV, then Tausert,

Merenptah, Khonsu-ardus, Uazmes, Saptah, and the White Queen—a bust unnamed. While I was on these for my partnership, Quibell was clearing the walls and galleries of the Ramesseum for the Research Account. For the first time at Thebes, work by the cubic metre was started; the people liked it greatly as they could earn much more by harder work, and we used to begin half an hour before sunrise.

Before long, I found that the local people's allegiance to their relatives among the dealers was not to be won by bakhshish, for I heard from Newberry, at Luqsor, that a block of Tausert had come over there. I knew there was only one deposit of the queen worked by a local man, and next week I began to promise him much higher bakhshish on all he found, so that on pay day everyone stared at him for his great success, ten times the usual wages. Just as I had the money in my hand I looked full at him and said: "When you bring me back the stone you took last week, I will pay you."

He protested innocence; I told the whole story, and he collapsed, amid the jeers of his friends. I had a very hard week's work out of him and his boy, worth more than he got for the stone. I then, January 13, cleared off all the local men, and recruited fresh workers from places two or three miles away: after that there was no leakage.

The great discovery was the large triumphal inscription of Merenptah naming the Israelites. The site of Merenptah's temple was disastrously dull; there were worn bits of soft sandstone, scraps looted from the temple of Amenhetep III, crumbling sandstone sphinxes, laid in pairs in holes to support columns. I was tempted to leave it as fruitless; then came the half-length figure of Merenptah, a fine portrait work, and

in the last corner to be cleared there lay a black granite stele, over ten feet high and five wide—on it a long
inscription of Amenhetep III, which had been mostly
erased by Akhenaten, and then piously re-engraved by
Sety I. On looking beneath it, there was the inscription of Merenptah.

I had the ground cut away below, blocking up the
stele on stones, so that one could crawl in and lie on
one's back, reading a few inches from one's nose. For
inscriptions, Spiegelberg was at hand, looking over all
new material. He lay there copying for an afternoon,
and came out saying, "There are names of various
Syrian towns, and one which I do not know, Isirar."
"Why, that is Israel," said I. "So it is, and won't the
reverends be pleased," was his reply. To the astonish-
ment of the rest of our party I said at dinner that
night, "This stele will be better known in the world
than anything else I have found," and so it has proved.

The most interesting group that we discovered was
a hoard left by an Assyrian armourer, with a bronze
helmet of Assyrian form, and many steel tools, the
forerunners of a modern carpenter's outfit (Manchester). The foundation deposits of Tausert and of Saptah provided an enormous number of bright blue pottery scarabs and small models, but otherwise there was
not very much discovered.

Quibell found also the deposits of the Ramesseum,
but the most interesting result of his work was a buried
tomb passage cut in the rock in the XIIth dynasty, and
a box of papyri in it, almost reduced to cobwebs by
slow oxidation. These were eventually entrusted to the
care of Dr. Gardiner, and Ibscher of Berlin came over
to unroll one papyrus. He succeeded in fixing it on
celluloid film. The rest were then taken to Berlin for

Devastated is Libya, Hittites are quiet, Canaan . . .
Israel is laid waste without seed, Palestine . . .
King Ba-ne-ra-Meramen, Merenptah, Hatep-her muat

MERENPTAH PHARAOH OF THE EXODUS
PART OF TRIUMPHAL STELE WITH NAME OF ISRAEL

him to work on. As now unrolled, there are a dozen important works—the greatest part of what literature there is of the XIIth dynasty. One by one, as published, they are being presented to the British Museum by the British School and Dr. Gardiner.

By March 4 I left, after clearing the six temple sites. Quibell stayed on for a couple of months and finished off the Ramesseum.

Knowing Egyptian dawdle, I gave notice over night at the ticket office that I should need twenty tickets for Bedrasheyn next morning, for the first train. The office opened late, and a crowd of local people blocked the way, till the train was almost starting. Then I asked for my twenty tickets for men; impossible in the time, was the reply. As it was quite usual to pay the guard for tickets on the train, I pushed my men in. The station master hauled them back, and they had to come a day later, when after all they were given a single ticket for the whole batch. One good man in consequence was so knocked up by night exposure, on changing trains, that he lost his season's work. Such is Egypt.

I called on Maspero on the way, and was in London March 20. I had to finish writing up Naqada and Koptos, besides lecturing. By May 8, Duncan returned from Mesopotamia. I had been desired by the Philadelphia authorities to find two men who could undertake to continue their excavations on the return of Haynes. I proposed Duncan, who was a Semitist, and knew excavating, and a new volunteer, Geere. They went out to Karachi, up to Baghdad, and with difficulty out to the work. There Haynes refused to yield any material or means to them, and compelled them to return next day with him. There are other instances of Committees entirely neglecting to give legal powers to men whom they lightly send on months of travel, and who have to return empty-handed.

On the death of Reginald Stuart Poole, the Yates Chair of Archaeology was vacant at the College. A Committee was appointed to see candidates, and the two considered were Jane Harrison and Ernest Gardner. It was my duty to draw up the report, which I did as impartially as I could. The committee were on the point of naming Jane Harrison, but I remarked that, though an authority on religion, she had not as wide a view and knowledge as Gardner, and that carried the day. I had then the pleasure of over thirty years' association with Professor Gardner, as my nighest colleague, working in with plans for teaching, seeing him Vice-Chancellor of the University, and having him as chairman of the British School of Egyptian Archaeology.

By June 22 our boxes arrived, and the exhibition was held during July. Through the summer there were negotiations for my again excavating for the Exploration Fund.

## CHAPTER IX

## DESHASHEH, DENDEREH, HU, ABYDOS

"Stand still, stand still, O Time!—
  And let me rest in present blessedness,
  Let the sweet fulness of contentment spread
  Far, into fuller hold on every sense."

"Shall I stand still and pause for thy delight
  While all the world is working for relief,
  While men are longing for my rapid flight
  To lift the load of pain and dullest grief?
  Not so, if I stood still ye now would be
  Remaining in the primal vacancy;
  Pains come with all the pleasures that ye see,
  That have made man that is, and is to be."

By now I had fairly recovered from my illness; my father had bought himself an annuity out of settled property, and transferred to me the rest of the small savings of two grandfathers; besides the College work, I was to have—for the only time in my life—a small salary for work in Egypt; and a good deal of lecturing and writing helped my resources; thus, at forty-three, I could think of marriage.

Just then a lady came to the exhibition whom I eyed from room to room; by curious hap soon after, she came to the College frequently to do drawings for Henry Holiday, the artist. Sundry talk followed, quite fit for College walls; but at last a walk to the British Museum gave space for a talk on going to Egypt. My weekly journals that winter went through my lady's hands. The next winter our honeymoon was in Egypt.

This book is not a personal record, except as regards work. I will only say that it was entirely due to my wife that the resources of the British School were raised, to enable work to be carried on by me and our students; much of the facsimile drawing and plans were hers, and latterly the chief management, and paying, of hundreds of workmen. So much followed on Mr. Holiday's drawings being done by Miss Hilda Urlin.

In the autumn I was trying to urge Professor Myres to the idea of a weekly journal on antiquities and anthropology, to be called *Man,* as a parallel to the journal *Nature.* It did not seem practicable to run such a venture, and I was asked to agree to transfer the title to a succursal for smaller papers and reviews of the Anthropological Institute. At the autumn meeting of the Egypt Exploration Fund I appeared again as their excavator. The chairman had the "Batavian grace" to refer to me as the returning prodigal son. As the Society was not renowned for economy, it was really a case of the *père prodigue.* I was asked back because the Society was in low water and wanted to placate the American subscribers by having things found to distribute.

Leaving London November 17, 1896, with the new student Geere, we were in Cairo November 24. On December 1, we put up tents at Behnesa, but it was not till the 12th that my permit for digging arrived, and with it an effendi to watch us. Grenfell arrived on the 14th, and he settled here with Hunt on the 20th. I was trying in all directions for early remains, but could not reach any.

On the 22nd then, I handed over the site to Grenfell for papyri, and went on a searching tour. An example of railway management arose. Aly Suefy had a donkey, which he took by train; when he got out, no one would open the cattle truck; his donkey went on to Girgeh, the terminus then, but no letters of his could get it back from whoever had appropriated it. I took up the quest, and at last got some pounds of compensation for him, as he had the receipt to produce. A poor fellah has little chance in the effendi world.

Here I learned from Aly how to go about the country at night; we got out at a station at sunset, and had to cross a dozen miles to our camp. He said: "Do not answer anyone when they say good night in passing; then they will think we are thieves out for a robbery and be afraid."

There was one village to go through; we passed the outer guard too quickly for him to note us; in the midst of the village the main guard sat round a fire which blinded them, and we raced by, at over five miles an hour; they caught sight, and hailed us; on we went; then they began firing after us, but we were at a safe distance; the outer guard "did not wish to make his wife a widow" (as an English watchman said), and on we went. At a canal, the boat was on our side, so we ferried over with a stick, and came into camp after everyone had gone to sleep.

By January 9, 1897, I had cleared my things out of Behnesa and settled into some huts at Deshasheh. For a week or two, I had visitors, Miss Oldroyd and her nephew, young Borwick. A Bedawy woman asked if they were my wife and son. I replied no, I was not married. "But why not? Children are sweet." (*Ayyal helu.*)

I began to dig on January 14, finding wells of small tombs. Geere and I cleared out dozens of tomb shafts of the Vth and VIth dynasties, finding little in any of them. The contracted skeletons here showed that the prehistoric habit lasted on into the end of the Old Kingdom. In one coffin, hollowed out of a tree trunk, were many linen garments, closely like the modern qalabiyeh, very narrow, and with long, tight sleeves. It would seem that the low sleeveless chemise of the monumental figures was a survival in art, but was not the actual dress at that time.

Our main work was in copying two rock tombs covered with sculpture, by full-sized dry squeeze and drawing. Much of it had been hammered over and scaled away, and only fragments of figures were left, but from similar figures these could be restored.

Happily the most important scene was nearly complete. This represented the siege of a walled town by Egyptians with Bedawy allies. A long ladder was used to scale the wall, and sappers were at work underneath it. The Bedawyn had broken into the town, but were shown as defeated by the women and children. The Egyptians were driving off captives bound together, and a girl that had been shouldered was holding on very carefully. This is the oldest siege piece known, probably referring to North Arabia. One small tomb had, lying before it, a reed mat and on it a coarse bowl, exactly the objects of the *hetep* sign, proving what was the source of the form.

At last we worked over a large levelled area of rock, on which had been built a great mastaba tomb. All was swept away; there remained a patch of dust in one corner. On clearing that we found a square pit, leading to a little chamber containing several statues, some damaged, but two almost perfect and of fine work of the Vth dynasty. Cairo took the most complete, but

SCENES IN A BESIEGED CITY
WOMEN FIGHTING INVADERS, 5TH DYNASTY

the finest carving was one now in the British Museum (Nenkhetef). After packing, I left March 14, 1897, and sailed on the 20th with Dr. Schechter, the Rumanian, who was active over his clearance of Jewish MSS. in Cairo. He had humour, and said: "There is no difficulty about miracles. I come from a country where miracles happen every day."

Our Messageries steamer at night ran ashore on an island with a lighthouse, near Marseilles. I went up on deck with a lifebelt on; a Frenchman in my cabin would not look for his, but said *"où est mon parapluie?"* On deck there was not one other person with a lifebelt, yet none could get free of the ship if it foundered, as we were penned in with a wall of tomato cases, and an awning over the top. I edged to the bows and sat there, ready to slip off ashore if the vessel filled.

However, we were all taken off in a tug from Marseilles next morning. The French papers said the vessel had grounded in a fog—the official truth; the real truth was that I could see for miles around when I went on deck, and probably the watch had been dining too freely on the last night of the voyage. One thing I secured in my pocket when we struck, the ebony negress, now in University College, which I had bought from old Aly Arabi.

The summer was passed in writing and finishing plates of Deshasheh, also writing up lectures on *Religion and Conscience*. For that I got statistics of Conscience Money from the Treasury; these showed that the amount exactly followed the distribution law of probabilities logarithmically; that is to say, there were as many cases of $\frac{1}{2}$ or $1/10$ of the average £5, as of 2 or 10 times the average. The periods of tenderness of conscience, and other curious illustrations of the mind,

were also investigated. The exhibition was during
July. In September the Liverpool meeting of the British Association was held, and I gave one of the popular
lectures, to show what high civilisation might be at-
tained without inscriptions.

On November 29, 1897, my wife and I left, and
reached Cairo on December 8. We had out two new
students, my cousin, Arthur Mace, and N. de Garis
Davies, the former mainly on excavation, the latter on
copying. David MacIver joined us on February 19. In
Cairo, De Morgan had left, and Loret was in his place.

"Loret wants to screw me into new and disadvan-
tageous—almost ruinous—terms. So I went and saw Sir
John Scott (Chief Justice) and Sir William Garstin,
who is President of the Committee which Loret had
persuaded to pass the new terms. Garstin sees the ab-
surdity of them, and will summon a fresh Committee
and alter them at once if he can do so. Nothing could
be more friendly and cordial than he was. . . . Loret
is already out of touch and disliked by everyone—
Museum people, officials and natives. Brugsch said to
an Arab that De Morgan was but a small devil but
Loret is twenty devils, and this has gone the round of
the natives.

"I hope we may get up to work in a week or so; but
one can never anticipate what official delays may be.
Certainly Loret will not relish, after trying to thrust
an agreement down my throat, being obliged, by superior power, to rescind it. I shall probably gain his re-
spectful hatred in place of his officious arrogance. Sir
John Scott cordially hoped that I would stand out and
urge for proper terms. I could not have more authori-
tative backing.

"At last I got a letter from Garstin on the 14th saying that Loret agreed to set aside the new clause about their taking all royal objects. So next morning I went down to the Museum, saw Loret, who took his defeat with easy assurance. . . . The great question of the division of things remains now where it was before Loret's new move; the Museum to have anything up to half, but not to take more unless they pay the expenses of the work."

Loret demanded of me a complete set of my publications. I replied that most of them were out of print; then I ought to print more, was the retort. We then went to Nagh Hamadi, the train terminus, and on by a native coal barge for two days, finally walking ten miles along the desert to Dendereh for lack of wind.

Work began on December 20, by clearing up large catacombs of sacred animals to gain room for our men. The animal burials had all been burnt, and the fire had raged there so that the brickwork of the tunnels was half melted. There were some bronze vessels of Ramesside date, and a jar full of Roman glass mosaic pieces from a disused shrine, besides some pieces of blue glazed papyrus-plant models of the XVIIIth dynasty; but nothing of importance for history or art.

The main subject of work was the cemetery from the IIIrd to the XIth dynasty. It had been handed before to Girgis, the dealer, and he found the tombs all empty, which accounted for my getting the site from the Museum so readily. But my object was to clear the east face of each brick mastaba, and there get the sculptures, in some instances six or eight stone panels from the false doors. We reaped a rich harvest of sculptures across the dark ages, beginning from the Vth dynasty, and passing through all the degradation of the VIIth to Xth, till the revival in the XIth dynasty. The style and peculiar forms of hieroglyphs were essential to publish, and so they were all photographed.

When I first walked over the site, there were still lying on the tops of some of the mastabas the original offering pots of the VIth dynasty, unmoved since that time, sand-worn but perfect. In one of the largest mastabas we found the enormous lid of the sarcophagus forming part of the chamber floor; on breaking through we saw that it had been rifled at the period of burial, for a tunnel ran under the mastaba from outside, straight through the side of the sarcophagus.

The architectural use of large brick barrel vaults to the passages was the earliest example of the arch on such a scale; one, in particular, I drew and published, and it is still the typical illustration often quoted. A very wet tomb of the VIIth dynasty had the great stone sarcophagus of Beb, built of slabs, almost a chamber, covered with long religious texts, roughly cut. The stone was so rotted that a finger could be stuck into it, and if left to dry it would crack and break up. So the wet slabs were laid on the sand, and covered with about four inches of sand to allow of slow drying; thus the stone contracted equally inside and out, and was preserved.

After a week or two the sand was brushed off and then my wife lay on the ground copying 20,000 signs in hieratic, cut in all degrees of accuracy; the worst cutting one could revise by the traces of the ink writing around it. A Ptolemaic cemetery had very small chambers in the rock, and we obtained many inscribed stone labels and steles.

"Loret came to Dendereh, and sent up for me. I found him in the temple, which he and Mme. Loret and her brother and Legrain all went over in very touristical fashion. I pointed out our work about a quarter of a mile off, but L. did not seem in the least inclined to look at it, or to take any particular interest in what was found. They spent about an hour and a half over the temples, just like green tourists, and never wished to see anything else."

I offered to show Loret a place in the temple, where I suspected another subterranean chamber but he would not pay any attention to it. From the known plans I saw there was room for another hiding-place, and on searching the pavement about there I found a stone slightly sunk, as if the thickness did not quite match the others, or wooden sliders below had decayed. Of course I might not touch it, and no one in authority would. Loret was entirely under the direction of a young effendi, Aref, who wore a great cloak turned back to show a brilliant scarlet lining, by which he would strike an effect half a mile away.

We had an exploring trip over the desert north of Dendereh and saw many sites which seemed desirable.

We left Dendereh April 2, 1898, in a hot spell, such that men refused to use camels through the day: we started at dawn, and got to Qeneh early. Shut up in the waiting room we escaped the furnace outside, and left by the night train. Mace stayed a month later, packing up. By June 20 the boxes came, and exhibition was during July.

On November 14, 1898, we left, were in Cairo 24th and at Abadiyeh by the 29th. There I worked for a month, helped by my wife, Mace, MacIver, Miss Orme, Iles (later in Sudan) and Miss Lawes. This region for some ten miles was covered with various cemeteries, all of good period for learning early ar-

chaeology. It was a useful training ground, and produced much of the prehistoric ages and of the VIth to
XIIth dynasties. The barbarous invaders who came
after that time were first recognised here, buried in
shallow circular graves and hence called the Pan-grave
people.

From Abadiyeh we moved down stream to the end
of our concession at Hu, a nome capital. I was hoping
to work on the temple site, but found that the whole
ground, though bare hillock, had been lotted up and
claimed among the villagers. There was no public land
left except a small market place. This land-grabbing,
though quite unprofitable, is a great hindrance to
work, and the English inspectors of later times used to
have a perpetual fight to keep off claims. If in the
hands of a native inspector, as at Behnesa, he simply
sells up the site to all comers, and reports private land.

There was a large cemetery, but partly clogged by
a modern cemetery over it. The period was of the Old
and Middle Kingdoms. The Roman fort is in fair condition, and our huts were built against the south wall.
The most important objects were a fine dagger of King
Suazenra (XIVth dynasty) kept at Cairo, and a well
modelled plaster mask of Roman age, which agrees remarkably with the skull, shown in superposed photographs. (D.P. XLII. Brit. Mus.) The whole account
of the season appeared in *Diospolis Parva,* along with
the first arrangement of prehistoric ages in sequence
dates. This new system has been accepted here and on
the Continent, and provides a scale for the preservation of any detail of dating which can be ascertained.

By March 9, 1899, we left Hu, doing Italian archaeology on the way back; Mace and MacIver continued later. The slate palettes I had packed very

carefully before leaving, but the box was left behind, and never recovered; all the fine ones vanished, and one or two of the commonest I got hold of next season. When our things were being selected at the Museum, there were two large vases, a porphyry and an alabaster. One was taken, the other put back in our boxes. Then, openly, Daressy walked over to the box, took out the other vase, and carried it in to the Museum; the robbery was so barefaced that it intimidated Mace, who was in charge, and he abandoned it.

We had three amusing little orphans in the work. The eldest, who had a waist cloth, was hardly old enough to hold a pick; the second could just carry a basket, and wore only a cord round his waist; the youngest, who wore nothing, did two or three hours a day toddling with a light basket on his head. The men commonly called them "the rats." Orphans are well regarded; one in Sinai went to and fro on the camels which he inherited, helped up each day by an uncle, and so earning his living.

During four years there had been the great scandal of Amélineau's work at the Royal Tombs of Abydos. He had been given a concession to work there for five years; no plans were kept (a few incorrect ones were made later), there was no record of where things were found, no useful publication. He boasted that he had reduced to chips the pieces of stone vases which he did not care to remove, and burnt up the remains of the woodwork of the Ist dynasty in his kitchen.

The things taken to Paris were scattered as pretty presents by his partners, and finally the greater part were sold by auction. Even Maspero described him as *un bête puante*. It was the usual French work, but with total indifference to what became of things. We had gone over in a previous year to see the ground, like tourists, had been entertained by the sheykh, and bought a few things from him "as souvenirs," which showed us who were his dangerous retainers.

Loret was now retired from Egypt. He was a man of limited vision; when I told him of a place being pillaged he remarked: *"C'est impossible! il y a un règlement."* He had by this time proved too unsuitable. He was given another post in France and the only man to save credit was Maspero, back again. He insisted on being Director of all the Museums at £1,500 a year and expenses, and had his way, for no one else was available in France. He evidently did not encourage Amélineau continuing to his fifth year, and gave me a permit for Abydos, irrespective of the running concession.

We left London November 17, 1899, and were at Abydos by 30th. In this season we had Mace, MacIver, Garstang, Wilkin and Miss Johnson in the work. Baron Anatole von Hügel came to work the caves, but hurt his hand and had to leave in three weeks. A delightful visit of a week was that of Francis Galton and his niece.

We began on the Royal Tombs at once; all but one had been turned over already, and the richest part of the ground was the top of Amélineau's rubbish heaps, which had come from the bottom of the chambers. It was a race of my men to turn over this surface, which was rich in fragments of vases and inscriptions. Of course I was giving good bakhshish, and got all the scraps most carefully brought up. Amélineau had left a clump of alabaster in the village, which we brought in to our stock, and found some fine pieces of inscription among it. The best ivory tablet of his work went, through a dealer, to MacGregor.

Altogether we cleared the tombs of Zet, Merneit, Azab, Semerkhet, and Qa, four of the eight kings of the Ist dynasty, and a queen. This was the first recognition of their full identification and historical position. Beside the royal tombs, over three hundred graves of the servitors were cleared and planned; but the contents had all been scattered without record before we arrived. I drew all the jar sealings, and they give the most important light on the official organization. The mass of pieces of ivory and wooden tablets and stone vases supply much more light on the times, and fifty gravestones give the titles and names of the court.

By March 16, 1900, we left, and were in London on the 24th. I pushed on with the sixty-seven plates as quickly as I could, and had them in the plate printers' hands by April 18, wrote the text and passed the proof of index June 22. Thus seven months from beginning work the full publication of results was ready for the opening of the exhibition. When Dr. King came from the Museum to see the things, he remarked: "I suppose you will be publishing these some day." "The volume is before you," was the reply. On June 12 I was at Cambridge, to receive the honorary degree of Litt.D.; and G. F. Watts invited me to sit to him in September.

At the Dover meeting of the British Association I met Bennet Goldney, who was stirring to buy up St. Augustine's, Canterbury, for historical preservation. He told me that years ago it was noticed that a bay of the crypt of the Cathedral was walled up. One morning there appeared a hole in the wall, no one knew how. When the Clerk of the Works died, it came out that he had land in the North worth £80,000, "the

connection of which with the plot one sees." It is supposed that the treasures of Becket's shrine were there
concealed.

The insensate greed of governments and authorities
has ruined untold treasures. If only "finding is keeping" had been the rule (provided that the police or
the post office were informed), we should not have
heard these frequent stories of irrevocable loss, such
as the treasure of Battle Abbey. Happily the Treasury
has now consented to the finder having full value if
finds are handed up for examination.

By November 10, 1900, we were off. We saw the
marvellous loan collection of MSS. and cathedral
treasures in the Paris exhibition, the last day. We were
at Abydos by the 25th, and our party spread on both
sides. Mace remained with us, and we had my wife's
sister, Amy Urlin, and Miss Orme; Garstang worked
at Beyt Khallaf; MacIver and Wilkin worked at
Mahasnah. The clearing of the Royal Tombs of Mena
and Den went forward from November 28, and the
arm of the queen of Zer was found, hidden in a hole
in the wall, with the gold bracelets in place. The lads
who found it saw the gold, but left it untouched and
brought the arm to me. I cut the wrappings apart, and
so bared the bracelets all intact. Thus the exact order
could be copied when my wife rethreaded them next
morning.

When Quibell came over on behalf of the Museum,
I sent up the bracelets by him. The arm—the oldest
mummified piece known—and its marvellously fine tis-
sue of linen were also delivered at the Museum.
Brugsch only cared for display; so from one bracelet
he cut away the half that was of plaited gold wire, and

he also threw away the arm and linen. A museum is a dangerous place.

The whole of the group of Royal Tombs was now cleared, and one—of Queen Merneit—had escaped the ravages of Amélineau. At the tomb of Khosekhemui, he had not in his ransack touched the objects hidden by a soft wall crushing down, and there we got the pieces of the sard and gold wand or sceptre, and the gold-capped vases. I had found all that could be recovered, after the clearance by the ravagers, ancient and modern. To ensure not leaving a hidden tomb, I "gridironed" the ground by walking to and fro in lines a few feet apart, and verifying that there was no patch of sand without a scrap of native concretion showing at every two or three feet; there was no hole sanded over.

Later, Legge persuaded the Fund to try to discover more; large clearances of desert were made, only producing a few scraps which had been widely scattered by destroyers; tombs were remeasured to search for errors in our plans, but the only difference found was in the length of a broken wall, probably knocked about since: the workmen were told that they must find another tomb, but there was none that answered nor regarded the appeal. As Sayce said to me: "If they had tried to give you a testimonial they could not have done better."

A considerable part of our work was the sorting over the fragments of stone vases, and reconstructing the forms. In this, of course, we were crippled by the best pieces having been carried away by Amélineau; we had only the fragments which he had overlooked, or which he had "reduced to chips," as he boasted. The alabaster and slate fragments were of such enormous quantity that it was only in peculiar forms that we could hope to distinguish the pieces that fitted.

The thousands of fragments of granite, basalt, volcanic ash, porphyry, quartz, limestone and breccia were first sorted into groups sufficiently distinct in quality to leave no question of the allocation of any piece. Then the whole of the fragments of one group were spread on a length of tabling in our courtyard; the pieces of edge were put along the top, those of the middle below, each placed with the axis vertical, those of the bases at the bottom. Each fragment was then taken, the angle of its fractures with the vertical was regarded, and every fracture at that angle was compared with it.

This is a ready test, as out of 180° there are at least eight directions which catch the eye at once. After trying thus every possible fit, the piece was set aside. From the reconstructed pieces, and from pieces sufficient to prove the shape, I then drew five hundred forms, with also a couple of hundred duplicate references, and so could trace the changes of work and of fashion in each reign.

These, by the close dating, constitute the standard of reference for all vases of the first two dynasties. Often an actual contact could not be found, between two pieces whose quality showed that they belonged together. I made a stand whereby the pieces of brim were placed edge down, centred on a set of concentric circles, and the piece of base could be slid up and down on the same axis until the contours of the two pieces fitted, thus enabling the measurements to be taken for drawing. See *Royal Tombs* II, VIII A.

Another large matter was the collection of all fragments of clay sealings of jars. Here again we had none of the largest and most complete. Every scrap was collected, and sorted over, to place all the impressions of each seal together. Then by lamplight these were examined, the fitting of the design traced, the number of repetitions on a cylinder seal fixed by observing small irregularities, and finally, with compasses, each sealing was drawn out to double scale. This work occupied me each evening while the smokers were away talking in Mace's room. More than two hundred different seal designs were thus secured, and they form the picture of the official world and organisation of the early dynasties, of which scarcely anything else is known. The drawings were borrowed for the Cairo catalogue.

Around most of the Royal Tombs were lines of graves of the retainers, who were probably sent to the blessed fields of Aaru to aid their master. In other countries and ages, it has been looked on as scandalous for a follower to shirk his duty just when his lord most needs his company. Sometimes the name was written in ochre on the wall of the grave; more often a small tablet of limestone, a foot or eighteen inches high, was put over the grave. The persons thus commemorated were mostly women, some being captives. These tablets were much scoured by the driving winds, and so eaten out on the face that often they were unreadable. For photography, they were largely restored by covering with sand, and then sweeping the sand off until the relief was just seen above it.

The great quantity of fragments of inscriptions, which we found on stone vases and ivory or ebony tablets were also crippled by the removal of so much before: but every piece was published in photograph, and many drawn, so that it should be possible in future for those taken by Amélineau to be connected and to regain their *état civile,* or original sources. Such was the result of our being permitted to go over ground of which it was reported that "every Arab knew that it was exhausted."

Had I been allowed to work at Abydos when I asked for it in previous years, the whole of the remains would have appeared together, and we should have known much more of the early dynasties. It should be recorded that the Exploration Fund has allowed all the pieces of carved stone vessels, and fine stone not joined up, to be taken to Brussels by Dr. Capart in hopes of connection with those he had bought.

While at Abydos we made a tent trip as far as Manfalut, and in that district saw a large walled enclosure, empty, and without any original gateway, similar to three enclosures or camps named before in the Delta. This class of structure needs clearing and placing historically, but as it promises little return, no one will undertake it while the Government's claims are so onerous.

The danger of misjudging character was painfully seen this year. There was a man in the work who, from his face, I much mistrusted. One of my friends considered that therefore he should be rewarded by trust, and, on my leaving, the doubtful man was kept about to help the packing. As result, there vanished all the carnelian necklaces of Khosekhemui, the crocodile-hunt sealing of Den, a quasi-Indian figure that I had bought, also a statuette of Yusef, of Hyksos age, and a batch of fine ushabtis. The next winter this man turned up wearing some clothing of mine, conclusively marking out the thief, but my friend persisted that I was hard in my judgments. I have had at different times to lay down that ours was not a reformatory society, but our business was to secure things.

We left on March 18, 1901, and had the interest of seeing S. Zeno's body at Verona in that wild festa on April 12. In a meeting of the Board of Studies in History, May 1, the teaching of the history of art was discussed; the scope of ideas on the Board may be seen by the proposal that the history should begin at A.D. 1500. I remarked that we had done nothing but copy since then; dead silence. Then someone proposed 1400.

The exhibition was during July, and a new public feeling appeared; instead of only caring for things of beauty or remarkable appearance, people hung over the tables, fascinated by the fragments of the Ist dynasty. The historic meaning and importance had an astonishing effect; some workmen would spend their whole dinner hour in the room. In the autumn, I was working out the series of sequence dates of the prehistoric age.

About this time, a friend who was on the Council of the Royal Society, talked with me on my possible chance of entry. The next thing I knew about it was a request for an outline of work and publications, and before long, to my surprise, I was elected without any waiting. The meetings twenty-five years ago were useful all round, stating the principles and results of work; but latterly the papers have started at such a technical level that only specialists in each department can grasp them. Two days I ever remember. One was that of Hales' account of photographing the calcium in the photosphere; in discussion Sir David Gill was asked to speak; he rose, "worr-shipful admiration" was all, but enough to fix the memory. The other day was when the Curies showed a solution with the mysterious property of being always 2° hotter than the surroundings. Little did anyone dream of the world of physics that radium was to open to us.

We were again in Cairo by November 26, 1901. As this year some of our previous workers were in fresh positions, we had out as students, Mace, Weigall, Caulfeild and Christie; Robert Sewell from India came for a short time. I built new huts further back in the desert, to be healthier, and move out of the way of the dust of the work in the great temple site. While I was attending to the great temple, Weigall was on the great enclosure of Senusert III and its subterranean building; Mace was on the pyramid of Amenhetep I, four miles to the south, all for the Fund.

For the Research Account, Caulfeild was on the temple of Sety I, and Christie doing facsimile drawings of important scenes there. On the great temple site nothing much had yet been done, Mariette's work having been on the box-like enclosure between the walls, where the great mass of funeral steles were placed. Gradually clearing over the great area we came upon some fine tombs of the Ist dynasty; these were all planned in detail and the vases published. The tombs of the XVIIIth dynasty which we removed, provided some larger private figures, Ptahemua, Unnefer, Amenhetep, and Rahetep, otherwise Pa-ra-hetep.

In this season and the next we cleared the plans of the successive temples of the Ist, IInd, IIIrd, IVth, Vth, VIth, XIth (Mentuhetep and Sankhkara levels), XIIIth, XVIIIth, XXth and XXVIth dynasties, all superposed one over the other. Discrimination of the twelve periods of building in fifteen feet depth of brick and mud wash was a tedious matter. To detect brick-

IVORY STATUETTE OF KING, 1 : 1
(British Museum)

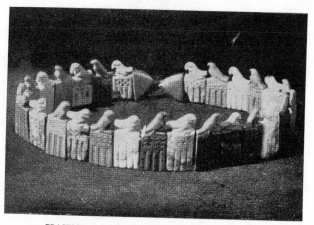

BRACELET OF GOLD AND TURQUOISE, 1ST DYNASTY

work, the only way was to cut clean sections with a dinner knife and examine them with a magnifier; if the little holes left by decayed straw dust lay horizontally it was a bed of mud wash, if the holes crossed in all directions it was a kneaded mud brick.

In the lowest temple level we touched on carved ivory in the mud at the bottom of a chamber. Gently working round it, the patch of ivories in mud was delimited, about a couple of feet across. I cut deeply around and under it, and cleared in front of it, laid a box lid flat before it, and then with a heavy lug dragged the soft mass complete on to the box lid. This was carried to our store-room and kept for a fortnight to dry. I then dissected the mass with nothing stronger than a pin and a camelhair brush.

All of the ivory figures were thus obtained entire, without any fractures. Some could be left thus, such as the old king in his quilted robe, now in the British Museum; others which were more fragile were bound tightly with thread and then soaked with paraffin wax. Thus was revealed a very naturalistic school of delicate ivory carving, happily dated by part of a glazed vase of Mena of green with brown inlay. Many green glazed figures were also found, mostly of baboons.

The fine ivory work was evidently continued, for in the IVth dynasty temple there was found a small seated figure, under three inches high when complete, with the name of Khufu on the front. Unhappily the head was broken off and lost by the digger. I stopped his work and set the diggers to sift for the head where the earth had been thrown. After three weeks of sifting, the head was recovered. Though the face was only three-eighths of an inch high, like the tip of a little finger, it bore the most amazingly powerful portrait of the all-masterful king. When magnified, it might be supposed to be a life-size statue.

In the temple of Khufu there was a chamber about twelve feet wide for burnt offering. In this was a great bed of vegetable ashes, with hundreds of little forked pieces of burnt clay, which might be a symbol for the forelegs of animals. These seem to be the substitute for the sacrifice of animals which Khufu abolished when he "forbade them to offer sacrifices." The various temple buildings were identified mainly by the foundation deposits. In the earlier levels a great quantity of flint implements were found, which are dated during the Ist dynasty by their levels.

Of the more usual historical material were some large slabs of royal decrees of the Vth and VIth dynasties, temple sculptures of Mentuhetep III, columns, a statue of Senusert III, a gateway of Sebekhetep III, a stele of Antef V, many slabs of a temple of Aohmes, and at the end some fine bronze hypocephali and sets of amulets from the cemetery. The finest carved coffin lid of the XXVIth dynasty, cut in very hard silicified limestone was taken for the Cairo Museum; it arrived there smashed into three pieces though the stone is of the hardest, and it is difficult to imagine how it can have been so maltreated.

Besides the work on the great temple, two outside excavations were done by our party. I observed on the desert, south of the cemetery, a block of stone. Randall MacIver went to examine it, and gradually cleared a complete temple site, dated by the lower part of a seated statue of Senusert III.

In the following year Weigall was set to examine two great pits further south; they marked where large subterranean tombs had been quarried, and showed

IVORY STATUETTE OF KHUFU, 3 : 1, 4TH DYNASTY

still the passages and enormous blocks of quartzite sandstone. Other apparent mastabas were searched, but only chips were found in them; then walls appeared near by; the whole site puzzled us. Sitting poring over it, the idea broke on me of a gigantic enclosure, about 500 × 300 feet, symmetrically behind the temple of Senusert. This we traced out, and in it a wide pit full of sand. This led deep down to a long passage which ended in the top of a deep chamber beautifully lined with stone.

On the opposite side of the chamber, as high up as the entrance, the passage continued, and was plugged with granite blocks. Quarrying round these, plunderers had reached a long passage, in the side of which was a great granite sarcophagus. This had been hidden by a lining of quartzite sandstone slabs which extended for some three hundred feet further. The builders hoped that the robbers would only search far on in the passage, and so not observe the sarcophagus at the beginning of it; but every block of lining had been forced out in search of passages. After all, was Senusert ever buried here? Or in his less magnificent brick pyramid at Dahshur?

Further south, on the edge of the desert, a pyramid of Aohmes I was examined. It defied previous explorers as well as Mace and ourselves. Far behind it was a square mastaba opened by Currelly, which was a shrine containing a splendid great stele of Queen Tetashera, worshipped by her son Aohmes. Then a terrace temple was found at the cliff further back. A pit on the desert near by yielded the entrance to a winding passage nearly five hundred feet long, with a hall of eighteen pillars half-way along it.

All this was cut in the rock, and seems to have been

for a duplicate tomb of the king, like that of Senusert III. This great rock cutting explained the pyramid, which was entirely composed of rock chips of the same quality; it was the means of thus hiding the tell-tale chips which would have been a token of the great work underground. Similarly, two great dummy mastabas contained the chips from subterranean passages of Senusert III.

By March 18 we left, after the division was settled, while Mace and Weigall wound up the work. I had in past years been observing architecture in Italy, and this year we visited nearly all the churches containing pre-Lombard work. This tour established that the interlacing patterns with rounded curves were all pre-Lombard, and those with angular bends were Lombard.

Looking at the curved interlacing on Syro-Hittite work, the basket-capital of Justinian, and wicker screens of modern Kirghiz, it seems to belong to North-West Asia, and to be due to working in willow, so frequent there. It first appears in Roman mosaics after the Dacian war of Trajan, who brought back many captives. The Lombard angular interlacing must be due to working with a less elastic material, more like rush-work. The purely Scandinavian style of objects from the tomb of the first Lombard Duke—Gisulf —were a striking evidence of the continuity of their art.

We also visited that astonishing example of very early gesso work, carrying on the classical tradition, at S. Pietro al Monte near Lecco, which is very little known. During the summer I was writing up the volume *Abydos I*, with the series of five tombs of the Ist dynasty, and the early temple sculptures.

By November 19, 1902, we were off, and in Cairo on 26th. Weigall had gone on, to see after our premises at Abydos, but he was engaged otherwise this year. The students who continued with us were Currelly, Ayrton and Miss Hansard (Mrs. Firth). Hugh Stannus came out to plan the temple work, Miss Murray, my colleague, came to help with the Osireion. Miss Eckenstein and Rawnsley were also out.

The clearance of the great temple was finished down to the basal sand, for most fortunately the Nile was so low that the water level had never risen since last season, and we were able to push on in dry earth at once. Twelve successive rebuildings of the temple were traced out. To distinguish the mud brick walls from the same material washed down by the rain was difficult; sometimes on drying, the lines of mud mortar would appear, or differences in the colour of bricks.

Abydos was not a happy place as regards the people. They had been accustomed to pillage for generations, and they resented intruders. One stormy night a man carried off a statue of over a hundredweight from our courtyard. I tracked him and made drawings of his feet from various impressions, as the toes were peculiar. I got a local man to tell tales which led to identifying the thief. He was arrested; at the police court his feet exactly tallied to my outline. I heard that it cost him £40 in bribes to get off, and nothing more was done. The statue is probably at the bottom of a canal.

Another time a man came in the dark and shot at close range at the first person who came out of our mess-hut, which was my wife. Happily she escaped. As an Englishman had been murdered at Baliana, we invoked having a resident policeman, in a hut at the end of our row, who was changed every fortnight. The people showed their feeling by plundering our Qufti men of all their money one market day, beating the policeman who tried to protect them. I reported about one of our men who was badly beaten. A police officer came over, professing great indignation. He went to sleep at the omdeh's and next morning took a very different view. Witnesses were summoned and squatted at the feet of the officer. After cross-questioning, the police officer dictated to his scribe what the evidence was. "No no, I did not say that," protested the witness; he was given a kick and told that he must be quiet. As soon as it was all written the officer leaned forward, grabbed the witness' seal, tore it off his neck, and sealed the false deposition. Such is the method of collecting the written evidence, which is usually all that the judges see.

Our beaten man was ordered to go over to the police court, eight miles on donkey, for a doctor to examine him. There he was locked into a room, where the doctor looked in and said he must raise ten francs before he would be let out. Luckily there were some of his companions within hail, they put together the sum demanded, and then the door was opened and the man was told, with a kick, to be off.

One of my men fell ill; I gave an order that he should be sent off at once to his home, but they concealed the case and left him till he was much worse. I then sent him home, by three or four men who carried him. Unhappily he died at home. Then the doctor came down on the family to inquire—this is what an Egyptian dreads more than death itself. He said that unless they paid him five pounds he would record the case as murder, and they had to raise the money.

I reported the matter to Surgeon-Major Gallwey. He ordered a native inquiry, and they concluded that the man had died from the fall of a wall upon him in his work. I at once requested that the reporters should be prosecuted for perjury, but nothing was done. Whenever accusations are made against an Egyptian, his only idea is to invent some story which will throw blame on the accuser.

Beside the temple work, the old fortress of the IInd dynasty, the Shunet ez Zebib, was cleared over, and the name of Khosekhemui was found to occur. The foundations of a second fortress were also discovered to the north of it. A third fortress was always well known as the Coptic Deir, the date of which cannot be examined. At the back of the Sety temple there was an enclosure wall, with a gate opening on to the desert towards the royal tombs. Within that wall I noticed, in the last year there, a slight hollow space; digging down, the men said they were on native soil, but I proved it to be made ground; this happened again, and at last we touched bottom at forty feet down. The view of this digging is the frontispiece in *Methods and Aims in Archaeology.*

Expanding this hole, we reached the sides of a long hall inscribed by Merenptah, and referring to the worship of Osiris. The workmen were managed by my wife, and Miss Murray and Miss Hansard copied the inscriptions. We were evidently not at the end of it when the season closed, but as the other important work at Abydos was ended, we did not think it worth while to continue there for such a very heavy and unprofitable site. I named the publication *The Osireion.*

Since then M. Naville has worked it out during several years; it was finished by Dr. Frankfort. It proves to be a religious cenotaph for Sety I, of interest from the Osiride view, but not of historic importance. Meanwhile we went on to one more Egyptian site before we began our campaign in Sinai.

## CHAPTER X

## EHNASYA, SINAI, YEHUDIYEH

WE left Abydos on April 6, having spent four seasons on the Royal Tombs of the Ist dynasty, and the great temple site, Ist to XXXth dynasty, a most fruitful search for the earliest dynastic civilisation, which remains as the main source for that subject. Coming down country, the bottom of our engine dropped out on the line, and the train was immovable. We waited till a train met us, exchanged passengers, got a fresh engine and reached Cairo at 3 a.m. instead of 8 p.m. As an Egyptian train is made up with second class in front and third behind, the reversal made confusion at every station, by all the passengers finding that they had to run to the other end of the platform. I pointed this out to a station master, and urged him to telegraph down the line to reverse the passengers, but he was incapable of a new idea. At one station there was only one passenger, asleep, as we were then six hours late. The guard stirred him up, he rushed to the wrong end, then began rushing back again, lastly the train went on just before he could get in.

We returned by Greece, and had the exhibition as usual in July. During the summer I was writing *Methods and Aims,* and *History III.* During the packing of the things after the exhibition, there was a mysterious disappearance of all the worked flints, a piece of painted pottery with kudu figures, and other things. None of these reached the places to which they were allotted; yet they were not at all enticing to a stray

thief. If anyone identifies these, which were all published in *Abydos II*, the present positions of them
should be reported.

When I saw Maspero on November 27, 1902, I
asked him whether I might undertake two pieces of
work at Saqqareh, neither of which anyone else would
covet. One was the great enclosure on the desert, supposed to be connected with the sacred bulls; the other
was the fortress in the valley south of the village, which
I knew to be of the Ist dynasty or earlier. I noted "Maspero was very cordial, and agrees to our having an
excellent position at Saqqareh next year." I made arrangements accordingly, promising to give several
lectures in Cairo on behalf of a hospital.

When I came out again, reaching Cairo November
27, 1903, I went to Maspero, and was met by the news
that the Committee would not grant what he had
promised to me. This threw me on my beam ends, for
I had pledged to give charitable lectures in Cairo; I
must keep within reach, and yet my site was refused.
Of all places near, Ehnasya seemed to promise most,
historically, as Naville had found a great portico there,
but had not gone further.

So, being deceived over Saqqareh, I switched off
plans to Ehnasya, reaching there December 1. There
we had Currelly, Loat, and Ayrton. The first two
went on to the desert to try the cemetery at Sedment,
where they got nothing, though we had a rich year
there later on; from there they went on to Gurob,
where Loat, who was an expert on fishes, tapped a
cemetery of enormous fish.

I excavated with my wife and Ayrton, clearing back
into the Ehnasya temple site. The successive buildings
of the XIXth, XVIIIth, and XIIth dynasties were

traced, and earlier burials found beneath the site. The main prize here was a gold statuette of Her-shefi dedicated by an obscure king of the XXIIIrd dynasty of whom a stele has since been found.

Strange to say, this was pitched upon for a *casus falsi* by an opponent. He declared that I had forged it, by casting from a glazed figure. The process was impossible. He even persuaded Rylands to take up the story, and to show a photograph of it as my forgery, to visitors at the Society of Biblical Archaeology. I was only informed of this at first hand under a pledge of secrecy, so I could not proceed for libel.

This queer story shows how—having failed in the attack on me at the Royal Tombs—there was no length to which the opposition would not carry their spite. As it was Ayrton who dug the figure out of hard mud, and I never knew of it till it came up to our hut, the story was the more ridiculous.

I tried hard to reach another temple site at Ehnasya but could not get any result. After the division of things, Ayrton found a colossal granite triad; this Maspero took without any offset to us; it is now in the outer gallery of the Museum. I published a large series of Roman terra-cottas and lamp types in addition to the annual volume.

Not seeing more prospect here, and having, at great inconvenience, gone up to Cairo four times for promised lectures, for we were twelve miles from a station, I then left on February 25, visited Loat, and on 28th left Cairo for Dessuk and Buto. We had sent on boxes of bedding and provisions well in advance, fully marked in big black capitals, both in English and Arabic, for Dessuk. The railway policy was illegible, but we expected to find our supplies there. None came, for they had been sent to Alexandria.

For a week my wife and I lived in a small tent pitched on a high wall in the marshes. We had evening dress and a camera without plates, but were without bedding or night things. But we dug here and there, and settled that the water level in the temple area covered everything up to the XXVIth dynasty level, all the older stuff being therefore inaccessible. Further, the early site had been plundered out in Roman times, before the Delta sank; they had sawn up limestone blocks for paving, and scattered pieces of Ist dynasty stone vases on the surface. I sank a deep shaft through the wall, hoping to reach deposits but could not.

Therefore, going on to Alexandria, I lectured and went back to Cairo. There, on March 7, Maspero was still agreeable to my having the Saqqareh site; it was only the Committee that objected. I went at once to Cromer, and he said that Garstin (as head of Public Works) should go to the meeting that afternoon and settle it for me; I only had to send in the formal application through Maspero.

I went back to the Museum, and told Maspero that it was settled, and I was to apply. He pushed over a sheet of official paper for me to write on, saying: "You may write what you like," and swung round in his chair with his back to me, an attitude which I knew before with Grébaut. It was only too evident that Maspero was the obstruction, and the Committee was only Jorkins; he was merely intending to play civil to me and to get the matter refused. My application came to nought, though backed by Cromer and Garstin. More of this in future years.

Leaving Egypt March 10, my wife and I spent three

weeks in Sicily, walking much in the hills. The Capella Palatina leaves one of the deepest memories in life; the harmony of the Norman, Arab and Byzantine art is perhaps the greatest triumph of the Middle Ages. In the summer I was working up the plans of Ehnasya and writing; the July exhibition was held as usual, and the volume of *History III* was finished.

The prospect of working up the Egyptian monuments in Sinai had tempted me for long, and now Currelly was ready to bring over my men from Koptos, so we settled on that region, leaving London November 18. Besides Currelly we had Philip Button, a lad who passed on to Navy Medical Service, K. Frost, who was killed in the war, running a machine gun single-handed, and given a military funeral by the Germans, R. Weill (who had catalogued the copies of the Sinai inscriptions), and during parts of the time, Montague Porch and Miss Eckenstein.

For the first six weeks my wife excavated at Saqqareh, copying mastabas, and had the Misses Hansard, Eckenstein and Kingsford there. One Sunday, some drunken Frenchmen tried to force their way into her huts, and were stoutly resisted by the cook boy. They went on to the official house and began to smash furniture and fight the native guards. Carter, then inspector, was fetched, and he very rightly allowed the guards to defend themselves till the police could come. The indignity of letting a native resist a Frenchman weighed more than the indignity of being drunk and disorderly, in the eyes of the French Consul, who demanded an apology from Carter. With proper self-respect, Carter refused to apologize for doing his obvious duty. For this he was, on demand of the French, dismissed from the Service. This was perhaps the dirtiest act of the subservience to French arrogance.

Our party went down from Suez December 3, walking and camelling. On December 9, we were at Maghara. Here we found that a box supposed to contain food, held other stores, so we were short; our camels had all left, as no man is allowed to monopolise wages in Sinai; the sheykh was absent. A pushful Bedawy, Khallyl, offered camels to fetch water and food, and I wrote up an Arabic contract and signed it to satisfy him.

The whole bother arose from our Consul at Suez knowing nothing of the district; had he been in touch with natives, he would have got hold of the sheykh who was there in Suez. I had, on hearing how things stood, to send back a messenger to get a Consular contract with the sheykh. Two days after we arrived, we got up camels with stores from our cargo boat which had gone down the coast from Suez.

Owing to our not being yet under the sheykh, we were pillaged at night, losing our store of treacle (needed for men's rations), new stove, and, worst of all, the quarter-mile roll of *Times* paper for making squeezes and copies. What the Arabs could do with this was a mystery; no scraps were ever seen about the place. I had to write up to my friend the editor of the *Mokattam,* in Cairo, to let us have a stock of paper, which was weak and brittle compared with *The Times.*

Old Abu Ghaneym the sheykh remembered Major Macdonald who, about 1862, tried to revive turquoise mining, and lived there with his son. The old sheykh was marvellously hardy, sleeping under the stars every night by our tent.

By December 18, Currelly arrived with twenty-seven men from Koptos, having marched them more than eighty miles to the Red Sea, got a mining company's steamer to carry them over, and then marched up to Wady Maghara. We had, of course, to feed all our party, as nothing could be bought there, except an occasional goat. The serving out of rations every morning was done by Button, 80 lbs. weight of flour, rice, lentils, sugar, oil, and onions having to be weighed out. Our men were very reasonable, asking for rather more in the cold weather, and then later declining so much.

Our main stores were sent down by boat, but we had to get flour and other things supplemented by camel from Suez, six days' journey each way. So it was needful to keep count a fortnight ahead, to make sure that we should not find our thirty-six people run short. Our water supply was kept up by two camels, making two journeys each day, from sources which the Arabs kept secret to themselves, springs in the granite; the water was quite good.

The first matter was to copy all the inscriptions, by wet squeeze on small ones, by dry squeeze and drawing on the large ones. A few years before, a mining company, run by Mr. Hoover I am informed, had been here to search for turquoise. Their men had bashed up or destroyed the sculptures abominably, and a relic of their occupation was an immense steel safe, locked, which they had never required. It would not pay to convey such lumber back to civilisation, so for thousands of years that safe will stand up in that gaunt valley, a monument to futile destruction. After our work was over, Currelly was asked to cut out and remove all the sculptures to the Cairo Museum; Semerkhet, the oldest, only remains, highest and inaccessible.

While at Maghara, a Sudany policeman came in, saying that the sheykh had sold a turquoise with warranty; it had proved bad on cutting, but he would not return the money. So the Sudany had come to get £17 out of that utterly barren valley, with only a few thorn bushes in it. He was a splendid man, tall, with hook nose, and black to the roof of his mouth. After half an hour he came in again, and shook a little bag, saying: "I have got it." The old sheykh was none the worse in person for the extraction.

Then the policeman asked to sit down and write. For an hour he went over his report and all his papers, with the patience of a humble clerk; then when all was packed in his wallet, he went out and rated at the Arabs till they shook. Such men, when suitably educated in the Sudan, may well prove to be the masters of North Africa some day.

Having finished at Maghara, we went over to Serabit by a way not recorded before, winding along the valleys till we pitched camp about 300 feet below the Serabit temple, where we began work on January 11. The primitive sacred cave on the hilltop had a small court and pylon built on by Hatshepsut, in front of which a long chain of rough chambers had been gradually added on each side of the path. These had all fallen by decay of the sandstone slabs, and we had to clear them out. Further, a shrine, dedicated to Sneferu and other kings by Hatshepsut, was on one side of the court, covered with sand and chips.

The inscriptions were in many instances weathered away into mere holes in the sandstone, but others were in perfect condition. The high wind made copying difficult. Sheets of paper had to be lashed to the boards at every inch or two, a sheet held by one side would be torn away in the gale. Lumbago also was a penalty from the chill.

The animal life was a puzzle; there were only a few desert plants and no water on that plateau, half a mile above sea level; yet rats were about, and we daily put our lunch on the top of a pillar to save it. Down in the valley there were spiny porcupine desert rats, who would eat through baggage. Another surprise was to see camels browsing on thorn bushes one or two hundred feet up, walking along the ledges of the cliffs. I have seen a camel drag a burning thorn bush off a fire to eat it, with thorns like nails, which the camel's mouth is proof against.

I noticed some strange inscriptions on statuettes and tablets, which were partly imitations of hieroglyphs, but partly in the old Mediterranean signary. They were evidently a jumble of signs acquired by the local workmen, just as are found in Egypt, and used for writing.

The later discovery of highly developed Phoenician writing at Byblos of 1300 B.C., finally puts it out of court that the Sinai writing was a precursor of the Phoenician. It is merely a local barbarism. All the wild theories of Grimm about it depend on his adoption of the natural cracks in the stone as being engraved signs. Now that Kirsopp Lake has gone to Sinai and removed the rock examples, which I left in place, they can be studied at Cairo. I had proposed removing all the Egyptian inscriptions, but as Maspero could not grant enough return for such a costly and wearisome enterprise, we left them alone, and only brought portable pieces.

There was one drenching day and night of rain, and

after it we ran out to see all the desert valleys rushing torrents. Our old sheykh had settled himself near us, with the shelter of a pile of brushwood to windward. He did not seek shelter in our men's tents when the rain came, but took off most of his clothes and rolled them up to keep dry. He then lay out all night on the bare rock, in his shirt, soaked by the storm. I expected to see him dead next morning, but he was just as well and croaky as ever. The men never seek shelter in Sinai, except ledges of rock; the tents are only for women and children.

My reliance on one helper was shaken when he remarked in my surveying that he did not need such things as a box sextant, he only needed to hold a sheet of paper flat, look along it in different directions, and he could make his plans, *voilà*. One day I searched for fragments of a great stele which were widely scattered, and succeeded in building it together, as I described that evening. Next day, as he went some way before me, I saw him turn over a small stele (which I knew) and look at the lower side inscribed. He dropped it on the ground and broke it. That evening he brought in the pieces and said that he also could find pieces of steles and restore them. Our party understood the man after that. *La gloire* is a fatal temptation.

By March 18 we left, and camelled up with all our baggage to Suez. From there I sent my men back by train to Quft. I had a hunt to find the list of fares at the station, it was hidden behind a cupboard. Seeing the official fare, I then gave my men money for their return; but the clerk gave them tickets far short of Quft, and cheated them all. This was a favourite trick on the railways, as the fellahin could not read their tickets; so, long before their destination, they were told by the guard who collected their tickets that they must get out or pay for a fresh ticket to take them on.

Another railway trick was not to open the ticket window till the train approached; then, while a dozen hands were holding on to the grating, each person was only too glad to get his ticket, and rush to the waiting train with short change or none. When the Nationalist state gets its Mussolini, perhaps such stories will be out of date. From Cairo I posted fourteen thick rolls of drawings to London. It is much safer to post drawings and photographs, registered, to England than to risk theft or loss of baggage on the way.

In London, matters were coming to a head. I was told later, by a friend in the British Museum, that it was settled that as the Americans were now safely attached to the Fund, I was to be turned off. Maunde Thompson, as chairman, had not the patience to work me out, and so John Evans took that position. In 1900-1 he had been in Egypt, and I had been much astonished to hear that he had been saying what he could to damage me in official eyes.

Then in 1904 the Fund had raised its subscription to two pounds to drain supplies, and had broken its agreement with me that I was to have half the excavating in my hands. On May 9, 1905, the Committee met, and the President said that he cancelled my agreement, and none of the Committee objected. It was stated that they had not money enough for a season's work, though soon after they arranged for Naville to go on.

A Sub-committee was appointed to deal with me. It met on May 11, when the President proposed my going about England touting for the Fund at £100 a year, without any certainty of my excavating. The agreement was "suspended" until the Fund should be able to renew it. I replied that I did not intend to cease excavating. The proposal was urged three times, adding that any money that I raised should be allowed to me to spend. I replied that, if so, I did not see why I should raise it to go in their hands, instead of directly for my own management.

In this emergency I could only fall back on the small student fund, the Egyptian Research Account, and I invited several of the Fund Committee to join that and work with me, in order to keep up some link of management. They replied, however, that they could not do so without the consent of the Fund Committee. I then announced definitely at my first lecture on May 18, that I was going to work on the small basis of the Egyptian Research Account, and on the 20th I resolved to start a large new Committee to manage it.

Thus the breach was forced on me by breaking, and then withdrawing, my agreement, refusing to allow me to excavate, except with money which I raised, and by the members whom I knew being hindered from working with me separately. After working entirely in the interest of the Fund for nine years, I found myself at the age of fifty-two turned off by intrigue, without any means of continuing my work, and having to begin over again to get public support for it.

That summer we were organising, and the Fund made a claim on their subscribers that they could not withdraw without a year's notice, an unheard-of position in a voluntary society. It had been agreed that as there was much to say about Sinai, I should publish a popular volume on my own account (*Researches in Sinai*), and prepare the inscriptions for publication by the Fund. I worked at both, and as the only size of plate which would do for a uniform scale of publication was that of *Deir el Bahri,* the Committee agreed to that. I was to arrange plates accordingly.

After I had done a good deal, the size was ordered by the Treasurer to be reduced; as I declined to break the Committee's decision, I then rolled up all the copies and deposited them in the Fund office, till a suitable settlement might be reached. There they remained for some years, until Professor Peet and Dr. Alan Gardiner took up the matter. They collated older copies and squeezes where available, for editing the texts, but no inquiry was made as to which of our five people had drawn, and had verified, each of our copies. The whole of the material of our expedition was then issued solely in the names of the editors, and without getting any of the names which should have been initialed to each copy.

There were other activities in 1905. We went to the Archaeological Congress in Athens, and I urged the need of museums having all ancient gold and silver work electrotyped, and a complete set of electrotypes distributed to every museum. That would enable gold work to be kept more safely out of sight, and save it from the losses which occurred in several museums; it would also greatly help study by having all the electrotypes together. Cecil Smith warmly approved, but we could not stir interest among the curators. The cost of the work would probably have been paid by many American museums buying whole sets.

For our July exhibition of Sinai, I had an accurate model made of the Serabit temple and monuments, but could not get any museum to take it off my hands, though there was much public interest in it. Dr. Capart came over to London and stayed with us, and later we went to visit the Hood collection at Nettleham. By the end of August, Currelly bid us good-bye, and kept on with the Fund. I was working up the Sinai book until the next expedition.

Thanks to my wife's energy, and my friends rallying round my work, we succeeded in raising enough to have out three students, and so continued excavating on a larger scale; this was aided by our receiving nothing personally from our newly started British School of Archaeology in Egypt, then, or at any other time.

Thus we could get off on November 17, 1905, having arranged with Duncan, my helper at Naqada, and two new students, Butler-Stoney and Gilbart-Smith. I asked for Tell el Yehudiyeh and the Wady Tumilat, but Maspero would not let me go as far as Tell Maskhuta as Cledat was supposed to work that for the Canal Company. We began at Yehudiyeh with thirty-seven men from Quft. There I cleared the top of the mound, and found the scraps of walls which belonged to the Jewish temple of Onias; I also delimited the mound all round, finding the great stone wall, the original stairway, and the ovens at the base.

All this enabled me to see that it was a model of the Temple hill at Jerusalem, entirely thrown up artificially over the Passover ovens of a great sacrificial feast. A scrap of accounts for bricks named an Abraham. The site of the decorated temple of Ramessu III was searched over, but the destruction of it, thirty years before, was too complete to leave us anything.

Seeing a white line on the ground I traced it, and found it ran far. Digging along it showed that it was a plaster face to a sloping earth bank. At last I traced out a great square camp enclosure of earth, with a raised entrance; later, a stone wall had been built around the foot of it, and the space filled in. This tallied with the account of the Hyksos fort, which later had a wall. From the wall the Jews obtained all the stone for the flanking of the great mound for Onias. This camp enabled me to identify a similar camp at Heliopolis, and in a later year the Hyksos fortress of Bethpelet in Palestine; these are now accepted as belonging to a system of earth-bank camps, from Central Asia down to Palestine.

The cemetery we worked for some graves of the Hyksos age, finding much of the black incised ware and scarabs associated; this put the classification of such things on to a firm basis. We then moved to Retabeh, which had been condemned as Roman. There was nothing Roman visible, and at last it appeared that the latest work there was of the XIXth dynasty.

This was an important result, as it renders the theory of this being Pithom entirely untenable. A large slab was found of a temple wall, with Ramessu II slaying an Asiatic. The lines of an earlier fort were traced, and beneath the corner of it was a burial of a small child, the Syrian foundation deposit. I went further East, and copied and wet-squeezed a granite stele of Darius. As there was nothing much wanted for the Museum among our things, I offered to Maspero that we should contribute by paying for fetching the Darius stele to the Museum. This was accepted, and it is now invisible in that dim place.

Duncan was working with Gilbart-Smith or Butler-Stoney at various sites, the most important of which was Saft el Henneh, where was a wide cemetery, mostly very shallow in sandy tracts. I went to see him there; we walked over distant parts, and then, not knowing the distances, I just lost my train back to Retabeh, twenty miles away. It was sunset, and only filthy native houses near. So I had to walk back along the railway at the end of the day. At Kishlak, about 9 in the evening, I found a Greek shop, and went in for some bread. The Greek looked scared, no train had been in for hours, and here was a stranger in the dark in the midst of the desert. "Where are you from?" he said; "My own work." "But where are you going?" "To my own place." I could not let anyone know where, or I should have been stopped by the guards. I bolted out into the darkness again with my bread, and went on, in the edge of cultivation to avoid hyaenas (who will pull a man down at night on the desert), and as soon as I heard dogs ahead in a farm, I had to skirt round in the desert. I got back by 2 a.m., having covered half the length of Wady Tumilat at the end of the day.

I went up four times to Cairo to give lectures for some charity. The trains were amusing on that line. The inhabitants did not take tickets, but tipped the guard. There were inspectors to go round and see tickets; I was told a guard would say to the inspector that this was a fat train, and he must have a share of the inspector's tips. Thus tickets were needless. I would not tip for having baggage weighed, so at no place did I get it done in time for the train. I had always to leave a man behind to bring it by the next train.

At one place I went twenty-five minutes before the time. No one was in the station; even the booking clerk had gone off to market, leaving the office open. When the train was seen coming in, the station master sauntered out of his house. I demanded to have my things weighed. "You should be here in time," he said. "I have been here twenty-five minutes." "Oh, you should be here half an hour before." Such was the

Tumilat railway. It was a regular custom on all Egyptian lines, to give a shilling to the weighing clerk, who put down the weight at half or three-quarters the amount. The Government were heavily defrauded—and may be so still—but I never could get my men to avoid this custom.

When I had down a large party of Quftis for the Delta work, I met them from the night train at Cairo, to get their tickets for the Delta. The hall for third-class tickets was a seething mass of waiting passengers, trying to get tickets in time for the various morning trains; the ticket clerks were slow and indifferent, as the later the passenger the less he looked after his change. I elbowed my way through to the office I wanted, but so slow was the issue that I saw most of the people would not get tickets in time.

Though I always took my turn in the crowds at stations, for to claim privileges is odious, yet here were twenty men at stake for a day, so I pushed in at the door of the office to get all the tickets at once. I doubt if any Englishman ever saw the scandal of most of the passengers not getting tickets in time, as such third-class business was always left to a native servant.

Altogether this was a satisfactory season; the objects of the Hyksos age were fixed, the fort of Retabeh was dated, the doubt about Pithom settled, the Hyksos fort defined, and the temple of Onias planned. We left the work on April 8; I lectured at four places on the Riviera, and was in London April 25. I had a model of the hill of Onias and temple site, also of the Hyksos fort, for the exhibition. At this, Duncan helped, and a new student Ernest Mackay, who was twenty years later to dig up the oldest civilisation of India.

The volume on the year's work was written up by

July 17. I was at the British Association at York, and next preparing the Huxley lecture on *Migrations*. I was invited to accept the honorary LL.D. at Aberdeen in the celebrations there on September 20th. The Strathcona banquet was immense; he had invited every graduate of that University, and 5,000 were present in a vast tenting. No one could hear over more than half the space, so conversation was general, no matter what the speeches might be. It was the limit for a feast, and rather beyond. Sixteen lectures about the country and various writing filled my autumn. The Huxley lecture has remained as the set of charts of post-Roman migration to which students are referred.

## CHAPTER XI

## RIFEH, MEMPHIS, QURNEH, HAWARA

A PROMISING part of Egypt was that south of Asyut, as there were important inscriptions of the Middle Kingdom at Dronkeh, which Griffith had copied. I therefore applied for this district. But before that there was a short work to be done at the south side of Gizeh where some great mastabas stood, which were not already taken in concessions. This year my wife was detained in England, and our last year's men were none of them continuing in the work. So I started with Mackay, Ward of Edinburgh, Rhoades and Gregg.

At Gizeh I settled in to huts on November 30, 1906, and in a week our old friend Miss Hansard, now Mrs. Firth, came with her husband. They were soon persuaded by Dr. Reisner to join him, and left me in a month. I had ninety-two Quftis at work; we cleared up the mastabas which were of the IInd dynasty, and thus occupied the hill before the pyramids. Some fine things were found, especially a long slip of translucent flint, polished, like a huge paper knife, kept in Cairo.

The more important tomb was a mastaba in the plain, which Daressy had cleared, without any plan. We got out sealings of Zer (middle of Ist dynasty), the plan of the outside, and the circuit of graves all round the mastaba. Though all had been robbed anciently, there were many good things, especially for dating. It was most desirable to work this for comparison with Royal Tombs of the same age, and it showed that the civilisation was alike at Abydos and Memphis.

I published all the contents, and desired to include those which Daressy found; but he was away, I could not see them, and nothing more has appeared about them—another blind end in the Museum. Many small tombs of the IVth dynasty had stone lintels which we brought away; and a late cemetery of the Ptolemaic age provided 2,000 skulls from which Prof. Karl Pearson has got the best defined characters of late times.

The cenotaph of Khoemuas, south of the pyramids, we worked over, finding many of his ushabtis, broken. (U.C.) On the crest of the hill there was a sandy hollow, and clearing into this we found much of a great mastaba with inscribed chambers of the Saite age. We copied it all, and I asked Maspero to let me bring the complete chamber to Cairo museum, and distribute the incomplete chambers to other museums at his choice. He refused, saying it was a fixed monument.

So I had to bury it again, but not for long. It was soon an unfixed monument in the hands of the dealers; all was scattered and lost and we got nothing for our trouble. It is folly to suppose that inscribed stones will be left in place if unguarded.

On January 2 I attended the Cromers' farewell party. January 9, having done what I could on the unallotted part of Gizeh, I left for Rifeh. There I worked with Ward and Mackay, while Rhoades and Gregg attended to the large Coptic site of Balaizeh to the south. Rifeh proved of much interest, as a main source of the house models or "soul-houses" which were provided for the deceased, at about the Xth to XIIth dynasties.

The dwellings of early times have all vanished, but in the models were preserved every stage, from the Bedawy shelter propped up with two sticks, to the two-

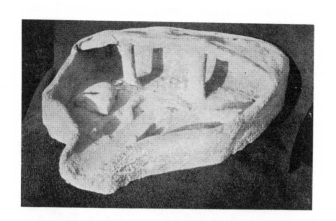

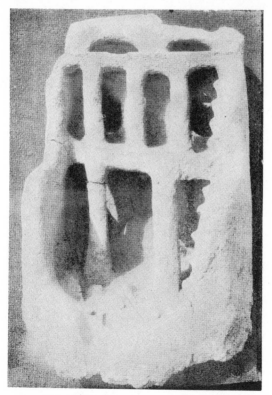

SOUL HOUSES, FROM TENT TO HIGH HOUSE

storey house with arched rooms, and furniture. For the history of early architecture they are invaluable. Such models were placed at the side of the grave, so that the soul when it wandered forth should find its comfort at hand. Those that remained on the surface became worn by sand-blast; but when a tomb was robbed the model fell in, and so was preserved. Besides these we got a series of pottery from the Old to the Middle Kingdom. Several interesting things were found, such as an ivory wand in form of an arm covered with net-work, also tombs of the IXth to XIth dynasties were excavated.

The cliffs were a mile away and I was anxious to make a thorough clearance along a seam of fine stone, in which tombs were likely to be found. At the end of the season, a tomb was reached with a very fine sarcophagus and figure coffin inside it, richly painted, accompanied by statuettes and fine boats for sailing up and rowing down the Nile. The whole group is in Manchester.

While there, I wished to be friendly to the Coptic community settled at Dronkeh near by. So, one day, Ward and I went up with a modest offering of jams. The sheykh was away, but his little daughter, certainly not over twelve, received us in a most dignified and pleasant manner. Some years later we found the girl of a Coptic police officer reading the lessons in the church service. There is none of the scandalous shamefaced manner of the Mohammedan seen in Coptic ladies and children, as may be noticed in the family groups attending service.

A Coptic village is clean and well swept, the women sitting at work in the doorways and chatting across the street. It is on the level of a civilised Mediterranean

land, and not like the filthy confusion of a Mohammedan village. The same difference is seen in Cairo;
the Coptic main road, the Fagallah, is well repaired,
planted and watered. The great Mohammedan boule-
vard Mahomet Aly has the pavements broken and full
of holes, and dust and filth heaped up in all the corners. Egypt will never be a civilised land till it is ruled
by the Copts—if ever.

By March 20 I was in Cairo, inquiring about the
land laws and hiring of land for excavations in view of
work at Memphis. I left on the 26th, did five lectures
on the Riviera and was in London April 14th. On the
26th our son John was born. The usual exhibition in
July, and preparation of the volume *Gizeh and Rifeh*
occupied me till October 13th. Much lecturing, and
writing articles, filled up my time.

The importance of the great temple sites of Memphis and Heliopolis as possible sources of historical
documents—such as the Palermo stone—had made me
wish to see some thorough search. The difficulties were
considerable; the ground was nearly all cultivated, and
the search must be always below water level. The cost
proved to be £300 an acre, and long and tedious negotiations were needed with the owners.

After six years of such work, with small returns, a
blow was struck at it, Maspero having a law passed
that all antiquities in private land were the property
of the Government. This would halve the small returns which we got. The existing antiquity law was
designed for work on desert land, where there were
no over-head costs, or for accidental discoveries in private land. Where such heavy costs of hiring land and
pumping were necessary, some compensation was
needed if the Government claimed objects. My protest

to Maspero was never answered; the war broke out, and the mounds of the Memphis site were given to American work, although we had housing there for ourselves and the men, and had sunk a good deal of earnest money to acquire future rights of using the private land.

The Museum had already gained by our work the colossal alabaster sphinx of Amenhetep III, which we had found and raised as a public monument. This disregard of all our claims to continue there was in marked contrast to the treatment of the Egypt Exploration Fund which, having neglected Abydos for ten years, was considered to have a lien upon it, when we asked to work a part of the ground.

This outline will explain in general the course on which we entered in 1907. To work Memphis the season should be as late as possible, for the subsidence of the water. Hence it was necessary to fill the earlier part of the season by short work further south. A ruined temple was known at Athribis near Sohāg, so I applied for that region, and also to work Memphis.

On November 14, 1907, I started, the students being Mackay and Ward as last year, also Gregg and Hill, and Schuler, a German architect sent by von Bissing. We began by settling at Deir el Abyad, December 2nd, in order to find the meaning of ruins near the monastery. These proved to be of the fourth century, by the pottery; we found part of an uncompleted town, containing the traces of a large limestone building which had been entirely removed.

The conclusion was that a basilica had been built here under Constantine, and part of a town by it; that it had been injured in the Julian reaction, and that under Theodosius an adjoining site was adopted, and the much larger Deir erected, using all the material from the earlier basilica, especially the carved bands of decoration, which were set up with disjointed pattern in some places. The great granite shrine of Nepherites had also been removed from the temple of Athribis, and cut to pieces to make granite paving slabs. This could not have happened before Theodosius.

After a week I moved to Athribis, and a week later our party settled there. The temple proved to be entirely Ptolemaic, and to have the peculiar feature of a peristyle court surrounding the whole, probably due to Greek influence. I copied much of the sculpture; this contained a detailed shrine of Min resembling the Punite huts, and suggesting the source of that god; this would well agree with his importance at Koptos, the place of entry of the Punite dynastic people. We copied the very rare examples of zodiac horoscopes of Roman age, painted on tomb ceilings. Some rock tombs of the IVth or Vth century at Hagarseh were also fully copied and published.

On January 1, Ward and Schuler went to Memphis to begin building our house; but German ideas did not fit with Egyptian conditions, and there was hardly a habitable room by the 27th when I moved there. The weather was remarkable; on January 8 we had 89° in the shade, and on February 14 only 46°. Wainwright came to join us on January 21; he had inquired about such work when I met him at Bristol in October. All our party were united here by February 15. The people were entirely impracticable about private land, and we could only begin on waste land.

Thus we worked out the western pylon of the great temple, finding many tablets engraved with ears, to

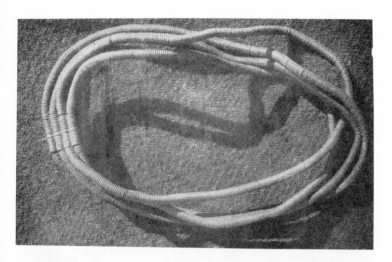

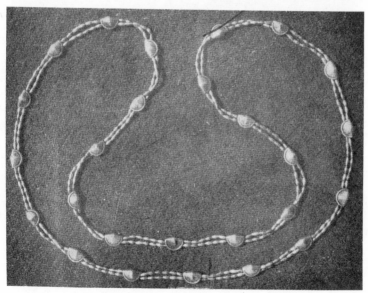

GOLD NECKLACES AND GIRDLE, 2 : 3, 17TH DYNASTY

entreat the hearing of the god. To the south of the great temple was probably the original Apis temple, but around that we only found sculptures of Sa-amen of the XXIst dynasty. A most unexpected result was the discovery in a particular part of the city ruins of many pottery heads of foreign types. Large kilns, and many glazed shards of the first century, threw light on the methods of pot making.

When this season was drawing to a close, Carter joined us for three weeks. I left at the end of April, and was in London May 5. The Memphis material was being worked up all the summer, before and after the July exhibition. The Congress of Religions at Oxford asked for an address on Egyptian religion, in which I dealt with the great variety of aspects of the subject, outside of the usual text-books.

A consideration of the trend of social changes was published in *Janus*. A long run of fourteen lectures about the country filled the autumn. The writing of *Memphis I* was finished November 15, and *Personal Religion* on November 9; *Arts and Crafts of Ancient Egypt* also appeared, and has since been translated into French and into Czech.

On November 20, 1908, my wife and I left, and were by December 7 settled in a large unpainted rock tomb at Qurneh, with huts for our party of Mackay, Wainwright, and Brian Hatton, an artist to whom G. F. Watts wished to give opportunity in the East. Within three days we found two important steles of the Antef family, relating to their political gains in Egypt.

At the end of the year we discovered, in a small valley, a burial in open ground of a *rishi* coffin of about the XVIIth dynasty. It was accompanied by furniture and vases in network slings, most of which were very fragile. I coated them with collodion, and so succeeded in bringing them away safely. On the body was a collar of strings of gold rings, a gold girdle, and bangles. The collar is of the greatest interest as it is of the same family as three much more elaborate collars found in Sweden, of a style the source of which is entirely unknown. Further, the Egyptian collar and bangles are made on a weight standard of 160 grains, and the Swedish collars are on the same standard—the *necef*, which belonged to North Syria.

Where in Asia this style originated is yet unknown, but the Egyptian example is doubtless due to the Hyksos influence. The whole set was remitted to us by Maspero on condition that it was kept all together; it was exhibited in London, and I mounted each of the jars with slings in a separate bell glass, with cotton filter, to preserve them from dust, as they were too fragile ever to be cleaned.

It was the largest group of goldwork that had left Egypt, and in recognition of our London subscribers we offered to present it to South Kensington Museum. We waited a fortnight for reply, and were then told that the condition of keeping the group together would not suit the museum arrangement. We then offered it to Edinburgh, but said that they had no such claim on us, and they ought to help the work if they took it.

The Royal Scottish Museum at once applied to the Science and Art Department for a grant of £100. That Department referred to their Museum authorities. So then, for the first time, a Museum man came to inspect it. He whispered under his breath, "We did not know it was such a fine thing," and reported that the

SUMERIAN

INDIANS

SPANIARD

MODELLED HEADS OF FOREIGNERS. MEMPHIS

Department should give £100 to Edinburgh to secure it, after they might have had it in London for nothing.

I have tried repeatedly to get the most important things fixed in London, and it is no fault of mine if London has not got them. In 1921 the finest Egyptian statuette was reported twice to Cecil Smith, but he did not reply, for S.K. was too much occupied over a mock-Chinese lacquer bedstead. However it is now in British Museum.

On one of the highest peaks at Thebes there was a building, reputed to be a temple of Thoth. On clearing it, we found that it was the *sed heb* chapel of Sonkh-ka-ra of the XIth dynasty, with a cenotaph coffin and a seated figure in the festal robe. Though only fragments were obtained, it was of great interest, as a separate chapel for this ceremony was then unknown. Later we found—on the highest ground again—a similar chapel for Senusert II at Lahun.

The store chambers of Sety I were cleared, and several tombs copied. My wife then left for England. We closed rather quickly as there was plague in Upper Egypt, and we wanted to get our men down to Memphis.

By February 10, 1909, we resumed work at Memphis. The main excavation was that of the Palace of Apries, on the top of the large northern mound. The walls of the large court and chambers around it were standing several feet high, and the broken columns and capitals lay in the court. Much scale armour was found, mostly of iron, and lesser scales of bronze for the fingers. In a hole in the floor of a workroom was a beautiful handle of silver with a gold and bronze head of Hathor (Cairo). Large alabaster vases were found smashed up and buried in a hole, probably destroyed to prevent their being taken by the Persians (U.C.).

The chief prize was the series of limestone slabs of a great gateway of the XIIth dynasty, with scenes of festal ceremonies which the king performed to ensure the fertility of the country. Having drawn all these, full size, I could realise the perfection of the work, far finer than any of the XVIIIth or later dynasties. This conclusion was reinforced when, some years later, I published a study of the similar scenes in each period. Then it was clear that the details of the Memphite scenes belonged to the earlier time, and were quite unknown in the XXVIth dynasty. (*Ancient Egypt* 1925, 65.)

Of remarkable interest was the discovery of many terra-cotta heads, modelled, not from a mould, which represented many different types neither Egyptian nor Greek. These were only found in the foreign quarter of Memphis, and belonged to the Persian age. In the first year the matter seemed to many people almost too strange for belief. The second season convinced all that we had here the figures of Indians, Persians, Kurds, Scythians, Hebrews, Sumerians, Karians, Greeks of Asia Minor, Macedonian, and even Spanish or Sardinian portraits. A very few pottery bodies were found, and those of Indians.

The reason for such a passion for ethnic figures seemed quite inexplicable; but a custom in Tibet, described by Gabet and Huc seems to throw light upon it. At an annual Buddhist festival, figures are modelled of all the races to whom Buddhism has been preached, that they may all have part in the festival. When it is over, the figures are all thrown away. Such a custom would exactly account for the Memphite

HEADS OF UNKNOWN RACES. MEMPHIS

heads, and for the whole figures being Indian. That Buddhism was preached in the West, a century later, is recorded by Asoka, and the presence of Indian heads here, and the large numbers of Indians in the Persian army, give quite enough ground for such a festival having been held.

Some fine lotus capitals of the Old Kingdom were found re-used, and many interesting slabs of sculpture. In the evenings at Memphis, I drew the plates and wrote up the volume of *Qurneh* by March 9.

On April 21 I left Memphis, and was in London on the 29th. There a long and difficult task was the re-arrangement of the whole collection at the College in new cases, which sufficed to place on view most of the material. This consisted of the small collection made by Miss Edwards, and much more subsequently presented to the College from our work; also of a great amount which belonged to me, from my own work and purchases. All this was afterwards taken over by the College.

The exhibition was held as usual, but I could not be present owing to a sharp attack of a kind of influenza, for which I had to go into the country. The book on *Arts and Crafts* was finished August 14, and our daughter Ann was born August 27. By September 13 the new cases at the College were completely arranged, and on October 21 the volume on the *Palace of Apries* was finished for press. Over a dozen lectures about the country occupied the autumn, and of course my regular two series of College lectures were given as in every year.

On November 28, 1909, I was again in Cairo, and settled at Meydum by December 2. Mackay, Wainwright and Benton Fletcher were with me. We had a sad case with us for a fortnight,—a man who seemed all right in London, but he became strange in manner, and we concluded that he was drugging. I had actually been given no home address by which to warn his family. As he lost the respect of the men, I persuaded him to go off to Luqsor, where I warned a doctor to look after him. From there, his hotel packed him off to Cairo; at Cairo the hotel sent him to the Consulate; and the Consul promptly put him in an asylum. Months after, a relative of his said about him that he had been out of his mind before. Such misfits are very awkward in a small desert camp, and one cannot ask for a certificate from every sane person. Families are too apt to try to shirk their obligation, as I saw in other cases.

The funniest thing was when a man who joined us and was very un-useful, confided to me after a fortnight that he was come out to seek for a commercial opening. I said if he wanted that, he would not find it in the desert, and he must go to a town. He went up to Luqsor, spent all he had in buying rank forgeries, and had to get the Consul in Cairo to save him by demanding restitution from the dealers.

At Meydum our business was to find the chambers of the big mastabas, to open the rows of large pits west of the pyramid, to clear up the small pyramid, and to try if there were a shrine on the inner face of the pyramid behind the coating. These matters were all settled. Wainwright stayed on after I left, and Bushe-Fox joined the later work on a cemetery at Gerzeh.

The largest mastaba in our area was blocked by an immense stone plug, but we tunnelled in, only to find that it had already been tunnelled at the weakest point, evidently while the plan was well known. It contains a fine sarcophagus of red granite, better wrought than that of Khufu. We removed the head of the destroyed mummy, which had evidently been unfleshed, as the atlas vertebra was reversed.

At the pyramid, we obtained many quarry dates on the stones. We ran a tunnel in the sand bed beneath the outer casings, but had to tunnel in rock for the inner part; no trace of a shrine was found on any coat of the pyramid. The terrible destruction of the sculptured tombs made Maspero desire us to remove them; that of Nefermaat and Atet to Cairo, Rahetep to be divided among museums.

The chamber of Atet was found, buried below a mass of mud poured in liquid to close it. The wooden door below was perfect, the tombs had never been entered. But inside, the workmen who closed it had broken up the whole mummy into splinters and rags, certainly from spite and not only for plunder. While here, I worked out the detail of the portions of the Synoptic Gospels which are in identical order, as indicating the earliest documents, on which they were all built up. This appeared in *The Growth of the Gospels*.

By February 6, 1910, I was at Memphis, and attacked the high mound at the north end of the site. There I had uncovered the palace of Apries, with walls up to ten feet high, and the central court still had the limestone capitals of large columns lying in it. I wanted Maspero to have the walls made up in the gaps and the whole preserved to view, but he declined, and it has been left to the usual destruction. To test whether earlier buildings underlay the platform, I sank a pit forty feet deep in the court, but found it all solid brickwork.

Mackay had a persuasive patience in negotiations with the natives, and after days of talk we at last got some plots of land hired in the temple area by March 6. Although the Government had peremptory powers to excavate anywhere, we were left to wait till the third year before we could make terms and begin our real work. The water level, even as late as March, was within three feet of the surface. We used powerful rubber pumps, which would discharge sludge.

By putting a drain cut along the middle of a plot of land, and then lowering the surface gradually, our pumps would reduce the water level three feet, or to six feet below the surface; but the land must not be lowered an inch too much, or it became water-logged and could not be worked. To keep pumps going, I had a double gang for day, and the same for night—each gang to work for a quarter of an hour, and then rest while the others worked. Thus the men were always fresh for it.

The night gang had to produce the ground dry in the morning. Having gone six feet down, pits about ten feet square were sunk, with one man baling for each man cutting; the baling water went into the pump drain. So soon as they reached the base sand they could go no further, as the water flowed in too freely; this was about eight feet down, or fourteen feet below the field. Then the gang had to enlarge their hole at the sides till sunset; when done, the channel was cut and the hole filled with water, as it would be sure to fill up in the night.

Next day, another pit was sunk at the side of the previous, leaving a foot of the stiff clay between the pits. Thus gradually a whole acre could be cleared sufficiently closely to find any blocks of stone; but any inattention to levels, and cutting the top clearance too deep, flooded the whole ground and stopped work, as one of my students found to our cost.

This work was undertaken solely to search for historical material; but we only got a few blocks, which did not help us. The largest matters were the colossal alabaster sphinx with perfect head of Amenhetep III, which we raised and left as a public monument; and a granite sphinx, with head badly weathered, of Ramessu II, which was by the north gate (now in Philadelphia).

I found the old north wall; it was marked out by the modern path, because it was higher and more solid ground. As Herodotos said that the north gate was built by Moeris, I searched for it, and had the satisfaction of finding the fallen lintel with the name of Amenemhat III. No doubt the Greek's other attributions are correct, but I was not able to verify them. The Aramaic dockets from foreign parcels, and Persian sealings, were an interesting by-product of this year's research.

By April 13 I left, and was in London on the 21st. Mackay left three weeks later. The usual exhibition opened on July 4. During the autumn, I finished off *Meydum, Historical Studies, Egypt and Israel* and *Revolutions of Civilisation,* and began to arrange for the Herbert Spencer volume extracts, and left them with Tedder. The volume on civilisation I had long been planning, but waited till I had the opportunity of a Royal Institution evening to bring the subject forward, April 28, 1911. Twenty years afterward that book is still in constant demand, and has been reprinted several times. It has brought me friends of various nationalities. The usual number of country lectures had to be fulfilled in the autumn, and I gave three lectures for charities in Cairo.

For the next season, Maspero had pressed on me to go to Hawara again. The *sebakh* diggers had cleared much from the cemetery, and more portraits were being found. I also aimed at more extensive work than I could afford to do in earlier years, especially on the labyrinth ruins. Accordingly I left on November 22, 1910, and was at Hawara by December 4.

Here was another example of the trouble caused by meddlesome clerks. When in Sinai, the bill of lading for our food stores was sent, not to the agent at Suez as I ordered, but registered to me, care of the agent. Hence a form had to be sent five days down to me and five days back, for my signature, before anything could be touched, while we were short of food.

Again this year my railway policy for food boxes was registered to Fayum; I was at Hawara expecting food that night, and only got a form to fill up for a registered letter; so I had to go on chocolate and a little native bread for two days. It is necessary to give very dogmatic directions to avoid the registered letter nuisance. Whenever an official sent me a letter, and I had sent perhaps twenty miles to post, I had to send twice twenty miles again, and wait two days, because the letter was registered.

People also seldom realise that the railway delivers nothing in Egypt, and will not give up anything without the original policy. A man sourly inquired why I had taken no notice of a large lot of flints which he had sent to me, months before; he said he had the proof of sending, by the receipt he held. That was the very paper without which I could not claim them, and I never even knew of them. To claim them at last would have entailed some pounds for demurrage, even if they were found.

On December 13, Mr. Stopford came to help me, as a civil engineer on holiday, and was of great assistance at Hawara. Mackay and Wainwright were mostly engaged on Meydum, finishing the pyramid and other work. In the Hawara cemetery we soon found more portraits, and altogether equalled the output of twenty-four years before. One of the most interesting was that named "Hermione Grammatikē," the only portrait of a teacher that is known, looking a typically studious and meek schoolmistress without a trace of show or ornament. As soon as I saw it I said it must go to a women's college, and so it is now in the library at Girton, a patron saint of learning enshrined, body and portrait. Another remarkable portrait was that of an ancient lady, Demetris, at the age of eighty-nine.

In the labyrinth, much digging was done along the side of the pyramid. There I found two colossal granite shrines, each with two figures of Amenemhat. Also several heads of statues of the gods, the only such figures as early as these. Three were the crocodile-head of Sebek; one of the tree-goddess with vegetation rising from the head, reminding one of the late terra-cotta figures of a goddess between trees; another was a bust of the king. Other pieces of sculpture were fragments of a group of the king between four goddesses, and a list of the Sebeks of various places. Portions of a row of tall lampstands, carved with flames on the top, had been placed before a shrine.

In the cemetery we found two fine mummiform figures of hard white limestone, evidently representing the deceased persons; from their style, descended from the Old Kingdom tomb statues, but merging into ushabti figures. They prove the descent of the ushabti figures from personal statues, and that idea continued until the change in the XIXth dynasty, when the figures represented slaves for the future world. I tried hard to trace the source of a large mound of yellow marl, which had evidently been taken out from a great subterranean working; that was not found, but a curious building was reached, with human offerings under two corners; one was part of a woman with the head far removed, and the other the legs of an old man.

On March 4, I moved to Memphis, and started work there with Mackay, Hayter and Stopford, while Wainwright and Bushe-Fox came later on. Having so many on the digging, I left March 22 and from April 1 was clearing up affairs in London. An editorial friend kindly worked over the questions about colour plates for our mummy portraits. The most obvious firm quoted to me £1,100; my friend got track of a firm further back, which quoted £800; then he traced marks of another firm which quoted £600. The agent of the last whispered faintly, "We have estimated for these twice already"; so the others were only profiteers.

We closed with the last firm, and had the work done to our great satisfaction. After the War, I got estimates for such work from the Continent, and among specimens of work sent in by Orell-Fusli, of Zurich, were several of my plates; so, after all, there were three stages of agents in England, doubling the price to those who prefer a fashionable publisher. This was like the story of the contract for the first iron-clad; the first estimate was half a million, but as it was entirely new and risky work, the costing department thought it safer to say a million; that, for safety, was doubled and yet doubled again, in higher departments, before it reached the Government.

An interesting Whitsun at Clodd's brought touch with Bury again, also Ray Lankester and Sir Mortimer Durand. The Coronation on June 22 brought us to Westminster; and I tried to impress my boy of four with it, as a memory to carry on to A.D. 2000. The sketch of Goth and Roman ideas in *Three Hours* appeared in the *Nineteenth Century;* it was roughed out in my berth while sick at sea, and written up, sitting on the Palatine overlooking the Forum. I sent it to Thomas Hodgkin for criticism, and he accepted it cordially. He wrote that it expressed the character of the two peoples, and he ended, "Were you not really there?" The dinner in honour of William Penn at Stafford House was a curious mixture of interests. I was John Murray's guest, and sat where I raked Kitchener side-ways. He seemed by far the most decisive person in the room, not even the overflowing Lord Charles Beresford could have stood up against him.

All this summer, the looking after colour copying of portraits for publication, College collections, Encyclopaedia writing, the *Formation of the Alphabet,* and writing part of my future architecture volume, filled up the time. I had done three lectures for charity at Cairo, and had a dozen more lectures up and down the country when I reached home.

## CHAPTER XII

## TARKHAN, LAHUN, THE WAR

By November 28, 1911, we were again in Cairo; this year's students were Mackay, Wainwright, Engelbach, Elverson, and for some weeks Lawrence—brightest of companions—little dreaming of his Arabian fame. In view of the importance of Middle Egypt, it seemed more desirable to work over the country from Cairo southward, rather than to take up distant places which involved time in travelling. For this purpose, I had finished what was yet unoccupied land at Gizeh.

South of that, the land was reserved by the Museum and Dr. Reisner, as far as Dahshur. Mackay had worked the sites between Dahshur and Lisht, which was in American hands. Meydum, Lahun and Gurob I had already worked, but we returned to finish Lahun later. Next Sedment was to be examined, Deshasheh was finished, and the further stage was Oxyrhynkhos. On the eastern side we worked Shurafeh and the district, and then moved on to Atfih. After beginning there, Mr. Johnson protested that he intended to dig for papyri, and begged us to desist. We accordingly withdrew to Tarkhan on the west; but Mr. Johnson only worked for a week or two and then abandoned the site.

Unfortunately, while waiting for a ferry in a wind, I got a chill, which ended in an operation, and kept me laid up for six weeks. All I did was planning the site at Shurafeh. Our party worked out the Byzantine fortress, and got late Roman and Arabic things.

240

Mackay examined the great dam in the valley south of Helwan. As our people were stopped from work at Atfih, I did not rejoin them till they had moved over to Tarkhan on the west side.

The cemetery proved to be of the Ist to the VIth dynasty, and mainly of the beginning of the Ist; there were also some late burials of the XXIIIrd. The principal results were in the private remains of the Ist dynasty, the beds and mats, sandal trays, baskets, and timbers from wooden houses. There were jar sealings of Nar-mer, large copper tools and a spearhead, and an alabaster amulet case in the form of a scarab, doubtless to hold a scarab beetle as a sacred emblem.

On February 25, 1912, after six weeks at Tarkhan, I moved down to our wet site at Heliopolis. The plan of the temple area was worked out, and special attention given to the eastern end where Schiaparelli had found sculptures of the IInd dynasty beneath a structure. This structure he modelled as a ring of earth, pierced with parallel tunnels running all round in it. After exhaustive search, with Quibell and others as witnesses, the only conclusion was that the tunnels were entirely cut by Schiaparelli's workmen without his noticing it. My own men made similar tunnels to search the ground for sculpture. The bank I traced all round, and examined at many parts; by March 20 it was seen to be another great square earth camp of the Hyksos like Yehudiyeh. I then hired some land near the obelisk and cleared it to the bottom, finding pieces of another obelisk, of Tehutmes III. A wild-cat story about a great site in the desert led me off on a ramp of eighteen miles donkey and twelve miles walk, but it proved as baseless as all Arab tales. Meanwhile others of our expedition were going on with routine clearance at Memphis.

On April 18 I left for London, in order to arrange the College collections, particularly scarabs, beads, amulets, flints, and stone vases. In the summer and autumn, photographing and writing the Catalogue volume of *Amulets* took up much time. The *Corpus of Prehistoric Pottery* was another long job. The exhibition was held from June 24 to July 20, and entailed the usual work.

In August the Chairman of the British School died, to my great regret; my cousin, Sir Robert Hensley, had possessed engineering knowledge and business faculty which made him much valued in public work. By the middle of November, I had finished the plates and writing of *Tarkhan I*. All the summer I gave half an hour a day of lessons to our boy of five, who had already learned reading, figures, and maps without any teaching. When we left for Egypt again, he went to school at five and a half.

By November 23, 1912, I left with Horace Thompson, and by December 4 we were at Tarkhan with North and Campion. Engelbach had gone to a cemetery at Gerzeh. My wife came out for two months. The previous year we had cleared the tombs on the hills, and I had tapped a wide valley between, and found tombs under the sand drift, but closed them again, not to draw attention.

Now we laid out an axis line down the valley, divided by cross lines for planning, and began with gangs to turn over the whole ground, which was thick with tombs. Each contained pottery; alabaster vases and beads were frequent; metal and gold ornaments had been taken away anciently. The period was about the beginning of the Ist dynasty, and hence the skeletons were important.

Unfortunately the ground was wet, and an unknown amount of the lower end of the cemetery ran under water level and could not be reached. What could be done was to measure the long bones in place, and take out the skulls in blocks of sand. These were laid face up in the store-room to dry; after a fortnight the faces were dusted with a brush and slopped with melted paraffin. When cold, the face was turned down, the back dusted and paraffined. Then the sand was tickled out of the inside and, holding the skull by the sides, I dipped it at the back into a pot of hot paraffin so as to half-fill it, then turned it over so that the paraffin covered all the inside and finally drained out below. Thus coated inside and out, the skulls were quite strong for travelling.

I photographed them all on shelves sloping towards the lens, so that only the edge of the shelf was seen; each skull was set in azimuth so that a ruler touching the forehead pointed to the lens; thus there is no distortion of the profile. The readiest way to level a skull is to cut a piece of soap (not too dry) so as to raise the base for the Frankfurt-plane level, with the jaw in position. A slight pressure beds the basion on the soap so that it is steady. A white sheet hung some feet behind the shelves gives a clear background. Thus there is no need to block out any part of the contour except the basion and tip of the chin. Remember always to have your pressed steel stewpans large enough to flood a skull with paraffin.

On working up the bone measurements, I found that the female distribution was a normal curve, but the male curve was double, showing that there were men of two races, while women were of one race. This stamped the cemetery as belonging to the period of invasion by the dynastic men without women. By taking out all the skeleton numbers of those under the minor hump of the curve, for each different bone, it was found what grave numbers recurred in each class of bone, and these constituted the extra amount of immigrating males, and could thus be extracted and examined apart.

There were some large mastabas on the ridge above the valley. These were carefully built, and the bays and buttresses of the brickwork had the same proportion as the height and width of the passages of Khufu's pyramid, but the meaning of this is not clear. Though plundered anciently, the cloths had been all cast aside in a heap and sanded over. This had preserved them quite clean and sound. From the various graves of different ages, we collected a large amount of dated linen. This was cut up and mounted on cards with dates, and distributed in pamphlet boxes to museums of textiles. The details of manufacture were carefully worked out by Mr. Midgley, and published with photographs.

One of the large mastabas had a wide court, and in that were low grave mounds; three of these together covered the skeletons of the owner's asses, and two were over box-coffin burials of human size, which only contained a pet goose and another bird.

The cemetery of Tarkhan enlightened us as to the house building. I had noticed before that the finely-wrought stone sarcophagi represented a timber house; now we found many house timbers used up for roofing graves: among them were all the kinds of pieces for framing the in-and-out recesses copied in the brick mastabas. I now realised that the brick mastaba was a replica of the timber house, much as brick models of funeral boats were copied from actual boats.

The timber hall of a chief had openings all along the side, with narrow doors to close if the wind were high; and these doorways came forward into the room, leaving between them a recess long enough for a man to sleep in. Thus the retainers slept around the hall in bunks between the doorways, clear of the draught. There was also a coffin in the form of a house, kept at the Museum by Maspero although there was a similar one there.

After three and a half months at Tarkhan, I moved to Memphis, and spent a month there organizing fresh work, which the rest of the party carried on after I left on April 17, 1913. Maspero stated that he had positive orders from Storrs to halve exactly everything found. So he proceeded to take half of each class of object, without any regard to the groups. Hence the whole grouping value for museums of this great cemetery of the Ist dynasty was destroyed. I tried to buy back the things, which were only to go to the saleroom; but the prices demanded of me were about ten times the value, as I was required to pay the fancy prices that tourists would give because of the saleroom guarantee. I said that the beads were only a few in each grave; that did not matter, they could be all strung up together for tourists. Such was the official destruction of the historic value of a unique site.

At Memphis much plain stone was found in the excavations, and in order to gain the guarding by the sheykh, I promised him my half of such stone gratis, so that he should have watch kept at night; of the other half I would pay the value to the Government. That was done, and I informed Maspero, who assented to me; but as soon as I left he sent orders to claim also the value of my half of the stone from the sheykh, so as to embroil me by falsifying my promise.

Mackay wrote to me for instructions, and I at once ordered the price of our half to be repaid by us to the sheykh, thus honouring our promise. The fiction about this was that the stones were on the footing of quarry stone (not being inscribed) and all quarries were Government property; but this ignored the cost of discovery which was ours.

I had planted some palms on ground which we had exhausted, in order to be able at some future time to exchange them for palms which we wanted to remove in excavating, and I informed Maspero. After I left, he denounced this as *une veritable usurpation,* though natives were freely allowed to plant upon Government property. I informed the Public Domains Department that the palms were Government property already, and solely for exchange. Antony defended me in this, and revoked Maspero's order to uproot the palms. Such actions behind one's back destroy confidence. A high official once remarked to me about Maspero: "The man's such a liar, you never know where you are."

In England, I had to continue arranging at the College, and begin the catalogue of weights. Though only a few dozen were known when I began work, I had collected about 4,500, of which 3,500 (mainly bought) were at the College. It was needful to expedite the weighing and I rigged up a chain balance, the first in England I believe, at least it was a new idea to Ramsay the chemist. An ordinary balance, without any modification, is used. A length of brass chain, doubled, is hung at one end on the scale pan and on the other to a vertical slider. As the slider is lowered, more chain hangs from the pan, the edge of the pan is read against the slider, which is divided in grains by trial. Thus no weights are used less than 100 grains, and fractions are read to 1/10 of a grain by estimation.

This chain balance is safe to read to about a quarter of a grain on some hundreds of grains; and the balance can carry up to five pounds. For heavier weights a long ancient steel-yard was used, the tip of it resting in the balance pan like any other object. This gave about a tenth of the total amount to be weighed in the balance, verified by frequent trials of modern weights.

This summer we had the Japanese archaeologist, Prof. Hamada, and he stayed with us for a time; his visit to England, to study all our methods of work both Egyptian and Roman, was the foundation of the very active school of Japanese archaeology, which has poured out excellent work adapted according to European methods. Happily the connection with England has induced Professor Hamada, and some of his pupils, to give a list of plates and some particulars in English in their publications, and so make them accessible to the west; these can be seen at University College. We have benefited by their series of publications, and we have the pleasure of seeing the pupils when they come to England.

This summer, the settlement of the collection was ended. The amount of material that I had acquired for study had, for several years, been more than could be arranged at the College; in glass cases, things were piled three layers deep, on sheets of paper. I then offered to the College either to work up a section at a time for publication, and then let that go to some

Museum, or else to hand it all over at cost price to the College, if space and casing were provided. That offer hung fire for some years, but at last things moved, and some contributions were given, mainly from Robert Mond; lastly, Walter Morrison came forward and gave the College nearly the whole amount.

I had estimated that I had spent in all ways £3,500 on it, and dividing the loss of interest between the College and myself, it represented £5,000 at the date of accepting the offer. There was no question that it was worth very much more, as prices had largely risen, and moreover I had collected from country dealers, especially from Girgis of Qeneh on his way to Cairo.

Thus at last, on July 29, 1913, the College took possession of all that I had collected; it has also received much from the work of the British School centred there. Since then, my object has been to publish catalogue volumes, not only illustrating the series in each subject, but discussing the dates and links with other collections, so as to frame a library of Egyptian archaeology; nine volumes have appeared, and there is more than that number still required.

There had been a talk for some time about the Exploration Fund publishing a journal, and various conversations had passed with Alan Gardiner, Walker the secretary, and Milne, as to the scope and method of such a journal, for I had pointed out that as the British School was doing most of the English excavations it was to be expected to join in any journal on the subject. These conversations dealt with practical details, apparently for a joint publication.

At last when co-operation seemed settled, and I was almost due to go to Egypt, the Fund management suddenly refused any joint arrangement. One of the

TREASURE OF LAHUN
GOLD PECTORAL OF SENUSERT III, LAHUN, 1:1

GOLD PECTORAL OF AMENEMHAT III. LAHUN
SHOWING THE DECLINE OF ART

Committee met me about then, and particularly asked when I was going to Egypt, to know when I should be out of the way. Some friends called, and quite innocently one of them asked when I was going: "Why, you are like ——, who asked me the same." "Oh, no, I did not mean it in that sense," was her reply, which was illuminating. I had not booked a passage until I should see this matter settled.

Having the answer, we at once called a Committee, and agreed that a journal was necessary for us, if the Fund had an exclusive journal to stir the public. I had done everything I possibly could with the Fund in frank planning of detail for some months past, without any reserve. But now action was suddenly forced on us. Printer and publisher were all agreed with quickly on November 7, the material was assembled, and by December 16 the first number of *Ancient Egypt* was issued.

Meanwhile I was at work on the second number. The Fund journal was not out till some time in January. Our success was ensured, the edition of 2,000 was exhausted, and the first number is now a rarity. I also had to write up *Tarkhan II*, which had been delayed owing to the journal question. Thus we did not get away till December 22.

The ship was a slow cargo vessel, and we were in Cairo on January 1, 1914. We had out on the work this season Engelbach, Mr. and Mrs. Brunton, Campion, Battiscomb Gunn, Willey, Frost (of chemical interest) and Dr. Amsden. The work was at Lahun where I was, and at Harageh a few miles off, where Engelbach managed. The other students moved to one or the other place for experience.

On January 12, I saw an undoubted portion of a

mock-sun and circle, a thing I believe unrecorded so
far south. We began clearing around the pyramid of
Lahun, having now exhausted all the ground that was
open to us between that and Cairo. When I was there
in 1889 I could not undertake any large work on a few
hundred pounds; now we settled to tackle Lahun on a
larger scale. On the south side of the pyramid, where
Fraser had found the well of entrance, we cleared several tombs of the royal family; one of these had the
main entrance to the pyramid concealed under floor-
ing slabs, the other entrance being only a workmen's
service hole.

On February 10 a tomb was being cleared which
had been plundered anciently; the sarcophagus was
empty, and nothing was anticipated. In clearing a recess (of about a cubic yard) at the side, which was filled
with hard mud washed down into the tomb, a few
rings of thin gold tubing were found, and at once reported. I turned out the local workers, and only left a
Qufti lad. As, owing to a strain, I could not go down,
Brunton went to see what the meaning of the place
might be. He continued carefully to cut away the mud
and found more gold work, and slept all night in the
tomb. I said the Qufti was not to go to camp till I saw
him. Near midnight he came up, and I promised him
£30 in any case, and much more if he said nothing.
That secured his silence, so that even his own brother
could not find out what he had.

For a week Brunton lived all day and every night in
the tomb, gently extracting all the objects from the
hard mud, without bending or scratching a single
piece. Everything as it came up I washed in plain
water with a camel-hair brush, so as not to alter the
natural surface, and then photographed it. I packed

the whole in a tin box by the 17th, and next day Campion took up the sealed box to the safe of the Museum. Our party were all warned not to talk or write about it, and there was no stir anywhere on the subject.

When we came to the division in Cairo, Maspero was startled, and said: "Why, you have got the Dahshur jewellery over again." We agreed on division, the Museum leaving to us all duplicates of gold work, but the halving left to us the silver mirror with obsidian and gold handle; Maspero coveted it, so I offered to resign that against all the commoner things that we had found. No one but my wife knows how we transferred the jewellery to London.

The only persons whom I informed of the find were the directors of three Museums, which had shared in our work before. Obviously the set liberated at Cairo should be kept together; but there were many Museums who were creditors to the work. The only course was for one Museum to indemnify the others by payment to us, so that the other Museums should receive compensation in other antiquities that we then, and in future, could provide. Of the three Museums, I named in writing to the British Museum £8,000 as the least value of what we had found, but no such amount to the other two Museums.

In a few weeks, exactly that valuation had been conveyed to dealers in Luqsor, a direct incitement to attack us by the many predatory parties who fought the guards at different places for objects of only a hundredth of that value. How the information was conveyed one may guess. The answer from the British Museum to my letter was that, if when they saw the things they thought they were worth it, they might be able to put hands on a couple of thousand—a ludicrous treatment of the matter, which closed that door.

When we had the jewellery in order, in London, I invited a few of the richest men who were interested, to come and see it privately. They were ready to see and admire it, but not one ever inquired where it was to go. The exhibition was crowded, with double the attendance that we had before, but no Museum showed any wish to have the group, and the Director at South Kensington said it would interfere with their purposes then in hand.

Then came the smash of all civil matters by the War. We waited to see what could best be done; the Committee left negotiations to me, with a condition that any English Museum was to have a preference of £2,000 over any foreign Museum. The only movement came from a patron of a provincial Museum, who could not come forward openly because of the feeling against spending during the War. I agreed to place the group on loan, and let him announce his gift at any future time. But that would not suffice—he wished to have the jewellery in his own hands. As a single hasty movement would ruin the pectoral by the inlay dropping out, it was impossible to entrust it to any private hands or house, and there would be the risk of loss by robbery. So the conditions closed that door.

Having waited for a couple of years without any response in England, we reluctantly accepted an offer from the Metropolitan Museum of New York, which was one of our contributing Museums.

After this, the then President of the Society of Antiquaries, who had never shown the smallest interest in this matter, made an attack on the management of the

GOLD CROWN OF PRINCESS SAT-HATHOR-ANT
TREASURE OF LAHUN

question. The apathy of all authorities in England, and the futile replies received from the British Museum and South Kensington, left no better course open than that which we took. The great importance of the finest treasure of Egyptian jewellery known, makes a clear account of the matter necessary.

Some people have objected to this and asked why not have presented it all to the British Museum. We had to consider our obligations to other places, and our obligations as a School to the present and future students. The value of the group was the equivalent of keeping three students in training during twenty years. The importance of such an opening nationally, in the absence of any scholarships for Egyptology, seems an investment for the future of the subject which we were only right in accepting. There was not to myself personally the smallest benefit one way or the other.

On July 21 my old friend Dr. Walker died suddenly. He had taken an active part in teaching Egyptian language at the College, and we greatly regretted him; he never knew what was in store. By August 4 the War fell on us. Engelbach, Gunn and Willey were all off to training at once. Brunton went on half-time training while he helped me over winding up the exhibition. I offered to gang Egyptians anywhere, or to do storekeeping and inspection; but I was ordered to stay by the College.

Thus it came about that my intention thirty years before, to sit down and write up Egyptian archaeology when I was sixty, was exactly fulfilled. My wife was occupied with organising work in war charities, and our interest in the changes was greatly increased by our taking in, for thirteen months, two Czech girls who had come to the Oxford Summer School and were stranded in England.

Through them and Professor Masaryk, we came in touch with all the situation. In spite of the arrogance of Austrians, there was no wish to break up the Austrian group, if each nationality could have equal liberty. When we described how Ireland had its own language wherever it desired, and nearly all officials were Irish, the Czechs said they had wanted no more than that from Austria. Had the Crown Prince lived, and brought on his policy for the subject states, there need not have been any disruption. His life, however, would not have suited the politics of other sinister forces.

During the War the fellahin in Egypt were stirred up by fanatical appeals to destroying many railway stations and telegraphs, as being Western innovations. For some years later, the Bedrasheyn station was a heap of ruin; trains only stopped as a favour, and by paying fares to the next stopping station, which hit the local travel of the peasantry heavily, and made them rue their folly. The possibility of such people being stirred to destroy their own property, either in Egypt, or the forests of Russia, shows how totally incapable they are of any political sense.

The War made an entire break of all my work in Egypt for five years. During that time I was at the College, doing regular lectures and working up material. It is useless to distinguish the various layers of work, so a summary of the subjects will best state the result of those dreary years, short of food and coal (we never had any butter, and could not use a fireless study) and in the perpetual uncertainty of the future.

The College collection arrangement had to be com-

pleted, and by June 1915 I was able to make it a public
exhibition with a handbook. The catalogue could then
go forward. The *Amulets* had been-issued just before
the War. *Scarabs and Cylinders with Names* followed,
giving transcription and translation of each, facing the
photograph. *Buttons and Design Scarabs* dealt with the
large, but little known, class of button badges mostly
of the VI-XIth dynasties; the scarabs of various subjects were classified for the first time.

For *Tools and Weapons* I had been collecting drawings during twenty-five years; these were made into a
*corpus* of forms by copying from all likely sources,
while all the College collection was photographed.
This has become a usual book of reference for types.
*Prehistoric Egypt* was mostly a photographic catalogue
of the varied objects, classified and described: the
*Corpus of Pottery* was issued with it. *Weights and
Measures* catalogued 3,500 weights at the College, also
those in the Greek Department of the British Museum, beside steel-yards, measures of length and of
capacity. The amount of material caused an entire
revision of metrology, following the historical order.
*Glass Stamps and Weights* was mainly on the Arab period, dealing with these more completely than in the
other great collections.

*Objects of Daily Use* gave illustrations of all the personal and toilet objects, jewellery, ornaments, head-
rests, furniture, ivories, music, games, toys, and
writing. These nine volumes were written during the
War, and published down to 1928. Others written but
not yet issued were stone and metal vases, ushabtis,
funerary, proto-dynastic, glass, glaze, and architecture.
There still remain to be written the catalogues of

beads, statuettes, moulds, foundation deposits, inscriptions, textiles and Coptic remains.

A large quantity of impressions of scarabs had been
collected by Mrs. Grenfell; on her death, her son gave
these to the College. Knowing how frail sealing wax
is, I cast all of them in plaster, put them on tablets,
and arranged them in two cabinets for reference. They
form an important annexe to the Scarab collection.
Some shorter subjects were worked out. The documents on British history down to A.D. 600, I arranged
in parallel columns, so as to see how much might be
original and how much copied. The details point to
the so-called Tysilio chronicle being the basis of Geof-
frey of Monmouth; and so much of Tysilio cannot be
derived from any known source, that it has strong
evidence of being based on a Gloucester chronicle during the Roman period. Other detail shows that the
British record and genealogies are better authorities
than the Saxon chronicle in the early period. (See
British Academy paper.)

Ptolemy's Albion I analysed into its component
material, finding the causes of its distortions, and gaining better definition of its meaning (Society of Antiquaries of Scotland). Some popular lectures were
issued as *Eastern Exploration,* and *Some Sources of
Human History.*

During our children's holidays we went each August to work up the great hill figures which had never
been seriously planned. Thus we recorded the White
Horse of Uffington, the Long Man of Wilmington, the
Giant of Cerne, and the Crosses of Buckinghamshire;
these were published together as *The Hill Figures of
England,* by the Anthropological Institute. More private matters were clearing up the letters of half a

dozen families that had descended to me, keeping all up to 1800, and only a small selection from those later.

The new responsibilities after the War, in Palestine and Iraq, brought about the appointment of a joint Archaeological Committee, run mainly by the British Museum,—nominated Societies being asked to appoint two members each. Though the Palestine Fund appointed members, yet the newly-born British School in Palestine also had two members; but as the Egypt Exploration Society was represented, it was said that the British School in Egypt (which had done most during the last twenty years) need not be represented.

However, the Palestine Fund nominated me; and after a couple of years the School in Egypt was acknowledged at the Museum. As very few members had had anything to do with practical excavation, I was fortunately able to represent the needs and difficulties of the actual work, about which the Committee legislated with the Foreign Office.

## CHAPTER XIII

## LAHUN, SEDMENT, OXYRHYNKHOS, QAU

And can I hold my soul, and not be tost
  Upon the seas of fruitless hopes and joys,
O'erwhelmed in this mechanic age, and lost
  To sense of inward life, mid shouts and noise?

We seek the barren double bloom, all show,
  Futile, without a scent, without a seed,
And lose the lasting life we ought to know,
  Springing from out the stem and soil we need.

ALTHOUGH it was difficult to secure passages even a year after the Armistice, we managed to return to Egypt, leaving November 19, 1919. Our workers this year were the Engelbachs, the Bruntons, Miss Hughes, Jefferies and Captain Miller. We left Cairo December 8; a general strike of cabs was started, and we had to get porters to carry baggage. The light railway in the Fayum took us to Bashkatib about a mile from Lahun pyramid.

Our work there this season was the clearance of the north and west sides in search of passages. Aly Suefy, who had been left as guard here during the War, noticed a very accurately inserted block of stone, and below it an inserted block in the rock floor, on the north boundary of the pyramid area. This looked exactly like the concealment of a passage, and we built a rough hut over it, to prevent anyone overlooking what we did. Then we cut it out, but found unmoved rock a foot behind. Then we took up the paving block, only to find some sand beneath it. Why such a mock

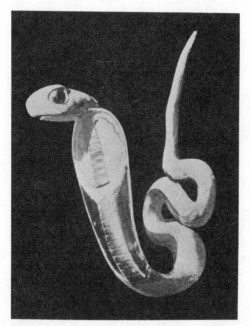

GOLD URAEUS OF SENUSERT III
FROM PYRAMID OF LAHUN

concealment was made seems quite unaccountable.

Just outside the pyramid boundary, we found a deep shaft which led to what was evidently a tomb of one of the royal family, beneath the pyramid enclosure, with a granite sarcophagus. We had the interior of the pyramid entirely cleared out, though only a little rubbish lay in it. By this thorough search we got the gold uraeus serpent inlaid with carnelian, which must have come from the king's head-dress (Cairo Museum). This was the only piece of a king's insignia known, until that of Tutankhamen.

The tombs all along the hill west of the pyramid were completely cleared and planned, but scarcely anything was found. A most interesting subject was the cemetery of the Ist to IIIrd dynasty near the railway. In it were many types of tombs—plain grave, square pit with offerings, chambered pit, stairway tombs, and deep shafts. The styles of pottery showed that many of these types of tomb were made at the same age, the difference being due to family habit and not to successive periods. This sets aside the following of tomb types as a guide to relative age.

The temple site at Kahun was completely searched over, and some tombs of the XVIIIth dynasty were found in the town of Kahun. The queen's pyramid, near that of Senusert II, was searched all over for any entrance; failing that, I had shafts sunk in the rock at opposite corners, and tunnels run in two most likely seams of rock diagonally under the pyramid, without finding any chamber. A curious private tomb of the royal architect Anupy was worked out; he had combined the old-fashioned sloping tunnel and chamber with the newer pillared portico and shrines of the

XIIth dynasty. Having exhausted Lahun, we left on April 12 and were in London on the 21st.

There was much to be done at the College in re-arranging the large reserves of material not exhibited. These were now placed in uniform ammunition boxes under the table cases. The pottery case needed clean-ing, and marking, over a furlong length of shelving. During the exhibition time I was working up the *History of Science* in Egypt. Though it was necessary to suspend the quarterly publication of *Ancient Egypt* in 1918-1919, we resumed it in 1920, and that occupied some weeks of time altogether.

Having now worked out all the unoccupied sites from Cairo southward to Gurob, the next place was Sedment, the cemetery of Ehnasieh. It had been worked by Naville, who found some fine objects, but published nothing, and left much behind which he did not care for. Later, Currelly had tried the site, and declared it exhausted.

We left on November 19, 1920, and were at Gurob by December 2; our party this year consisted of the Bruntons, Major Hynes, Captain Miller, Bach, and Montgomerie Neilson. After a sampling of what was left at Gurob, of no historic value, we were at Sedment by December 17. It was an awkward upland of desert, bitterly exposed to the wind on all sides. Finding two great craters of old tomb working, I pitched our own tents in one, sunk ten feet down, and put our Quftis into the other. Water we had to fetch about a mile from the canal over the ridge in the Fayum. The Bruntons were finishing at Gurob, and later passed our camp and went to the south end of our cemetery at Mayana.

The ground was riddled with tomb pits, and looked

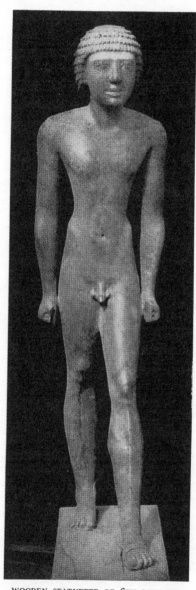

WOODEN STATUETTE OF 6TH DYNASTY
MERY-RA-HA-SHETEF

pretty hopeless; but we soon found things. A tomb of a
cavalry officer Pa-hen-neter gave fine glazed ushabtis,
and a beautiful black granite coffin lid which had been
stolen from a tomb of the XVIIIth dynasty. Then, an
immense tomb of Pa-ra-hetep, with many chambers,
was worked out; the granite coffin was too large to
extract, but by working down the sides of its hole, the
carving could be recovered by paper squeezes.

Much better results were found in undisturbed
tombs of the Ist and IInd dynasty: alabaster dishes,
copper pans, and pottery all in position, which I photographed and drew. Later there was the prize of the
season; a small rock chamber of a chapel had a pit in
the corner of the courtyard. About ten feet down in
this were three wooden figures of the owner Mery-Ra-
ha-shetef at different ages, the youth, the landowner,
and the elder; the youth is the most detailed and spir-
ited statuette of the Old Kingdom. (Brit. Mus.)

Below, the shaft went far down to a damp chamber
with a half-rotted inscribed coffin, containing an exquisite alabaster headrest; this and the skull are also
in the British Museum. Of the XIIth dynasty there
was no trace, but the XVIIIth flourished here, leaving
a large papyrus with the finest painting and gilding,
much broken (Cambridge), and an exquisite wooden
figure of a woman holding a toilet dish (Ny Carlsberg),
a group of perfect baskets with some very rare foreign
vases, and many other satisfactory objects. Mayana
also furnished, among other things of interest, a perfect example of the rare figure game-board, and a good
carving of a lion.

A pattern of Egyptian administration came before
us. Our cook was sent across the desert to distant shops
one day; men saw him go, and on his return waylaid

him in the dusk half a mile from the tents, thinking he was bringing money. Vexed at only finding some hardware, they kicked him brutally, and he was found in the dark lying stunned, and then was unconscious for two hours, while we tended him.

It was obviously the work of some of the lawless Arabs who had settled along the desert edge near us. The police were summoned, and took his depositions at once. Then there came a concourse of sheykhs, guards and rabble, eighty in all, to discuss whether the attack was within the Beni Suef boundary, which was not defined on the open desert. After a week, a similar concourse took place from the Fayum, to discuss whether the place was within the Fayum boundary.

These discussions satisfied Egyptian justice, no one was responsible, no one was arrested or examined. Had every Arab squatter within two miles of us been arrested at once, the cook could have recognised which of them attacked him, and the case could have been settled in twelve hours.

After we left, a pedlar was attacked there, beaten and stripped of all he had. When we arrived first, there was a very pretentious old Arab sheykh who boasted that he was over all the Arabs for miles around. The next time that I saw him, after the cook was attacked, I asked him what he was worth if he could not produce the villains, and demanded that he should do so. After that, he no more claimed afternoon coffee and long visits at our camp.

The really important historical result was that we had here the graves of the IXth and Xth dynasties of Heracleopolis (Ehnasieh) and though only pottery, coffins, and a few scarabs were the reward, these served to prove the style of that age, as distinct from the

VIIth-VIIIth, which were of button-badge Syrians.
Here not a single button was found, but several scarabs
with scroll pattern of early type. As nothing of the
XIth-XIIth dynasty styles were here, we had a very
clean section of the civilisation, clear of both the
earlier and later ages. Thus a type set was established
for a standard of comparison.

The Museum sent down Quibell and Wainwright
to divide the stuff. Fortunately for us, Engelbach had
found, the year before, a granite coffin of new form,
which the Museum man had neglected to extract from
under the water, twenty years earlier. As the lid was in
the Museum, the sarcophagus was wanted. Lacau tried
to demand it as already being Museum property; but
Sir Murdoch Macdonald ruled that it was justly ours,
and assessed it at £500. Hence this amount had to
come to our credit, and, for the only time, we had a
valuation assessment of everything, and secured a real
half of the values. The Museum got the largest of the
wooden figures, the finest painted stele of the XVIIIth
dynasty, and what else it wanted.

A new light was thrown on dealing with salted stone-
work. A large stele, weighing several hundredweight
was lying by our tents, with salt crystallized on the face
of it. A rainstorm came on, and, to preserve the sculpture, I hastily put an inch of sand over it. After some
days, when it dried, I found the sand hard with salt,
and when I broke it away the stone was so un-salted
that I could not taste a trace with my tongue.

This showed how to remove salt with wet sand, at
least from the face of stones. For getting it entirely out
of a stone, the way is to lay the stone, face down, on
sand kept permanently wet. The moisture will ascend
through the stone, carrying the salt with it, and evap-

orate on the back, leaving a crop of salt which can be brushed away. In this way salt, which is fatal if left in a stone, can be entirely removed without even injuring colour on the face of a block. In the salt soil of the Delta, granite on the surface is entirely disintegrated into separate crystals by the salt, and cannot be lifted without falling to pieces.

I left on March 14, 1921, the Bruntons taking my place, and was in London on the 24th. There I had to prepare the Rhind lectures on the Science of the Egyptians, which were delivered in Edinburgh, May 2 to 13. The exhibition in July was crowded, and in August we went to the Avebury district for antiquities. In the autumn I had to recast the first volume of the *History* to include the earliest dynasties, and to work out the rival rule under the XIIIth dynasty, when the frontier was fluctuating between Thebes and Asyut, and Edfu was a rival capital to Memphis. Various articles also had to be finished before I left.

I had a visit in England from the librarian of the Mitchell Library at Sydney, desirous of obtaining by purchase or bequest the papers and relics of my grandfather, Captain Matthew Flinders, for that Library. On inquiry, it appeared to be the right home for such national possessions; it contained the largest collection for the history of Australia, under Government care, and in a fire-proof building. I therefore proposed to give all the official papers, and most of the personal objects, and Sydney undertook to spend at least £2,000 on putting up a statue of Captain Flinders, who had planned his voyages and found his base of work at Sydney. Mr. Colton was appointed to be the artist, and he took much care to model the head from the minia-

COMB OF KING ZET, 1ST DYNASTY WITH
SUN-BOAT ON WINGS

GRAVESTONES OF SERVANTS, 1ST DYNASTY

ture and silhouette, with the result that I saw a likeness to the living members of the family.

I then handed over to the Agent-General in London the private log-book of the *Investigator* (except the second volume, seized and lost by the French in Mauritius), the letter books, private journal, and miniature (after having it copied for the National Portrait Gallery, and for myself), the cocked hat and sword, Navy badge, and the Captain's share of the *Investigator's* silver plate. Such things are the fundamental relics for Australian history; long may they remain as the foundation deposit of that continent. To present them there was a pious duty. I retained only the private letters and small personal objects.

To my great satisfaction, soon after, the Colonial Office found in store the missing second volume of the log. It was reported to the Admiralty, and referred to me as being private property. So I was able to have it restored to the companion volumes in Sydney, after being separated for over a century.

Leaving London on November 23, 1921, and visiting Luqsor, I was, by December 7, at Abydos. I had for ten years wished for the tombs found by Peet there, obviously of the Ist dynasty, but left unexplored. I asked to be permitted to work them, but was not allowed until the Fund formally renounced that site, an entirely new extension of claim. We had out Henri Bach, Montgomerie Neilson, Walker (of classical interests), Miss Caton Thompson, and Miss Morton, beside my wife and myself. We soon found the line of tombs, tracked it around a large square area, and then discovered two other such squares of tombs; the objects dated these to Kings Zer, Zet and Queen Merneit, or the middle of the Ist dynasty.

Though the tombs had been anciently plundered, there were many objects left in position. The ivory work included a comb of Zet with an entirely unknown figure of the solar bark with wings, also inscribed labels, lion gaming pieces, and a fine ram-headed wand. Flint knives of large size, and perfect, were not uncommon. Many copper weapons and tools were found, some with the name of Zer. Alabaster vases occurred in a few graves. It was altogether a very welcome addition to our knowledge of that period.

The positions of the skeletons in some instances indicated that they had been buried alive. The persons seem to have been court officials, all stunned, and buried at the royal funeral. There was no central burial within the square. The whole subject was new and difficult to explain, especially the position of these burials, at more than a mile from the Royal Tombs.

By February 13, we left for Behnesa, in order to carry on our clearance southward from Cairo. Again no early remains could be reached there, the deepest ground down to water level being Roman. We cleared enough of the great theatre to recover the plan of it; the form of the stage was new to us, and the complete development of a spiral stair with newel was not known till examples of much later date. The graves of Justinian age were cleared and planned, enough to show the types; the chapel graves with apse and Holy Table were noteworthy.

The custom of throwing away glass cups on the funeral mound, shows the idea that having once been used for libation to the dead, the living could not resume them. Many papyri were bought from dealers there, and our men found some of the earliest Hebrew papyri, of the second or third century.

Opposite to Behnesa we visited rock tombs at Sheykh Fadl and noticed Aramaic texts, written on a tomb of the Old Kingdom. These were later studied by M. Noel Giron, and found to belong to a family settled here as early as Tirhakeh, or in the reign of Manasseh, the earliest such settlement, presumably Jewish. I left Behnesa April 11, searched for a reputed sphinx on the east of the Nile opposite Gizeh, and was in London by the 25th, where I had to give a lecture on "The Status of the Jews in Egypt" on the 30th.

In June I was working up details of Sedment, and had Mr. Tait to stay, for reading the large collection of Greek ostraka at the College. A bad cold blocked my management of the exhibition, held in July as usual. In the previous summer, I had looked over Silbury Hill and wished to examine it. With Lord Avebury's permission, I excavated there from August 11 to 30, aided by kind help of Mr. Passmore. I tented with my son on the site, and saw the tent covered with ice in full sunshine, a record for that month.

The result of our work proved that the whole plan had been laid out of full size from the beginning, the layers of chalk rubble being quite flat, out to the edge. Levels were taken of the interior in the old tunnel. The size of the mound, and spacing of sarsens around it, proved to be based on the Northern fathom of seventy-nine inches, the basis of our land measures, which is now also known from Mohenjo-daro.

By September I had to work up the *Descriptive Sociology of Egypt,* the Herbert Spencer volume delayed by the War. Garstang had some idea that the French might accept my help at Byblos. I said that I would give my time if either (1) a budget of £2,000 a year were provided for the work, or (2) I would also find

£2,000 a year for the cost, if I might name the Museums to receive half the objects. Nothing more was heard of this plan.

In the winter of 1922-3 it seemed most needful for me to take up bookwork, as there were several volumes waiting, delayed largely by the great increase of wages to English printers, which obliged us to resort to printing in Vienna.

The issue of new and arbitrary conditions by Lacau was a repetition of what former French Directors of Antiquities had tried to do, by ignoring their subordination to the Ministry in Egypt, and trying to establish an autocracy. This attempt had been checked before—as I have recounted—by the strength of British management. Now that Britain was leaving much more to Egyptian direction, there was not the same check, and French autocracy was left uncontrolled. The terms which Lacau enforced were only based on his right to veto any application; hence, unless an applicant would sign the illegal terms demanded, his application could not proceed. The applicant was required to renounce all rights to any share of his discoveries, to send in names of his workmen to be sanctioned, never to see his friends without a permit from the Government, and not to put up any shelters or structure without submitting plans to be approved.

In this condition of affairs there was a general reluctance to continue work. The British School avoided work on any subject of interest to the Museum. The Fund and the Americans hesitated. I tried to pull all the forces together by a meeting on December 5, 1922, at the College, of Lythgoe, Winlock, Mace, Sir John Maxwell (Fund), Hall and Gardiner. A formula was agreed on hesitatingly, and shaped on December 8

with Lythgoe, that we demanded half share of finds as
before, or else free scope to work at Saqqareh if Lacau
was autocratic; if not granted we would work in other
countries. But this again crumbled away; each party
made compromises, bought over by promises of not
carrying out the new terms, and so nothing effective
was done.

The Fund work was heavily drained of its results,
the Americans held off for a time only, the British
School kept to its non-monumental anthropology, and
Lacau was left with the barren triumph of drying up
the works which had been so productive for the
Museum. It was a triumph like the Egyptian refusal
to accept two millions for an endowment for Egyptian
antiquities, and then doing nothing to make up for
the loss.

The completion of the volumes on Lahun II and
Sedment occupied much of my winter. The Herbert
Spencer work resulted in a popular volume on *Social
Life in Egypt*. The working up of the *Tombs of the
Courtiers and Oxyrhynkhos* also took much time.
Meanwhile in 1923 we sent out the Bruntons who
worked with Bach and a new student, Starkey, at Qau
and Hemamieh.

The principal discovery was the earliest Coptic MS.
of St. John's Gospel, only exceeded in age by the Greek
of the Vatican. This had been much worn in use, was
then doubled up, wrapped in old rag, and reverently
buried in a pot near a small Coptic chapel. In England
I was busy with unfolding, damping, flattening and
mounting it. We published it entire, with transliteration and full discussion by Sir Herbert Thompson.

A cemetery of the Old Kingdom was begun, and a
deposit of bones found, mainly hippopotamus but

some human, of great age, partly fossilised and stream-worn. These were so inexplicable that I went out next season for this subject. We held the exhibition of Brunton's and Starkey's results in July.

On July 25 I received the *accolade* and many kind expressions from my friends. In August we were going over antiquities in the Cheddar district, and I was fair-copying all the tables of college weights, to lithograph, instead of type-setting, which was too costly. In the autumn the *Religious Life in Egypt* was prepared, also from the material of the Herbert Spencer Sociology. I sent off the drawings for *Sedment* to be printed, and could leave London November 17, 1923.

By December 2 I reached Qau, and was joined by Lieut.-Commander Wheeler and Greenlees, while Brunton, Yeivin, and Bach were on Hemamieh ceme-tery. I began clearing up the great tomb of Prince Uah-ka, while Greenlees was making copies of the fragmentary inscriptions. The clearance and cleaning of the walls went on for two months, and, in course of it, we found the prince's eldest son's name, Senusert.

This was of first importance, as it linked the Uah-ka family with the XIIth dynasty. The period of the Uah-ka family was not fixed, till in London I worked out all names associated with Uah-ka persons on steles: also all names absolutely dated to the XIIth dynasty. These two lists were largely different, and the Uah-ka names were intermediate between those of the VIth and of the XIIth dynasty, and could not be of the XIIth dynasty. This fixed the Uah-ka period to the IXth and Xth dynasties. The XIth was a very brief independence after the Xth, so practically the Uah-ka and Senusert of the Xth dynasty led on to the XIIth.

The other rock-tombs were also all cleared and

planned, and their connection with the great tomb was traced out. The large cemetery of the Old Kingdom, a few miles to the south, was further worked out, and a great variety of pottery was found and drawn. Miss Caton-Thompson came and exhaustively worked out a settlement which lasted through the prehistoric periods that were already known, and had a lower stratum of a different character. Graves with the same pottery as that in the lowest stratum were also found.

At last it was necessary to give some name to this oldest civilisation, and I called it Badarian, after the name of the district Badari, in which it was found. The Badarian civilisation was the oldest then known in Egypt; it had finer pottery than that of any later age, also hardstone work and glazing. The skulls proved to be closely kin to the earliest Indian, and the later periods of Egypt all show increasing changes toward the Mediterranean types. It is certain that the Badarians were immigrants from a higher Asiatic culture, as their work steadily deteriorated in Egypt.

The question of quasi-fossil human bones was cleared up by finding another deposit. This proved that it was a religious collection of the bones, fossil and recent, of the sacred animal of the district, the hippopotamus, and the human bones had been gathered up with those of various other animals, some extinct, without discrimination.

In the great tomb of Uah-ka, the painting of patterns on the roof of the great hall was carefully copied. It proved that what is commonly known as the Greek fret and the scroll and palmetto were already in being as early as the IXth dynasty, at least 2,000 years before the Greeks; it was thus a great step in the history of design.

An illustration of native method occurred. A man reported an inscribed stone about three miles away. I went to see it, took a squeeze of it, and bought it for a few pounds; it was an Old Kingdom altar of archaic style, in grey quartzose rock. The man who sold it was only a tenant; his landlord claimed the money; they squabbled, and went to the police, who at once seized the stone for the Government, though I had bought it knowing I should leave it in Cairo. The police took it, about six hundredweight, many miles to the police station, and it was long before it reached the Museum.

On February 29, I left for Cairo, and spent some days about Alexandria looking up the site where flint knives of the IInd dynasty had been found: the ground was most unpromising for work. I then reached London March 12. The *Descriptive Sociology* claimed most of my work till the summer. Though the plan of the work was to be of extracts, so much was known that had not yet been written up, that I had in many sections to frame an outline of the whole subject from the prehistoric time onward. There was thus a large amount of original writing to be done for it. The compiling of lists of all the names of the Uah-ka period and the XIIth dynasty took up much of the summer and autumn, beside the classification of titles begun in *Ancient Egypt*.

All this spade work was essential for further progress, in history and in the subject of administration. Lastly the *corpus* of Old Kingdom pots occupied some weeks.

Next year, 1925, was a quiet time of working up material while the Bruntons were on the Old Kingdom cemetery, and Miss Caton-Thompson was excavating in the Fayum desert; Starkey had passed on to the Michigan work at Wushym, Bach had stayed in France, Wheeler and Greenlees were taken up by Reisner. I had to see to the proofs of the Coptic gospel volume, and to wind up the Herbert Spencer volume. The *Buttons and Design Scarabs* had to be photographed and described. The collection of titles and classifying them took up much time. A summary of results about the successive civilisations was begun, as *The Making of Egypt*.

On July 7, I was presented with a medal which had been founded by those who cared for my work; the firm aim of the artist seemed to have been his own virtuosity according to modern standards. The Badarian material was consolidated, and I worked out its sequence dating. In the summer we were at Brecon, partly associated with Dr. Wheeler's excavation of the Roman camp, and were making plans of earthworks in the district. Thus began a valued intimacy. The autumn was spent in working up the plans and description of the great tombs at Qau, though the publication was delayed for some years in order to fit in with Brunton's series of volumes on that district.

For 1926, the party at work comprised Miss Caton-Thompson, Miss Eleanor Gardner (geology) and also Carline for part of the time. Sandford came as a geologist to try to discover the sources of the very early human bones; he worked over a large amount of desert, but no evidence was reached about these bones. However a valuable result was gained in the observation of terraces of old high Nile levels, the 100-foot terrace being Chellean, the thirty-foot terrace Acheulean, and the ten-foot terrace Mousterian, remarkably similar to the terrace levels and styles of flint work in the Thames valley.

I was engaged on the *Weights and Measures* book, on the *Objects of Daily Life,* and on the *Hill Figures of England.* The most interesting event was the Great Strike, the greatest social struggle since 1649. The defiance given by the hand-workers to the head-workers was triumphantly answered by the head-workers doing the whole work, and proving their ability, while no serious violence marred the spirit of the challenge. All other countries watched the clash, Italy most of all, and each said afterward that none but our own people would have come through it as well. The menace of a social revolution was broken.

## CHAPTER XIV

## EGYPT OVER THE BORDER

On June 21 the Committee of the British School determined that, looking at the prospects in Egypt. it was now desirable to transfer our work to the Egyptian sites in Palestine—Egypt over the Border. The exhibition of Miss Caton-Thompson's and Dr. Sandford's results was during July. After the British Association at Oxford in August we went to Cardigan, as the district was one that required examination. For three weeks, with my son, I planned all the stone and earth works within ten miles around, helped by information from Mr. Hemp, the Inspector of Monuments. The wide area of the inspectorships leaves scope for collaboration in remote parts. *Ancient Egypt,* of course, claimed a good deal of time as usual.

By November 14, 1926, we left, and, passing through Cairo picked up half a dozen of our old Qufti men and brought them on with us to Gaza. Our party included my wife, Mr. and Mrs. Starkey, Harding, Mr. and Mrs. Risdon, and for most of the time Dr. Parker, who most kindly looked after the health of the camp. At Gaza we searched the district; the town wall was cleared in one part to twenty-seven feet high, Canaanite and Egyptian, but the ground was *wakf,* and could not well be dug out.

Opposite the C.M.S. Hospital, we dug down in a ravine through the modern cemetery, but only found Roman work at the level of the fields outside. The most promising place was Tell Jemmeh, nine miles south of Gaza, which could not be other than Gerar, a name which lingers in the district. The results at Gerar were the finding of six town levels, from 1500 to 460 B.C. each dated by Egyptian remains, and five of them due to Egyptian wars of which the exact date is known.

From these, seven hundred forms of pottery were obtained and drawn, and about as many other objects. Thus the dating of south Palestine was put on a much firmer basis than before. The iron furnaces and great tools proved that iron was commonly used at 1150 B.C., and iron knives started as early as 1350 B.C. At about 1150 there were many pieces of gold work, only one earring being found at any other date; this period of gold agrees with the abundance used by the Midianites of that time. At 950 B.C. there were many connections with Central Asian work, agreeing with the coming in of Shishak from Susa.

The evidence of abundant corn supplies, in the great granaries, and the sickles of iron and flint, give the reason for a Philistine occupying the place, as the Philistine did at Ekron in the rich grain district to the north. The export of grain to Crete would certainly be in demand, as it was rather later in Greece. Gerar was in those times the centre of trade and manufacture for N.W. Arabia, as Gaza is now.

Thus, historically, we reaped a rich crop of connections with other sources, and the work was most successful. The recording was on a new system of making the plans of each level and the drawings of each object completely linked together, and finishing the record ready for publication as the work went on. Thus five months from closing the work I could put the whole results in the printer's hands, beside attending to exhibiting, lectures, and current affairs.

As to position, Gerar was difficult owing to bad water. All of our party were laid by more or less, even though we fetched water nine miles from Gaza. At one time, out of five who were competent to manage the men, only one was fit to stand out in the work. For my own part I could scarcely eat anything owing to nausea, and I thinned away until skin hung on my bones like an old cloak; it took three months of milk diet afterwards to set me up again. The continual run of small illnesses has been unnoticed in this account, but on an average of various years, I have been disabled a month in each year, a considerable drain on working time.

We started the training of the Palestine Bedawy with half a dozen of our best men from Egypt, but they always wanted to claim all the bakhshish due for things found by the new men. One day a Palestine wag slipped into his digging a new brass bracelet; the Egyptian pounced on it thinking it to be gold, and claimed that he saw it first, so he earned a good laugh. Even the best of my Egyptian workmen cannot resist the temptation to squeeze another worker if they get a chance, either by sharing his bakhshish, or making him supply them with food for nothing. The Arab-Egyptian mind seems incapable of honest power, and all the sound men in office whom I have met are Copt or Albanian or Tunisian.

Leaving Gerar on May 7, 1927, I went up to Beyrut, and there made friends with the American College, saw Dr. Nelson who was on the Medinet Habu publication, and found one of the staff who would like to drive out to Byblos. On the way we picked up Heidenstam, the engineer of the Nahr el Kelb waterworks, who knew Byblos well, and had a large collection from there. The excavation was a piteous sight, the earth cut down through some eight feet of ruin (which needed search layer by layer) and thrown in lumps into trucks to be tipped into the sea. I heard that much had been recovered from the tip heap by a collector waiting in a boat at the bottom of the slope.

The French director M. Dunand was most obliging, and showed us many fragments of inscribed stone vases, but no uninscribed pieces to complete them. He did not seem to know his pottery, or to be doing plans, and an architect was sent there later to make plans of five years' work at once. No day-by-day plan of finds and details was to be seen. The workmen were obviously corrupt, a little jeweller's shop at the gates was evidently a market for things. There were no children to search the earth.

The only thing I could do was to write plainly about it all to Salomon Reinach, the President of the *Académie,* and responsible. He sent my letter to the Director of Antiquities for Syria. Later an account of the work was published by M. Dunand stating what care was given to details of work, exactly as I had said should be done, and rather later M. Reinach made an inspection of all the Syrian work and reported that it was as perfect as could be.

Yet in the *Comptes Rendus* it was freely admitted that gold statuettes and other jewellery had to be bought up; the leakages to the British Museum and to America were scandalous. Even when the authorities keep the objects discovered, they are put in the Beyrut Museum without any mark of source or registration, so that the collection is as intelligible and useful as a

dealer's shop, without any of the details of scientific
value. Still, there are pleasant posts for a French and
a Syrian keeper of the Museum.

I reached London May 19, and proceeded with lectures; the exhibition was opened June 23. In July, at
a lunch given by Mr. Squire, the Stonehenge Committee was formed, which in two years succeeded in buying up all the land round Stonehenge and preserving
its true surroundings. Working up the Gerar material
occupied me till September 21, when the last plates
and MS. went off. I was asked by an editor to do a
book on Egyptian Art, but after my doing a good deal
of it he threw it over. *Ancient Egypt* as usual occupied
much time, and I gave lectures on Egyptian Architecture in the autumn. My wife took a five weeks' cruise
to Brazil, to recover from a dislocated hip joint.

During winters in London I had been much delayed
by chronic trouble in the air passages, and two doctors
had done all they could with auto-injections without
any benefit. I was told my only chance of health was
to keep out of England for the winter. This winter it
was not so necessary for me to go to excavate, as
Starkey, Harding and Risdon had experience at Gerar
and Miss Tufnell was going also. As there was much
writing to be done, I fixed to go and winter in Rome
for 1927-8. Quiet and sunny quarters fitted me at 149
Via Sardegna. I had weekly reports from Palestine, and
could have gone over there in case of necessity.

The first matter needed was an index of the many
lists of titles which I had published in *Ancient Egypt*,
and this proved a long affair, owing to the frequent
changes in transliteration of the rarer signs. My main
work was a *corpus* of decorative motives, for which I
had been collecting somewhat during thirty years past,

and much wished to carry out. The library of the British School in Rome was an excellent ground for collecting all Mediterranean material; the northern sources I tapped afterwards in London, and so amassed over three thousand drawings.

The main purpose was to frame an instrument of research for the prehistoric times. Every drawing needed therefore to have its date, its place, and reference to the publication. Many good results soon appeared, and such a work will be more and more useful as it grows, and as fresh fields of research are added to it. It seemed to be the greatest need for the study of early times, and to promise considerable results immediately.

I met many friends in Rome, and often saw my revered Lanciani, with his wife, the Duchess of San Teodoro. My old fellow-worker, Randall MacIver, was most visited, and he lived close by; his great study of systematising Etruscan and early Italian archaeology was cordially recognised in Italy, by his presiding at the first Etruscan Congress.

Another strange interest was with John Marshall, who was struggling over the Dossena sculptures, which had been sold as antiquities. Marshall was just suspecting them, and probing the question. A typical piece I was taken to examine, and saw that it had been artificially treated. After my return to England the bubble burst, the dealers were run down, Dossena was exonerated, and was properly advanced for his undoubtedly fine talents, which rivalled the best early Italian work. Unhappily Marshall died suddenly before the final clearance of the affair.

Another matter which occupied me was the writing up of the various experiences in archaeology in the present account. Away from current business I could go over old diaries and letters and recall the course of affairs in past years. Many matters had stuck in the mind as vividly as on the first day.

Returning to London on April 22, the usual affairs at the College had to be carried on, and *Ancient Egypt*. The exhibition of results at Beth-pelet, obtained by our expedition, had to be prepared ready for July 2. Working up decoration from various sources was needed, to prepare for autumn lectures. After the British Association meeting at Glasgow I went to Bishop's Castle September 8, as that promised fresh work in surveys. Thanks to Major Sykes and others we managed to go over all the district, and left on the 24th.

On September 26 an important meeting was called by the Provost at University College, of about a dozen archaeologists (three from the British Museum) to discuss the need of museum space for all the branches of archaeology. Some came to object—officially—even said it was an insult to the B. M. to provide fresh accommodation outside. But the Royal Commission on Museums had just issued its report, showing that for fifteen years to come all the expansion of the British Museum was bespoken for the library alone, and nothing could be done for the urgent needs of archaeology. Finally the meeting resolved unanimously that we must press for great Archaeological galleries for all countries, if possible as part of the University buildings in Bloomsbury.

The next step was for the Archaeological Board of the University to formulate a scheme. This amounted to a claim for a building of about 1,200 feet length of galleries, 40 feet wide, to provide for Egypt, Palestine,

Iraq, early India, Northern Europe, classical casts, and mediaeval England. The matter was complicated by the anthropological interests pushing into the scheme, but at last it was agreed that each side should work its own plans, in conjunction.

Finally on November 7 a deputation of the Archaeological and Anthropological Boards met the Committee on Sites at the University. Sir William Beveridge presided, and stated that Universities had no business with Museums. His interest was bounded by books and social institutions. At last we were told that no plans would be looked at, but, if we put our requests down in square feet of gallery required, that would be considered. There the matter slept for a year, while various allotments of space were being made for other purposes. On the Archaeological Board asking then for some reply, the matter was further postponed by saying that all claims would be considered in future.

Meanwhile nearly a hundred boxes of Palestine antiquities were lying in the cellars of the College, all Woolley's Ur material except show pieces were shut up invisible, and no provision was possible for other countries. The alternative of all going to America came more into view, as England could not provide for housing all the work of English excavators.

On November 14, 1928, I left London for the Orient Express overland to Palestine, with Mrs. Benson and Lady Agnew. They branched off to Baghdad, and I went on to Gaza and Beth-pelet. On the way we had four days in Constantinople. There I found the disarmed crosses on the doors of St. Sofia, showing the Iconoclast origin of the dis-arming of the Cross, which I had found in Rome. The history of this Puritan movement, and its full outcome at Turin in A.D. 820, is the most interesting of the ecclesiastical subjects of the ninth century, and appears to be quite unknown and unsuspected hitherto.

We had rain all across the dreary rock plain of Asia Minor, and through the mighty gorges of the Taurus range, which make the Alps seem a mere play-ground. Having crossed the Mediterranean seventy-five times, usually in some misery, I settled that I would go by overland in future. By November 23 I was at Beth-pelet with Starkey, Harding, Miss Tufnell, and later Dr. Parker and Colt.

Our good friend Harold Wiener came over twice from Jerusalem with friends, and little did we think that he would be barbarously murdered by an Arab fanatic before the year was out; he was the most charitable, broad-minded of men, who only wished to help everyone. The fanaticism of Islam never worked a worse deed.

The principal results at Beth-pelet were on the cemetery of the Hyksos and Philistine periods. I had tried for years to reach the Hyksos remains in Egypt, and had only succeeded in finding half a dozen graves and two camps. Now we had two dozen large graves, containing more than a hundred scarabs, and the obvious course of decline in the work of these, from the style of the XIIth dynasty downward, gave the means of placing the material in its historical order. The immense ditch and defensive works around the hill fort were also of Hyksos age. Great quantities of the finest pottery, also daggers and other objects, gave us a full view of the civilisation of the time.

The similarity of the pottery to that of Byblos, while the Hyksos pottery in Egypt was purely Egyptian, showed that the Hyksos had no style of their own, but used that of each country; thus they were not a population but a ruling caste which adopted any civilisation which they met with, like the Arab and Turk. The Philistine tombs of five lords and their families covered the later Egyptian period, from about Sety I to the rise of David, as dated by the scarabs found with them.

For the first time such evidences of their civilisation were definitely fixed, and their burial customs ascertained, differing from the Egyptians or Syrians. From the Egyptian side there was a burnt casket, which had an engraved ivory panel, smashed to small chips. The whole of it we removed in a block solidified by wax, then dissected, and the ivory slowly recovered in London. The restoration of the fragments was a matter of many weeks, carried on by Harding and Colt. It gave us for the first time fine work of purely Syrian execution, though the motive of the scene was Egyptian, the Egyptian governor under Sety I, seated, with his various servants.

A very surprising matter was finding several places of flint working, and a flint hoe, of the Israelite period, about 1100 B.C. This agreed with the statement that the Philistines kept the use of metals to themselves, and would not allow weapons to the Israelites; but the precise survival of the neolithic type of hoe showed that the flint working had never been arrested until iron drove it out about 1050 B.C. The fort and immense revetment of Vespasian closed the history of the place. Altogether it was the most important year's work that there had been for the Hyksos and Philistine ages, which hitherto had eluded research.

The flint working around Beth-pelet was astonishing. It had been said that there were no chipped flints

SYRIAN ENGRAVING ON IVORY. BETHPELET

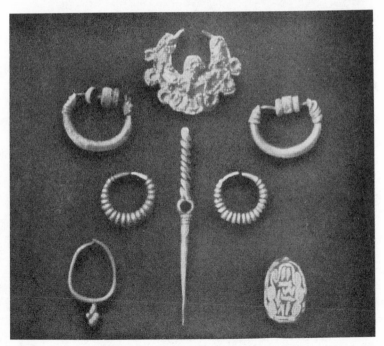

GOLD WORK OF HYKSOS AGE. ANCIENT GAZA

in the southern region. But our work boys brought up thousands of them from the Wady Ghuzzeh which ran past our tell. We selected over a thousand palaeoliths to keep, some of entirely new types; many were very heavy, and could only be held in both hands. Sorting these over impressed on me the meaning of the most usual forms; the heavy pointed flints must have been for breaking up the ground to reach the roots for winter food; the sharp-edged ovates must have been for cutting soft green summer food. Neither form is at all applicable to cutting wood, or any other use than food gathering.

To this day, the Bedawy who worked for us had to resort to grubbing up roots in order to live when the harvest failed by drought. Besides these river-worn palaeoliths, many sites of neolithic settlement were found. Only one was worked in that season, providing hundreds of microlith cores and pottery. The series of these settlements were left over for the next winter.

By April 8 I returned to London. Preparing lecture material, writing for *Ancient Egypt,* and working up the fresh position of chronology filled my time. The great step was taken of realising that the Hyksos XVth dynasty followed directly on the XIIth dynasty, and that there was no reason for adopting the variable year in understanding the celebrated papyrus about Sirius rising, but that the seasonal mid-winter year was quite as likely. Thus all the difficulties of the last thirty years in chronology were wiped out. Mackay's *Bahrein,* and Harding's Hemamieh tombs had to be edited and published.

The writing up of *Beth-pelet I,* and preparation of seventy-two plates of the last two winters' results, took most of the summer. The *corpus* of Palestine pottery, which Duncan was preparing, occupied a month of my time. The usual exhibition was from July 4 to 27 and required much attention in details. While at Caerleon during three weeks, with my family, I had to ink in and prepare for lantern slides the drawings of patterns for the autumn lectures. Altogether I was over-pressed with work before I could get away on November 16.

Our former working party was reduced for 1930 to Starkey, Harding and Colt, owing to reasons of health hindering others, and we had a new recruit in Eann Macdonald, who came with geological familiarity in flint research, to work the neolithic settlements. As I had by now seen the historical position cleared up, it did not seem needful for me to go on to the field work, for our party could develop the known lines further. Therefore I could have time for writing, which I much needed in various subjects, and for this I returned to my former quarters in Rome. There I had first to work up *Ancient Egypt* for December; the March MS. was lost in the post.

The collection of patterns was now published as *Decorative Patterns of the Ancient World*. The organising of all this, making up plates, and finishing for press was a long affair. Merely putting the numbering on them was five hours' work a day for over a fortnight. The final plan of the Beth-pelet site had to be put together. Lectures were given at the Archaeological Schools, and in other ways I had an interesting part in the life of Roman archaeology. In a charming day over Caere we were led by the excavator Comm. Mengarelli. I reached London again April 21, 1930.

Among the matters to be attended to was the application, a third time, for space for archaeology in the University building. The officials had announced that

SIR FLINDERS PETRIE IN 1930

work was to be begun, but could not supply any information as to how the requirements of two years ago were going to be met. A further strong letter was then sent in from the Archaeological Board. Our exhibition was delayed till July 9 owing to six weeks' detention of our boxes by the Palestine Government.

The attainment of fifty years since I began in Egypt, and twenty-five years' work of the British School, was marked by a show of historical Egyptian scenes, organised by Lady Newnes at the Hippodrome, which was crowded; also by Dr. Robert Mond giving a dinner to about 180 workers and friends of Egyptology, including forty of my former students, a most happy gathering of friends who had never all met before.

The annual exhibition was held, showing the results of clearing the Egyptian cemetery of the Ramesside age at Beth-pelet, by Starkey and Colt. Preparing publications and *Ancient Egypt* occupied the autumn. As bad colds much hindered my work, my lecture dates were put nearer together, and I was able to get away by October 24.

We went overland with three new students, Richmond Brown, Vernon, and Scott, visiting the Constantinople and Beyrut museums. We were met at Lydda by Starkey with the bad news that malaria was rampant at Tell el Ajjūl, and we must wait till it subsided.

We went up to Jerusalem, and had to stay there or at Gaza till November 26. The malaria being unreduced we could only undertake work by going back to Beth-pelet. There we cleared more of the Ramesside cemetery in the great fosse; also exploring the top of the tell in search of any pavement, but nothing decisive of a temple site was found.

By December 17 we could venture to Tell el Ajjūl,

where Starkey had had fever, though Miss Tufnell and Harding had resisted it. Mr. and Mrs. Colt arrived the same day. Royds had joined us before, and gave his valuable help in surveying. Dr. Parker came later, and kindly helped in attending to the health of ourselves as well as the natives.

Tell el Ajjūl is a great site of thirty-three acres inside the fortifications, at the side of the Wady Ghuzzeh. It seems to have been the Old Gaza, which was deserted about 2000 B.C., owing to malaria. The inhabitants sought a healthier site, four miles to the north, and founded the Gaza of Jewish and later times.

The condition of the city is unique; when abandoned, the tall houses crumbled down and buried the lower storey, so that the walls are still perfect up to six or eight feet high, and no later settlement obstructs our search. The latest dating of the city was about 2250 B.C., fixed by scarabs of the Hyksos Apepa I. Only a few little patches left by later squatters belong to any subsequent age.

The view of Canaanite civilisation of the Patriarchal age is most enlightening. The regular lay-out of the houses, the long streets, the neat shrines for prayer with places for ablution at the door, the quantity of foreign painted pottery, all show a high standard of life. The country was dominated by the Hyksos horsemen, but the civilisation was not due to them. The skeletons of horses found buried with their owners are a thousand years before any such remains in the Mediterranean area.

About thirty generations before all this, there was a virile people here, making great fortifications, and a long tunnel. Their tombs show that they were heirs of the neolithic people, but had acquired large copper weapons. Their works were abandoned, probably when North Syrians overran Egypt, and ruled as the VIIth and VIIIth dynasties, 3127 to 2912 B.C.; this city was then neglected as it had ceased to be a frontier defence.

The excavations this season were aided by New York University, through Mr. Colt's negotiation, thus renewing an arrangement in years long past with United States. The season had been a most promising opening of a great prospect of future work, which I hope to conduct in coming years.

The opportunity for discovery is wider than ever before. A great capital of the Bronze Age lies before us, without any need of removing later soil. The much earlier work of the Copper Age has been revealed; the Neolithic sites have been exposed, and linked into a series. The connections with Egypt enable us to place all this material in historical order.

Hundreds of men and children have been trained in the last five years and zealously preserve all that is uncovered. More students than ever before are wishing to enter the field, and those who join are of the most promising class for the future. The whole machinery of research has never been so well developed, and the only hindrance is insufficiency of means, for in the absence of any government help, the progress of researches depends entirely on the public. I trust that my experience of fifty years may still be utilised to the full, in such time as may yet remain for action.

# BIBLIOGRAPHY

Joint authorship marked with *

1877 Inductive Metrology
1880 Stonehenge
1883 Pyramids and Temples of Gizeh
1885 Tanis I
1886 Naukratis I*
1887 Tanis II, Nebesheh, and Defenneh*
1887 A Season in Egypt
1888 Racial Portraits
1889 Hawara, Biahmu and Arsinoe*
1889 Historical Scarabs
1890 Kahun, Gurob and Hawara*
1891 Lachish
1891 Illahun, Kahun and Gurob*
1892 Medum*
1892 Ten Years' Digging
1893 (pub. 1896) Koptos*
1894 Students' History Vol. I
1894 Tell el Amarna
1895 Egyptian Decorative Art
1895 Egyptian Tales I, II
1896 Naqada*
1896 Student's History Vol. II
1897 Six Temples at Thebes
1898 Dehasheh
1898 Syria and Egypt
1899 Dendereh
1900 Royal Tombs of 1st Dynasty
1900 Hierakónpolis I*
1901 Diospolis Parva
1901 Royal Tombs of Earliest Dynasties
1902 Abydos I
1904 Abydos II
1904 Methods and Aims in Archaeology
1905 Student's History Vol. III
1906 Religion of Ancient Egypt

1906 Researches in Sinai*
1906 Hyksos and Israelite Cities*
1906 Migrations
1907 Gizeh and Rifeh
1907 Janus in Modern Life
1908 Athribis*
1908 Memphis I*
1909 Qurneh*
1909 Personal Religion in Egypt before Christianity
1909 Arts and Crafts of Ancient Egypt
1909 Palace of Apries, Memphis II*
1910 Meydum and Memphis III*
1910 Historical Studies*
1910 Growth of the Gospels
1911 Roman Portraits, Memphis IV
1911 The Labyrinth, Gerzeh*
1911 Portfolio of Hawara Portraits
1911 Egypt and Israel
1911 Formation of the Alphabet
1912 Tarkhan I and Memphis V
1912 Heliopolis and Kafr Ammar
1912 Revolutions of Civilisation
1913 Riqqeh and Memphis VI
1913 Tarkhan II
1913 Amulets
1914 Lahun I, The Treasure
1915 Scarabs and Cylinders
1916 Tools and Weapons
1917 Prehistoric Egypt
1918 Corpus of Prehistoric Pottery
1919 Some Sources of Human History
1919 Eastern Exploration
1922 Student's History of Egypt, I. 10th edit.
1922 Status of the Jews in Egypt
1923 Lahun II, the Pyramid*
1923 Social Life in Ancient Egypt

291

1924 Sedment I and II
1924 Religious Life in Ancient Egypt
1924 Descriptive Sociology, Ancient Egypt*
1925 Tombs of the Courtiers*
1925 Buttons and Design Scarabs
1926 Ancient Weights and Measures
1926 Glass Stamps and Weights
1926 Hill Figures of England
1927 Objects of Daily Life
1928 Gerar

1929 Bahrein and Hemamieh*
1929 How to Observe in Archaeology*
1930 Decorative Patterns of the Ancient World
1930 Beth-pelet I*
1930 Corpus of Palestinian Pottery*
1930 Antaeopolis
1931 Ancient Gaza
Articles in *Dictionary of the Bible*, *Encyclopaedia Britannica* and much of *Ancient Egypt*.

# PERIODS AND DATES OF EGYPTIAN HISTORY

## NEWLY REVISED, 1930

|  | B.C. |
|---|---|
| TASIAN | ? 9000 |
| BADARIAN | |
| AMRATIAN | |
| GERZEAN | |
| SEMAINEAN | |
| I Dynasty | 4326 |
| IV " | 3747 |
| VI " | 3330 |
| VII-VIII (Syrians) | 3127 to 2912 |
| XII | 2584 |
| XIII EGYPTIAN, XV HYKSOS | 2371 |
| XVI HYKSOS | 2111 |
| XVIII | 1583 |
| XIX | 1318 |
| XX | 1195 |
| XXII Bubastite | 940 |
| XXVI Saite | 664 |
| XXVII Persian | 525 |
| Ptolemy I | 322 |
| Augustus | 30 |
| ARAB CONQUEST | A.D. 638 |

These dates are based on the annals of the early kings, the ancient lists of kings, the inscriptions dated in reigns, biographies and genealogies, epochs fixed by the calendar, the horoscopes, and new moons. All these sources are fitted together by means of the outline of Manetho's history compiled about 300 B.C., and checked in later parts by histories of other lands. A shorter dating, which has been fashionable, requires us to ignore much of the ancient records, by depending on one form of calendar only, that of the shifting year. In reality the Egyptians at all times had also a fixed year by mid-winter, and even two other calendars. The rejection of the ancient records, in order to follow a theory of one calendar instead of another, does not appear reasonable. The details of the chronology are given in *Ancient Egypt*, 1929, p. 33 and 1931, p. 1.

# INDEX

## A

Abadiyeh, 184.
Abu Ghaneym, 208.
Abydos, 185-202, 265.
Accuracy measured, 115-116.
— search for, 25.
Aegean pottery (in 1889),
   108, 109, 116, 118, 151.
— — dating, 139.
Aird, Sir John, 165.
Ajjūl, Tell el, 287, 288.
Akhenaten, 148-152.
Alphabetic signs, 108, 116.
Altar with Offerings, 102.
Aly Suefy, 152, 167, 177, 258.
Amarna excavations, 144.
Amasis, 73.
Amélineau, 185-189.
Amenemhat III, 87, 101, 159, 235,
   237.
Amenhetep I, 194.
Amenhetep III, 119, 172, 225.
Amos, Prof. Sheldon, legist, 40, 63.
—, (Sir) Maurice, 97, 104.
Amsden, Dr., 249.
Amulets found, 102.
*Ancient Egypt* started, 249.
Anen-tursha, 108.
Animal catacombs, 181.
Antef sculptures, 159, 160, 196, 227.
Antiquities, export of, 23, 34.
Antony, H. M., 246.
Aohmes I, 197.
Aohmes II, 60, 68.
Apepa I, 288.
Aphrodite, a modern, 169.
Aphrodite temple, 60.
Apollo temple, 60.
Apries, Palace of, 229.
Apse chapels, 266.

Arabi and American advice, 43.
Arabs at Pyramids, 32, 33.
Aramaic labels, 235.
— inscriptions, 267.
Arch used, 182.
Archaeological galleries decided on,
   281, 286.
Archaeology, growth of, 20.
—, in it by nature, 8.
Arian controversy, 112.
Army agitator, 43.
Artemidoros, Ti. Claudius, 59.
Artemidoros mummy, 89.
Assault on cook, 261-2.
Assyrian arms, 172.
Aswan, copying at, 79.
— dam, 165.
Atet chamber, 233.
Athens visited, 138.
Athribis, near Sohāig, 225.
Ayrton, E. R., 199, 204.

## B

Baboon of ivory, 117.
Bach, Henri, 260, 265, 269, 270.
Badarian civilisation, 271.
Ballas, 166.
Baring, Sir Evelyn (Lord Cromer),
   129, 144, 146, 169.
Barrel vault, 182.
Barsanti, A., 150.
Bastinado used, 110.
Bead collection, 137-8.
Bead-hunting, 109.
Beadwork preserved, 105-6.
Beb, coffin of, 182.
Bedawieh, 48.
Bedrasheyn station ruined, 254.
Behnesa, 176-7, 266.
Belim, Tell, 76.
Bes dancer, figure, 116.

# BRITISH SCHOOL OF EGYPTIAN ARCHAEOLOGY

THE school was developed by Professor Flinders Petrie, twenty-six years ago, from a small student fund begun eleven years earlier, to serve the following purposes:—

1. The excavation of sites for Egyptian history, latterly on the Palestinian frontier of Egypt.

2. The full publication of the results; thirty-nine volumes have been issued, and given to subscribers.

3. The training of students, who have passed on to government work, and to other researches, both British and foreign.

4. The issue of standard reference volumes on archaeology; ten have been published and others are in progress.

5. The issue of a quarterly Journal, *Ancient Egypt*, at a nominal price, seven shillings, to give account of foreign journals and books, and to supply articles on new discoveries.

Scholarships have been founded, for helping students. The *Gertrude Bell Scholarship*, 1928, is devoted to the general history and archaeology, especially the eastern connections of Egypt. The *Biblical Research Scholarship*, 1930, is also to secure the knowledge of actual remains, which must be the basis for reasonable study.

The extension of our outlook on the Canaanite, Hyksos and Philistine periods is essential to Biblical studies.

Both these scholarships require yearly renewal.

## A NEW CITY IS UNEARTHED

### Tell-el-Ajjūl (South Palestine)

by SIR FLINDERS PETRIE and Students of the British School of Egyptian Archaeology

OUR excavations in South Palestine have now brought us to the actual site of AJJŪL, home of the Hyksos, or Shepherd Kings.

This city, twenty times larger than Troy, lies on the ancient international road between Palestine and Egypt. It was strongly fortified, and with its ramparts and defences covered an area of fifty acres.

AJJŪL stands on a tell about forty feet high, commanding what was then a wide estuary, but is now a dry stream-bed of the Wady Ghuzzeh.

It was a key city and its harbour must have played an important part in the trade between Asia and Africa.

Our discoveries clearly controvert the popular notion that the Shepherd Kings were merely wandering nomads living in hair tents; here is evidence of centuries of settlement with brick fortresses, harbourage, and a system of weights and measures that show established commerce with Egypt and other countries.

AJJŪL was abandoned about 2000 B.C. probably owing to malaria, and a new settlement made at Gaza five miles to the north.

The city gate of Ajjūl stood at the N.E. corner over a rising cobbled road. Below this was the older gate with a complex of walls and trenches, overlooking a wide fosse 150 feet from edge to edge.

Near the gateway we found a tunnel, meandering out underneath the plain to a distance of 500 feet.

This may have been a sally port for escape or an ambush from which to attack those besieging the town.

Our excavations were concentrated upon the south corner of Ajjūl, on a bluff overlooking the estuary. We began this work in the present season and were able to complete two-thirds of an acre. The remainder of the city is as yet untouched.

We went down through three storeys of buildings and found rooms full of brick debris. Close under the ploughed soil the walls still stand 8 feet high. The doorways remain intact and we could walk through them as at Pompeii, passing down a main street and three side crossings.

We discovered and excavated eighty chambers in all.

Beside two of the larger houses there are shrines, white plastered inside, and approached past a low bench carefully embedded with sea shells set in the mud, and intended for foot-washing.

These ablutions must have formed part of the Canaanite religious ceremonial, the precursor of Jewish and Muslim rites. We excavated three kilns, an oven, and several store jars still in position in the corner, on the stuccoed floors.

The whole of the tell was strewn with Bronze Age potsherds. We found various smaller objects of personal adornment, and several scarabs of Apepa I, one of the earliest Hyksos kings; also some of Egyptian workmanship, naming officials of the twelfth and thirteenth dynasties.

We came upon a gold ornament, a bird of granulated gold work, with spread wings, lost by some lady of 2000 B.C. in a muddy street of Ajjūl.

Then there was a silver frontlet or head ornament

in position—the only one known—in a burial found in the town.

On the plain below we worked extensively through the season. The earliest remains were found in domed chambers of the Copper Age, and not much later were pit tombs belonging to the Bronze Age.

There were human remains in all the tombs—in some cases the master of the household buried with his asses. We found skeletons of the great horse which proves to have belonged to the Hyksos at this period, imported by them for riding; these horses had been buried most carefully.

Also in the tombs there were store jars for the deceased, bronze daggers, and a rapier, and much flat-bottomed pottery of a shape entirely non-Egyptian.

These excavations in the south corner of the tell and on the encircling plain of AJJŪL represent our full season's work.

There are three areas of the city which we expect to tackle shortly—areas which should contain the principal buildings and are likely to bring to light some new pages of history.

When the city of AJJŪL and the surrounding settlements are further laid bare, Sir Flinders Petrie hopes to find the remaining links connecting the Neolithic Age with early Egypt.

There is no Government grant for this work, and it depends entirely on donations and subscriptions from Great Britain and America, and on the honorary service of the Director and of the Organising Secretary.

Adequate support is urgently necessary, however, and we confidently rely upon all who have the interests of Egypt and Palestine at heart to see that our work is not delayed, at this interesting stage, by lack of funds.

Hon. Assistant Director and Hon. Sec.: LADY PETRIE,
UNIVERSITY COLLEGE, GOWER STREET, LONDON, W.C.1.